Daily Life in Anglo-Saxon England

Daily Life in Anglo-Saxon England

Sally Crawford

Greenwood World Publishing
Oxford / Westport, Connecticut
2009

First published in 2009 by Greenwood World Publishing

1 2 3 4 5 6 7 8 9 10

Greenwood World Publishing
Prama House
267 Banbury Road
Oxford OX2 7HT
An imprint of Greenwood Publishing Group, Inc
www.greenwood.com

Library of Congress Cataloging-in-Publication Data

Crawford, Sally (Sally Elizabeth Ellen)
Daily life in Anglo-Saxon England / Sally Crawford.
        p. cm. – (The Greenwood Press daily life through history series, ISSN 1080-4749)
    Includes bibliographical references and index.
    ISBN 978-1-84645-013-6 (alk. paper)
    1.   Anglo-Saxons – Social life and customs. 2.   Anglo-Saxons – Social conditions. 3.   Great Britain – History – Anglo-Saxon period, 449–1066. 4.   England – Social life and customs – To 1066. 5.   Civilisation – Anglo-Saxon.   I. Title.

    DA152.C76 2008
    942.01 – dc22

                                                            2008033706

ISBN 978-1-84645-013-6

Designed by Fraser Muggeridge studio
Typeset by TexTech International
Printed and bound by South China Printing Company

For Alice and Esther

Contents

Acknowledgements

A synthetic work such as this could not have been written without the published output of colleagues and field archaeologists, whose contributions I have acknowledged all too briefly in the bibliography and whose works I strongly recommend to anyone who wishes to know more about the period than I have been able to include in this book. I am grateful to the Institute of Archaeology at the University of Oxford and to the Centre for the History of Medicine at the University of Birmingham for supporting my research and to those who helped with or provided illustrations, who are acknowledged in the appropriate place. I owe a large debt to Tony Randall for helping me to see this book to completion by taking care of the burdens of daily life in order to give me time to write, and my thanks to Simon Mason and Liane Escorza at Greenwood Press for their patience, persistence and encouragement.

Preface

There is relatively little surviving physical evidence from 600 years
of Anglo-Saxon society in England when compared to the Romans with
their surviving physical structures – walls, roads, buildings and villas –
and the later Normans with their castles, cathedrals and monasteries.
Yet an Anglo-Saxon presence is everywhere. The majority of English
towns and villages were founded and named in the Anglo-Saxon period,
and parish boundaries and county names evoke an Anglo-Saxon past.
Towns which were founded in Anglo-Saxon times still have streets
respecting the original layout. The Anglo-Saxons have also left a legacy
of art, sculpture and literature. Artefacts from the Anglo-Saxon period,
such as the gold and garnet jewellery deposited in graves, or the
magnificent manuscripts created in Anglo-Saxon monasteries, are truly
outstanding in their beauty, craftsmanship and intricacy. Monuments do
survive, such as the great earthwork of Offa's Dyke, as a reminder of the
resources, control, power and ambitions of Anglo-Saxon kings, and the
modest Anglo-Saxon churches that were overlooked in the rebuilding
schemes of the following centuries nonetheless hint at the magnificence
of the important cathedral buildings pulled down by the Norman
conquerors. Such evidence is a reminder that the Anglo-Saxon period
was far from being a barbaric and insignificant 'Dark Age' falling
between the Roman empire and Norman Conquest.

Information about Anglo-Saxon life comes in two main forms.
Surviving documentary sources provide information about the complex
political history of Anglo-Saxon England, which was dominated by the
actions of war leaders, kings and churchmen. Archaeological excavations
from the late eighteenth century onwards have provided a significant
strand of information about the Anglo-Saxon past, including information
on Anglo-Saxon burials, settlements and material culture, much of which
corroborates and elucidates the written sources. What is striking about
the surviving evidence, however, is how much of it allows us a direct
window into the personal lives of the people who lived in England before
the Norman Conquest. The ability to trace the familiar, everyday and
personal in the life of an ordinary man, woman or child who lived over
a thousand years ago is one of the excitements of studying this period.

Both the archaeological and the documentary sources provide
incomplete evidence about the past, and any researcher attempting
to reconstruct Anglo-Saxon society is aware that they are only offering

a 'best-fit' version of the past, that is, a picture which best seems to fit the available evidence. In the course of this book, I highlight areas of debate – and there are many – and discuss previous and current interpretations. New evidence continues to be excavated, and new advances in the archaeological sciences, particularly in the areas of DNA analysis and isotope analysis, are providing fresh material for interpretation which may yet help to solve what are some of the most challenging unanswered questions in British archaeology. The fact that we still cannot be certain about many aspects of Anglo-Saxon daily life adds to the excitement and interest of studying a period which is both accessible and, in many ways, familiar, yet which still holds secrets and which may yet throw up surprises for the modern researcher.

The Anglo-Saxon period has attracted much scholarly attention, and books abound on its literature, archaeology and history. Inevitably, the history and lives of the elite have traditionally dominated the picture, but there is a growing interest in the minutiae of how people lived their lives on a day-to-day basis, as evidenced by the number of dedicated Web pages, reconstruction societies and reconstructed sites in England. Through a close study of the archaeological and documentary sources, this book will take the reader on a journey through England from the fifth to the eleventh century, shedding light on Anglo-Saxon ways of life and death; looking at houses, family life, health, food and clothing, crafts, economy, religious beliefs and legal systems; and providing a starting point for further study of this fascinating culture and society.

Chapter 1
The Anglo-Saxons in England

The Anglo-Saxon period in England, also known as 'Early Medieval' or, more romantically, 'the Dark Ages', is usually divided into three parts: early, from the fifth to the seventh century; mid- or middle, from the seventh to the ninth century; and late, from the mid-ninth century to the Norman Conquest of England in 1066. The roots of modern England – its geographical boundaries, language and aspects of its culture – were formed in the Anglo-Saxon period. There is still a vigorous debate amongst scholars about the actual ethnic make-up of the people whose language (Old English) and culture (Anglo-Saxon) dominated southern and central England from the late fifth century onwards. But broadly speaking, it appears that these people were made up of distinct and often warring Germanic tribal groups who had their origins in what are now the countries of Germany, Holland, northern France, Denmark, Sweden and Norway, including the surviving native British (known in Old English as *wealh* – the Welsh). One of these Germanic tribes, the Angles, gave their name to the land and the people who lived in it. As early as the eighth century, the Venerable Bede, an Anglo-Saxon monk, wrote about the *gens Anglorum* (the English People) when he wanted to write about the various tribal groups living in the country, even though he thought that people living in different parts of England came from different ethnic groups. According to Bede, the English came from three powerful Germanic tribes: the Saxons, the Angles and the Jutes. The people of Kent, the Isle of Wight and 'that part of Wessex which is still today called the nation of the Jutes' were Jutish, and the people of Essex (East Saxons), Sussex (South Saxons) and Wessex (West Saxons) were Saxon and came from that part of Germany known as Saxony, while the people of East Anglia, Middle Anglia and Mercia, as well as Northumbria, came from a part of the Continent which Bede called *Angulus*, and which, he claimed, was 'still deserted from that day to this' (Figure 1).

However, all these tribes communicated in the same language and shared a culture which was different to the cultures of the neighbouring Picts to the north, the Welsh to the west and the Irish across the sea. From Northumbria to Kent, the Anglo-Saxons built similar settlements, buried their dead with similar rites and used similar artefacts in their daily lives.

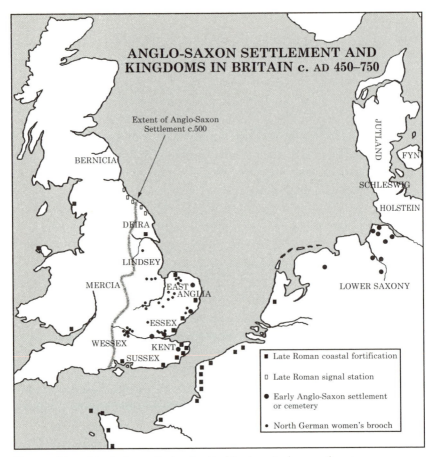

ANGLO-SAXON SETTLEMENT AND
KINGDOMS IN BRITAIN c. AD 450–750

Extent of Anglo-Saxon
Settlement c.500

BERNICIA

JUTLAND

FYN

SCHLESWIG

HOLSTEIN

DEIRA

LINDSEY

MERCIA

EAST
ANGLIA

LOWER SAXONY

ESSEX

WESSEX

KENT

SUSSEX

■ Late Roman coastal fortification

□ Late Roman signal station

● Early Anglo-Saxon settlement
or cemetery

· North German women's brooch

Figure 1 Map of Anglo-Saxon England and its kingdoms in the seventh century.

The 500 years during which Anglo-Saxon culture dominated England
have left an indelible mark on the landscape of England and on English
culture. Over the centuries following the Anglo-Saxon period, other
peoples and cultures have had an impact on the English language, so that,
over time, Old English became 'Middle English', and Middle English
evolved into 'modern English' – a language which has borrowed
widely from other linguistic sources, including French, Greek, Latin,
Scandinavian languages, Dutch, Spanish and Italian. The core of the
language spoken by 360 million people today, however, remains the
same as the language introduced to England by the first Germanic
migrants, and this is particularly true for the language we use to describe
the basic activities of our daily lives. An Anglo-Saxon lived in a *hus*,
sat on a *benc*, felt *hunger* and *lufu*, had a *wif* and *cild*, read a *boc* and

counted his *pennigs* and his *punda*. The 100 most commonly used words in the modern English language are predominantly Old English in origin. Here is an extract from an Anglo-Saxon poem entitled *Solomon and Saturn*, evoking the sadness of autumn and the inevitability of mortality, with a translation in modern English. The words and the emotion in the voice of the poet are accessible to the modern reader:

Lytle hwile leaf beoth grene,
For a little while, the leaves are green,
Thonne hie eft fealewiath, feallath on eorthan
Then they turn yellow, fall to the earth
And forweorniath, weorthath to duste.
And die, turning to dust.

Because the Anglo-Saxons spoke a language which now is retained in the language of our everyday lives, and because, as this chapter will indicate, so much of modern daily life in England – place names, parishes and parish boundaries, churches, villages – were established in the Anglo-Saxon period, a study of Old English texts can evoke a feeling that daily life in Anglo-Saxon England is relatively transparent and familiar, and that the Anglo-Saxon past is a less 'foreign' country than, say, the earlier Iron Age or the Romano-British periods. In some fundamental ways, this is true, but familiar words can be deceptive. In most European languages, the word for 'Easter' is a variant on the ecclesiastical Latin *pascha* (Passover). In English, however, the most important date in the Christian calendar is named after a powerful female pagan Anglo-Saxon deity. We know nothing about her apart from her name, *Eostra*, nor do we have any idea what rites and rituals were associated with her worship, but there she still is, embedded in the calendar.

As archaeologists and historians are beginning to realise, many of our old assumptions about the lives of Anglo-Saxons are having to be re-evaluated in the light of new readings and new evidence. For many decades, for example, early Anglo-Saxon settlements were interpreted as having been filthy, primitive collections of squalid huts, useful only for uncomfortable shelter. It seemed that the Anglo-Saxons using these primitive dwellings were not particularly tidy – archaeologists discovered that the earthen-floor pits of their huts contained quantities of broken pottery, animal bones and even the odd human burial, especially infants.

The idea that deposits of materials such as bones and pottery might have a ritual or sacred aspect to them is relatively well explored amongst prehistorians; but Anglo-Saxonists, perhaps lulled into thinking that the Anglo-Saxons were rather like us, had, until very recently, overlooked the possibility that such dumps of 'rubbish' in early Anglo-Saxon settlement contexts might have something ritual about them. In addition, it has been suggested that these 'huts' were not even primarily used as dwellings, and it is now clear that the idea that the whole purpose and function of Anglo-Saxon settlements was entirely 'domestic' needs re-evaluating. This, and other problems in understanding Anglo-Saxon daily life, will be explored fully in the following chapters, but this book can only suggest current interpretations and 'best-fit' explanations of the archaeological evidence. Modern excavations, and the introduction of new scientific techniques, are constantly throwing up new surprises, and it has to be borne in mind that many aspects of the Anglo-Saxon past are arenas for some of the most energetic disputes in British archaeology.

Early Anglo-Saxon England

Early Anglo-Saxon England began with the arrival of Germanic tribes in England some time in the fifth century, after the withdrawal of the Roman troops and the collapse of the Roman way of life. By around AD 410 at least, the Roman field army units had been withdrawn, supplies of imperial coinage had dried up and most of the Roman administrative structures had collapsed. Over the course of the fifth century, the Romano-British way of life was fundamentally transformed in terms of culture, settlement and society, and that transformation was brought about by the influx of Germanic migrants from the Continent. The incomers belonged to a pagan warrior society without a written culture, who brought with them a distinctive Germanic material culture, including new settlement forms, a new lifestyle characterised by small, self-sufficient, localised farming communities with no evidence of complex hierarchies or administrative systems. Their buildings consisted of huts with sunken floors (usually termed 'sunken-featured buildings' or 'SFBs' by archaeologists) and earth-fast timber halls (also known as 'timber-framed buildings' or, more accurately, since these structures were technically not built with timber frames, 'post-built structures'). The incomers also brought with them new types of art and artefacts and a distinctive burial ritual which included the deposition of grave goods with the dead. By the end of the early Anglo-Saxon period (documentary sources provide evidence for the names of the first kings), a written record began to emerge, and the process of Christianisation was underway.

There are a number of intractable problems associated with the coming of the Anglo-Saxons, which still vex archaeologists and historians, and which represent the most heated and difficult areas of debate in British archaeology: what was the date, nature and extent of the Germanic arrival in England? Was it a peaceful integration or a warlike conquest? What happened to the native British population – were they driven out of lowland England or were they incorporated into a new, racially mixed population? How many Germanic immigrants came to England – just a few leading warriors, or was there a large displacement of population from lowland Germany, Holland and Denmark? Why did the native British language become extinct in lowland England and why are we not speaking Welsh in modern England? These questions are still unanswerable.

The genetic identity of the people buried with Anglo-Saxon grave goods is also in dispute. The eighth-century Anglo-Saxon monk and historian Bede and the sixth-century British monk Gildas were consistent in asserting that the Anglo-Saxons were a warlike race, who systematically overran Anglo-Saxon England westwards from their first footholds in East Anglia and Kent. Both Bede and Gildas emphasised that the Anglo-Saxon takeover was violent and thorough, forcing native Britons to flee, while those who were unable to leave were either enslaved or killed. This story is reinforced by the archaeological evidence, which shows the characteristic settlements and burials of the Anglo-Saxons permeating rapidly westwards. It has been pointed out, however, that there would have to have been a huge number of migrating Anglo-Saxons to fill known sixth-century Anglo-Saxon cemeteries. The possibility has been raised that, rather than engaging in a ruthless campaign of ethnic cleansing, only a few powerful Anglo-Saxons came to England, and the archaeologically visible graves and settlements that we see are largely those of Germanicised natives, who simply adopted the culture and lifestyle of their new overlords. To some extent, the documentary sources offer corroboration for this theory. Both Bede and Gildas claimed that the first Anglo-Saxons were mercenaries who were invited to Britain by the tyrant Vortigern to protect the British from the raiding Picts and

Irish. Bede recorded that these first Anglo-Saxons were two brothers named Hengest and Horsa. According to Gildas's version of this story, one of the mercenaries married Vortigern's daughter, and some early Anglo-Saxon kings recorded in later genealogies had names with British elements, for example, Cælin/Ceawlin, king of the South Saxons. Archaeological evidence to support this tradition has perhaps been found at Dorchester-on-Thames, Oxfordshire. Dorchester was the site of a Roman town. There is some controversial radiocarbon-dating evidence to suggest the persistence of a Roman identity here into the fifth and even early sixth centuries. Just outside the Roman town, two burials were found in the Dyke Hills Iron Age ramparts which had grave goods dating to the early fifth century. One of the burials, a male, had weapons and a late Roman official belt. The Romano-British did not normally bury their dead with weapons, so was this man an Anglo-Saxon warrior hired by the Romano-British 'tyrant of Dorchester' to protect himself? The theory is attractive, but not without its critics (Figure 2).

One of the problems with the suggestion that a few powerful Anglo-Saxon warriors dominated a native British population is that, when two linguistically different cultures merge, it might be expected that some borrowing of language would take place and, in particular, some borrowing of place names might take place, especially where we would be arguing for a relatively high level of intermarriage between Anglo-Saxon warriors and native British women. However, not a single verifiably British/Welsh word entered the Anglo-Saxon language, and to this day, only a handful of Welsh words have found their way into the English language. Remnants of the Roman presence in England are recognised in Anglo-Saxon place names, because the old Roman towns and roads continued to be important places and routeways across the landscape. Place names with the Old English element *stræt* (street) are normally located next to a Roman road, such as at Stratford-upon-Avon (Warwickshire) and Streatley (Oxfordshire). *Ceaster* indicates a Roman town or fortification, such as Winchester (Hampshire), Bicester (Oxfordshire), Caistor (Norfolk) and Wroxeter (Shropshire).

Settlement names with Welsh elements in them are a comparative rarity in England. Welsh survivals attach more often to features in the landscape, such as rivers (Nene, Ouse, Thames and Severn) or hills (Wrekin, Wenlock and Chilterns), than to habitation sites. In addition, some place names with a 'wal' element (such as the many Waltons in England) may derive from the Old English word *wealh*, or 'foreigner',

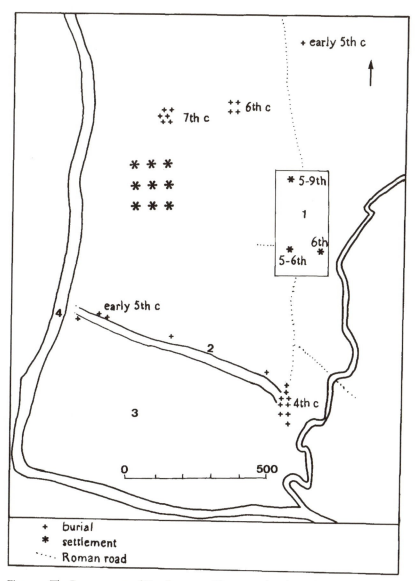

Figure 2 The Roman town of Dorchester-on-Thames and early Anglo-Saxon presence: 1, Dorchester; 2, site of Iron Age Dyke Hills; 3, site of Iron Age *oppidum*; 4, river Thames.

and have been interpreted as identifying the isolated settlements of the native British (Figure 3).

Future research, particularly in the area of DNA analysis and the chemical analysis of bones, may shed more light on the genetic origin

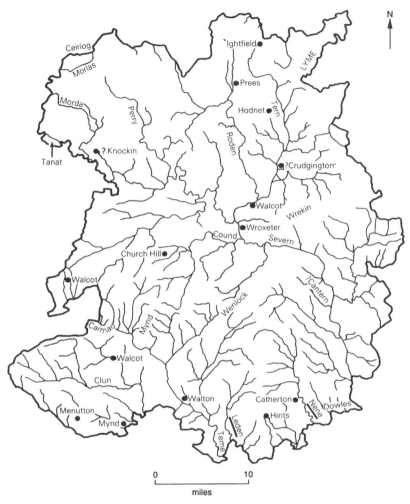

Figure 3 Shropshire: ancient Celtic names and names which refer to British people.

of the people living in Anglo-Saxon England. At present, what we can say with certainty is that, by the end of the fifth century, people whose language, art and culture were significantly different from the preceding Romano-British culture occupied large parts of southern, eastern and central England.

The origins of the people who settled in Anglo-Saxon England are open to debate, but broadly speaking, the famous statement by Bede that the ancestors of the Anglo-Saxons came from 'three very powerful Germanic tribes, the Saxons, Angles and Jutes' seems to be borne out by the archaeological evidence, though it is clear that other groups, such

(a)

(b)

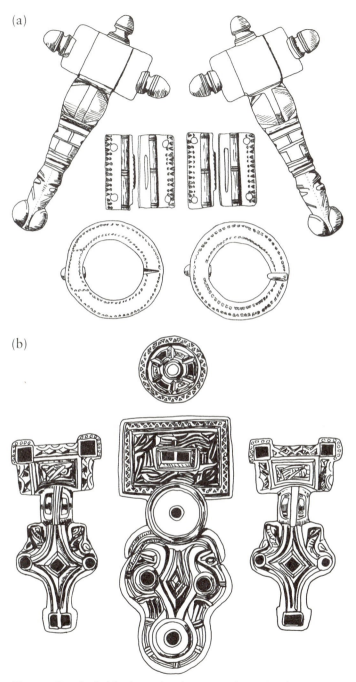

Figure 4 Female clothing items showing contrasting regional variation:
(a) Anglian brooches; (b) Kentish brooches.

as the Frisians, also had a part in the Anglo-Saxon settlement of England. Evidence provided by grave goods suggests that women's costumes, in particular, demonstrated tribal affiliations, and broadly speaking, distributions of female clothing artefacts relate to the tribal areas defined by Bede (Figure 4).

Middle Anglo-Saxon England

From AD 650 to AD 850, Anglo-Saxon England saw the emergence of competing kingdoms, accompanied by more-elaborate social hierarchy; the establishment of elite and royal residences; the creation of highly powerful and influential monastic communities; the dominance of the church in daily and political life; the expansion of local, regional and overseas trade; the introduction of an Anglo-Saxon coinage; and the rise of specialised places (*wics*) for manufacturing and trade. With Christianity came writing, and from the seventh century onwards, documents such as law codes begin to play a part in our understanding of Anglo-Saxon life, though the majority of surviving Old English documents date from the tenth century onwards. Through the middle Anglo-Saxon period, the kingdoms of Anglo-Saxon England played a significant role in the intellectual and economic life of Western Europe, and a relatively peaceful Anglo-Saxon England prospered. It was partly this prosperity that attracted the attentions of the Vikings, and towards the end of the middle Anglo-Saxon period, trade and manufacture began to decline under the onslaught of the Viking attacks.

The seventh to the ninth century saw significant changes in the cultural, political and religious life of Anglo-Saxon England. Small tribal units coalesced into kingdoms, and named kings appear in the historical sources. The emergence of an elite group is reflected in the archaeological record: while burial with grave goods had all but ceased for the majority of the mortuary population in the seventh century, there were a few very high-status burials with a spectacular wealth of grave goods. Burials of important males under raised mounds or barrows at sites such as Taplow (Buckinghamshire), Prittlewell (Essex) and, above all, the famous burial at Sutton Hoo Mound 1 (Suffolk) included lavish treasures which conformed to a new type of elite funerary ritual. High-status women, too, were buried with lavish grave goods, including gold and garnet crosses, such as the necklace found with a woman buried in the

1. Three circular sheet-gold pendants from Milton Regis, Kent.
2. Gold and garnet necklace from Desborough, Northamptonshire. Length 25cm.
3. Gold and garnet pendant cross from Ixworth, Suffolk.
4. Gold, silver and garnet composite brooch from Boss Hall, Ipswich, Suffolk.

Figure 5   Elite seventh-century Christian grave goods.

churchyard at Desborough, Northamptonshire, and exotic imported
bowls, such as the Coptic bronze bowl from Christian Egypt found
with the woman buried at Swallowcliffe Down, Wiltshire (Figure 5).

Whereas fifth- and sixth-century female jewellery and costume
emphasised tribal affiliation, the new high-status burials of the seventh
century emphasised affiliation to an elite and separation from the rest
of the population: elite women across the country were buried with
a similar repertoire of gold and garnet jewellery and other costume items.

High-status settlements, differentiated from ordinary settlements by their large halls, fences, enclosures and other architectural features, appeared in the landscape. These sites include settlements that can be matched to places named in the documentary sources. Yeavering in Northumberland, excavated by Brian Hope-Taylor, was known to Bede as *Ad Gefrin*, a royal palace belonging to King Edwin of Northumbria. It was at Yeavering, according to Bede, that the missionary Paulinus preached to the king and his people, leading to a mass baptism in the waters of the nearby river.

The role of Christianity in driving the emergence of kingdoms, giving authority to the new kings and leading to changes in burial ritual remains unclear, though there are causal links between the introduction of Christianity and the dramatic social and political changes that took place in Anglo-Saxon England in the seventh century. Christianity resulted in the establishment of monasteries in Anglo-Saxon England, and with them came the introduction of schools and the associated creation of books and manuscripts. Pagan Anglo-Saxons had used runes, a system of linear marks, but runic symbols were used sparingly and were not used to transmit complex information in any way that has survived archaeologically. It may be that knowledge of runic writing was a sacred art, restricted to a special few: the word 'rune' is cognate with the modern German word *raunen*, to whisper (Figure 6).

Where Anglo-Saxon monasteries have been excavated, such as at Jarrow (Northumberland), Whitby (Yorkshire) and Hartlepool (Yorkshire), it is apparent from the evidence found that they formed a focus for production and trade. Exotic imports such as wine vessels and glass have been found at such sites, and they were also producing

Figure 6 An example of runic writing on the back of a mended composite disc brooch from a burial at Harford Farm, Norfolk. The runes read, '[L/T]uda mended this brooch.'

manufactured goods such as manuscripts, textiles and metalwork, perhaps for trade. In other words, monasteries developed into 'proto-towns', supporting a population of specialists in manufacturing or trade who did not have to produce their own food. At the same time, secular proto-urban sites known as *wics* were being formed, which were probably controlled by kings. The best excavated of these sites, at *Hamwic* (modern Southampton), *Gypeswic* (Ipswich), *Eoforwic* (York) and *Londonwic* (the Aldwych, London), were planned settlements with streets, uniform housing and areas of manufacture. Archaeological evidence, such as pottery and coins from the Rheinland and Frisia, show that these sites were engaged in production and trade with the Continent. These were not full towns, though – royal and ecclesiastical functions were located elsewhere.

It may be that *wic* trading and manufacturing sites were under royal control or ecclesiastical control; it is difficult to distinguish the two in this period. The excavations of a settlement at Flixborough, Lincolnshire, exemplify the difficulty of differentiating between ecclesiastical and secular sites. Originally thought to be an unrecorded monastic site because of the number of styli and other writing paraphernalia found there, the function of the site was reinterpreted by the excavator, and though it is still a subject of debate, it is now thought to be a high-status secular site with some ecclesiastical functions. However, documentary evidence suggests that the majority of influential members of the church were closely related to the most important secular families – St. Hilda of Whitby, for example, was a Northumbrian princess and probably directly related to the man buried under Mound 1 at Sutton Hoo, Suffolk. St. Wilfred and St. Guthlac (who was a successful warrior in the heroic mould until he became religious) were from the nobility as well as being prominent in the church. The extent to which they and their relatives saw their religious lives as separate from their obligations to their aristocratic families is difficult to assess, and any discussion of Anglo-Saxon daily life from the seventh century on must take the role of the church into consideration.

Late Anglo-Saxon England

The late Anglo-Saxon period (usually defined as from c. AD 850 to the Norman Conquest in AD 1066) was marked by periodic violence as the

Norwegians and Danes attacked, and then conquered, the kingdoms of Anglo-Saxon England until only Wessex was left outside Viking control. The immediate impact of the Vikings, apart from the fear and shock caused by their violent raids, was economic. *Wic* sites failed, and trade and manufacture relocated to the relative security of former Roman towns. Through the course of the late Anglo-Saxon period, Viking raids, followed by Viking settlement, led to fundamental changes in Anglo-Saxon England.

By the late ninth century, all the Anglo-Saxon kingdoms except Wessex had been overrun and subsumed into the Viking world. However, under King Alfred the Great, the king of Wessex from AD 871, the Anglo-Saxons began to resist and regain control of territory from the Danes, culminating in the unification of England in one kingdom. Under Alfred, England was united under one king, but the territory was governed under two laws – the law of the English for those living to the south and the law of the Danes for those living to the north of the Thames, the area known as the Danelaw. The Vikings, however, continued to press Anglo-Saxon England, and from 1016, when the Danish King Cnut (also known as Canute) became king of England and married the Anglo-Saxon princess Emma, Anglo-Saxon England had a mixed Viking and Anglo-Saxon leadership. However, the population had been ethnically mixed since the first Viking settlements in the tenth century, particularly in the north and east of England, where place names with Viking elements such as – *by* and – *thorpe* are common.

Under the influence of Danish settlement, aspects of Anglo-Saxon England changed. Viking art styles were introduced, some aspects of Viking clothing were adopted, and there were subtle changes to some aspects of law and society reflected in the Scandinavian words which were added to the Old English vocabulary at this time – 'earl', 'law' and 'skirt', for example, are all Scandinavian introductions to the English language. Vikings were also influential in the establishment of towns in England, and they were catalysts for the beginnings of what has been described as the 'first industrial revolution' in England, when goods, particularly pottery and textiles, were manufactured on an industrial scale. Viking influence was probably responsible for the substantial wheel-thrown pottery industries that emerged in Ipswich (Suffolk) and Stamford (Lincolnshire). The Vikings promoted the urbanisation of settlements such as York, Nottingham and Stamford, while King Alfred, his daughter Æthelfled and her husband Edward promoted the

recommissioning of former Roman towns and the construction
of new, planned and fortified *burhs* throughout southern England,
so that no one would be more than a day's walk from the safety
of a *burh*. Some of these Alfredian *burhs*, such as Burpham, Sussex,
were superseded by later settlements located elsewhere; but many
of these towns, situated on important river crossings, are still central
places. Alfredian towns were perhaps the first real towns in England
since the collapse of Roman Britain. Late Anglo-Saxon towns such
as Oxford, Winchester, Northampton and Bridgnorth supported mints,
markets, production, administration and ecclesiastical functions and
were laid out with gravelled roads in a grid system – walls, gates and
intramural access.

In addition to the arrival of an influential Scandinavian population,
the Late Anglo-Saxon period saw major social and political changes.
A national system of administration was created, with an inevitable
burgeoning of legal documents, including writs, law codes, charters
and wills. Writing was no longer confined to the elite few. One of King
Alfred's achievements was to encourage schools and literacy, resulting
in the creation of texts as varied as books for children, poetry collections
and medical handbooks. This period also saw the evolution of small
estates controlled by local lords (a process associated with the nucleation
of villages) and the creation of parish churches and parish boundaries,
many of which survive and still inform the English landscape. The
manorial system which characterised the post-Conquest medieval
period had already taken shape in late Anglo-Saxon England.

Sources

Archaeology

From the fifth to the seventh century, Anglo-Saxon England was
effectively a prehistoric society, without a written culture, and our main
source of evidence comes from the archaeological evidence.

Cemeteries

Throughout the early period, Anglo-Saxon cemeteries are the single
most useful source of evidence. Analysis of the burial ritual and the
skeletal remains can give us a range of information about, for example,

Anglo-Saxon social structure, health, disease, diet, longevity and cause of death. The earliest Anglo-Saxons either buried or cremated their dead. On the whole, the decision to cremate or inhume seems to have had a regional (and possibly ethnic) distribution. Cremation was the most common form of disposal in Anglian areas to the north and east of England, inhumation was the predominant ritual in southern, Saxon areas of the country (though in both areas examples of both methods occur), while mixed cemeteries with balanced numbers of cremated and inhumed bodies occur in the Thames Valley and the Midlands. In the case of cremation, the dead were burned fully dressed, sometimes with accompanying animal carcasses, and the bones were collected and placed in the ground, sometimes in decorated pots, sometimes in bags or other containers. Cremation urns have been found containing fragments of more than one body, which suggests that several bodies might have been burned in one place over a period of time, then the larger bone fragments were collected for deposition in a pot. Fragments of melted metal and glass found in cremation urns show that some artefacts, probably associated with the burial costume of the dead, were burnt in the funeral pyre; but sometimes, additional small unburnt items, such as bone combs, spindle whorls, playing pieces, metal tweezers, knives and the occasional miniature artefact, were placed in the cremation urn with the ashes. Cremation cemeteries could be extensive and may have served a large area. Over 3,000 cremation urns have been retrieved from the cremation cemetery at Spong Hill, Norfolk.

The rite of cremation may have required specialist knowledge to ensure that the corpse was properly consumed by the fire and the amount of fuel required for the pyre meant that cremation was almost certainly a more costly method of disposing of a body than inhumation. The act of cremation, too, would have offered an impressive display for the onlookers, which was described in graphic detail in the Old English poem *Beowulf*: 'the greatest of funeral pyres curled up towards the clouds, roared in front of the burial mound: heads melted, wounds burst open, when the blood gushed out of the cruel slashes on the bodies'. Inhumations, by contrast, were less dramatic and perhaps less expensive, but because of the better survival of the bodies and their associated artefacts in the ground, inhumation cemeteries have received much more archaeological investigation and interpretation than cremation cemeteries and can tell us more about the age, sex, health and causes of death of the mortuary population, as well as their social status.

Inhumation cemeteries tend to be smaller than cremation cemeteries, typically containing less than 200 bodies buried over a period of one or two centuries. Most of the dead were buried in a supine position with arms and legs laid out straight, though, occasionally, one or more bodies are found in the same grave. Individual graves were rarely disturbed by having a second grave dug into them, which indicates that there was plenty of space for burial. The fact that later burials were rarely dug into earlier burials also suggests that graves were marked in some visible way over long periods of time. Unlike earlier Romano-British cemeteries and later Anglo-Saxon churchyard burial grounds, the early pagan cemeteries were not usually confined by any boundary ditches or fences, so that inhumation cemetery sites sprawl over an extensive area of land. Although thousands of early Anglo-Saxon cemetery sites have been located, their great area, coupled with the cost of conserving and storing the artefacts found in the graves, means that only a bare handful have been fully excavated. The majority of the interpretations of Anglo-Saxon burial ritual are based on the study of partial mortuary populations.

While many of the dead were buried without any recoverable grave goods, more than half of the excavated skeletons within a typical fifth- to sixth-century cemetery site will have been buried with at least one archaeologically retrievable object. The majority of the grave goods were associated with the burial costume, either as part of the fastenings of the costume, such as buckles, brooches and wristclasps, shoe toggles and pins, or they were items typically carried on the body, such as pouches, knives and keys. Some items, such as spears, shields and swords for men, may also have been part of a 'costume', but other items were deliberately placed in the ground to accompany the dead, such as food in bowls. It is assumed that the presence or absence of grave goods indicated the status of the person buried with them. Grave goods indicated gender, in that only men were buried with weapons, and only women with jewellery (though there are a few exceptions to the rule, and not all women, and not all men, were buried with gender-related artefacts), and there was some correlation between grave goods and the biological age of the person at the time of death.

A huge number of these early Anglo-Saxon furnished cemeteries have now been identified and excavated to some extent, and there now exists a significant body of data. Surviving grave goods have allowed archaeologists to reconstruct the kind of clothes Anglo-Saxons were dressed in at the time of their funerals, while pottery and metalwork have allowed a reconstruction of some of the early English trade routes, manufacturing abilities and ethnic identities. Grave goods have also been used to reconstruct social structure and social status within the burial population and are a valuable tool in reconstructing daily life in this pre-documentary period.

During the seventh century, the burial ritual changed: burial with grave goods became less common, and by the tenth century, burial without grave goods in church cemeteries had become normal practice. Even so, social differentiation, in terms of the location of the body in the cemetery, and differences in burial form, such as the presence of coffins, shrouds or stone lining, are all useful to illustrate social status, gender roles and hierarchies, and the skeletons themselves provide further information on diet, health and longevity.

Although (paradoxically) cemeteries provide the most important source of data for daily life in Anglo-Saxon England, there are some problems associated with the information they provide. First, there are very few examples of Anglo-Saxon cemeteries that have been fully excavated and published. The majority of known sites have often been found after partial destruction, through quarrying, road building and so on, and were subjected to only limited excavation, which means that there is only partial recovery of the total mortuary population. Many of the excavated cemeteries were dug before the introduction of modern archaeological techniques. Under these circumstances, any statistics derived from the excavation of an Anglo-Saxon cemetery represent best guesses. To take an example, the cemetery of Berinsfield, Oxfordshire, excavated in 1974/1975, and published in 1995, was in use from the mid-fifth to the early seventh century and has a mortuary population of 114 inhumation burials in 100 graves, and 4 cremation burials. Though the excavated population is sizeable, and even allows something to be said about possible family and household groupings within the buried population, the fact is that some of the cemetery was destroyed by quarrying before it was discovered, and it is clear from the plan of the site that the southern and western limits of the burial ground have not been found. It is possible that the excavated 114 bodies represent only half of the original cemetery population.

Not only have the majority of cemetery sites been only partially excavated, survival of skeletal remains and the objects associated with the burials is also variable and incomplete. In particularly acidic soils, bones may not survive at all – at Snape, Suffolk, for example, often the only signs of the presence of a body were discoloured grains of sand, which allowed shadowy 'sandmen' forms to be unearthed. Even where bone preservation is good, information about diet and disease, for example, is limited to conditions which affect bones. Chronic illnesses such as leprosy, trauma such as bone fractures or weapon injury, and birth defects affecting the bones are visible, but a sudden fatal infection which left no trace on the bones cannot be identified from skeletal evidence.

Grave goods, too, have variable preservation. On some sites, there may be good preservation of organic material, allowing discussion of Anglo-Saxon cloth and clothing, but excavation can only recover artefacts which have survived in the soil for 1,500 years. This poses acute problems for Anglo-Saxon archaeologists, where the status of the dead is inferred from the number and type of associated grave goods. At Snape, Suffolk, for example, where the soil conditions did not allow the preservation of bone, other materials not normally found in Anglo-Saxon cemeteries did survive. One burial had no grave goods except a pair of drinking horns. Drinking horns are normally associated with only the most important, elite male graves. Horns were found at Taplow, Bucks, and at Sutton Hoo Mound 1, Suffolk, for example, where the gold repoussé ornaments that decorated the horns survived in the ground and allowed the horns to be inferred. Because of the peculiar conditions of preservation at Snape, however, the undecorated horns survived to be excavated, suggesting that the burial was high status. Had the soil conditions been different, all trace of the horns would have perished over time, and the burial would have been classed by archaeologists as unfurnished, and therefore, low status.

Finally, Anglo-Saxon cemeteries offer only one part of what may have been a long and complex ritual. Any singing, feasting or other forms of ceremonial remembrance which may have been associated with a burial have left no mark in the archaeological record.

Settlements

In addition to cemeteries, settlements offer useful evidence for daily life in Anglo-Saxon England. Anglo-Saxons throughout the period built their secular dwellings exclusively with wood (King Alfred's will suggests that he had a stone-built palace, but if so, it was an exceptional structure) right up to the Norman Conquest, so the traces of their houses are largely ephemeral, consisting of post holes and pits, which mark out the location and probable size of the houses, but tell us very little about what they looked like above the ground.

So ephemeral are Anglo-Saxon houses that the first Anglo-Saxon settlement was not recognised or excavated until the 1920s, when Edwin Thurlow Leeds excavated some Anglo-Saxon pits at Sutton Courtenay, Oxfordshire, and correctly identified the material he found within the pits as Anglo-Saxon.

Like Anglo-Saxon cemeteries, early Anglo-Saxon settlements were randomly sprawling sites, unbounded by ditches or fences, spreading over several acres; so, like Anglo-Saxon cemeteries, very few of these settlements have been fully excavated. The distribution of excavated settlements is also uneven: they tend to be easier to spot and excavate on upland gravel sites rather than in clayey valley bottoms. So, the location of known early sites may have more to do with archaeological recovery than with Anglo-Saxon settlement preferences.

The majority of modern English towns and villages have their origins in an earlier Anglo-Saxon settlement, which means that unknown quantities of Anglo-Saxon archaeology either have been lost to modern development or are inaccessible. The problem is particularly acute for the middle and later Anglo-Saxon urban settlements which form the core of modern English towns. Small 'keyhole' excavations in the town centre of Oxford, often no more than careful observations by archaeologists as service trenches have been dug, or buildings modified, have revealed that fragments of the town from over 1,000 years ago still survive under the modern roads and buildings. In the tenth century, the road that is now the High Street was metalled, with channels or gutters for water run-off, and the town was so crowded that late Anglo-Saxon suburbs with cellars lay outside the town walls. Full excavation of such sites is out of the question, even assuming that evidence for the Anglo-Saxon period has survived later disturbances and urban activity. However, the size, structure and layout of excavated Anglo-Saxon settlements still allow much to be said about Anglo-Saxon social structure and domestic organisation, while artefacts associated with settlement sites allow a broader picture to be formed: hearths show the location of domestic activities; pottery and metalwork say something about trade, production, distribution and eating; and environmental evidence – seeds, insects, animal bones, fish bones and so on – allow us to reconstruct diet and agricultural practices.

Place names

In addition to their settlements and cemeteries, the Anglo-Saxons also left traces of their activities in the numerous place names of England. Place names are a valuable source of evidence because they map out the way Anglo-Saxons viewed their landscape, as well as helping us to identify places of ritual or other significance.

Documentary sources

Early Anglo-Saxon England was effectively prehistoric. Writing was introduced with the arrival of Christianity. The first recorded Anglo-Saxon kingdom to be converted to Christianity was Kent, under the influence of St. Augustine, sent by Pope Gregory, in AD 597. But Irish and Frankish missionaries, and contacts with Christianised society in both Ireland and on the Continent, are likely to have had an impact on Anglo-Saxon kings and kingdoms outside Kent. Texts begin to assume more importance in the reconstruction of Anglo-Saxon society, though even for the later Anglo-Saxon period, when documentary sources become more abundant, the archaeological evidence remains vital to our understanding of daily life in Anglo-Saxon England.

The main sources of information for the early Anglo-Saxon period are the writers Gildas, Bede and Nennius. Gildas was a British monk who probably died around AD 570, according to the Irish chronicles, and who probably lived and wrote in south-west England (though both where and when he lived are open to discussion). What is not disputed, however, is that he was highly educated and skilful in the art of Latin rhetoric and that he wrote a historically important religious polemic against what he perceived as the sin and depravity of the British elite at the time of Anglo-Saxon incursions into England: *De Excidio Britanniae* [Concerning the Ruin of Britian]. Gildas's work offers few names or places and even fewer dates. Perhaps the most valuable aspect of Gildas's writing is that he is evidence of the survival into the sixth century of monastic learning and culture amongst the British. Gildas must have been educated, and he was writing for an audience which was able to understand Latin. Although Gildas was almost certainly writing about events that occurred before his birth, his account of the Anglo-Saxon arrival in England is one of the very few texts to have survived from this period that has anything to say about the Anglo-Saxons, and it formed the source material for later Anglo-Saxon reconstructions of their early history, most notably Bede's account of the origins of the English people.

Bede (c.673–735), a Northumbrian Anglo-Saxon monk who spent his whole life from his early childhood to his death at the monastery of Jarrow, completed his *Historia Ecclesiastica Gentis Anglorum* (usually known as *The Ecclesiastical History of the English People*, but more accurately translated as *The History of the English Nation as a Church*) in AD 731. Like Gildas, Bede was writing with the intention of using his text to express God's work on earth. Like Gildas, Bede wrote in Latin for an educated audience, though later his work became the early medieval equivalent of an international bestseller, read throughout the medieval world, and it was also translated into Old English. Unlike Gildas, though, Bede was attempting to record a genuine history of his people (or at least their religious history), and, like a modern historian, he offers a guide to his sources to show that he has authority for his writing. The majority of his information came from oral histories, eyewitness accounts and records provided for him by other monastic houses across Anglo-Saxon England.

Occasionally, Bede made explicit the process of selection in what he chose to record, and there are some obvious gaps in his narrative, either through lack of sources or because Bede did not wish to record events which would conflict with his narrative. Bede was hostile towards the native British, for example, and was often silent about the role of the Christian British in the conversion of Anglo-Saxon England. Nonetheless, Bede's clear narrative, scrupulous description and assessment of the quality of his sources, and careful research to provide evidence for his stories, make his work justifiably central to any discussion of the early Anglo-Saxon period. Bede has provided us with a chronological outline to the period, and it is thanks to Bede that we have such a detailed knowledge of the political and religious framework of England up to the eighth century. It is also thanks to Bede that we can people the early Anglo-Saxon period with named characters, such as St. Hilda of Whitby, King Æthelbert of Kent, King Edwin of Northumbria and Caedmon, a monk whose devotional poetry was the first to be written in Old English rather than in Latin. In addition, Bede provided the western world with the dating system we use today. Although Bede was not the first to use a chronological system based on the birth of Christ, he was the first to use it consistently, and the widespread influence of his *Ecclesiastical History* led to the subsequent adoption of the system.

It is possible that Bede's work may have given us the name for the country and the language. In his history, Bede recorded a traditional story about Pope Gregory, which was central to Anglo-Saxon ideas about themselves as a Christian nation. According to this story, 'which has come down to us as a tradition of our forefathers', as Bede reports, Gregory was walking in the marketplace at Rome when he was struck by the appearance of some fair-skinned and fair-haired foreign slave boys who were for sale. On enquiry, he was told that they were heathens from Britain. He asked the name of their race and was told that they were Angles: 'good', he replied, 'they have the face of angels.' On being told that they came from the kingdom of Deira, he perpetrated another pun: '*De ira*', he cried, 'snatched from the wrath of God.' On being told that their king was called Ælle, he played on the name: 'Alleluia! The praise of God the Creator must be sung in those parts.' According to the traditional story, this encounter led Gregory to send a mission to Anglo-Saxon England when he became Pope. This traditional story played an important role in the Anglo-Saxon consciousness of their special place – not Angles but angels – within the Christian world. Later, in the ninth century, when King Alfred of the West Saxons brought all of England under his rule, he referred to himself as a Saxon, but he referred to the country and its language as 'England' and 'English'. Alfred was ruling in dangerous times, constantly under threat from the pagan Vikings, at a time when the Continental Saxons of Germany had a reputation for heathen savagery. Describing his people as English may have been a deliberate move to evoke the traditional story of the conversion of his ancestors and to align his people with an old story fundamental to the Anglo-Saxon myth of being a 'special' Christian race, in contrast to the Vikings and Continental Saxons.

Like any scholarly early medieval writer, Bede was conscious of the power of the written word, and of the need for histories to conform to traditional models, so that the actions of saintly characters such as St. Cuthbert and St. Wilfred deliberately and consciously echoed episodes in the Bible. To this extent, Bede was not writing history in the modern sense, and not all episodes need be read as being literally true. However, Bede was writing for an audience of Anglo-Saxons who would have expected to see their known world reflected in Bede's descriptions of peoples, events and places to find the narrative credible, and some

of his listeners and readers would have known the characters he
described. For example, Bede reported, in chapter 15 of his third book,
a miracle performed by Bishop Aidan. According to this story, a priest
named Utta had been sent to Kent to bring a Kentish princess, Eanflæd,
back to the court of King Oswiu of Northumbria to be Oswiu's Queen.
Knowing that his return journey, with his royal charge, was by sea,
Utta went to Bishop Aidan for a blessing. Foretelling a storm that would
strike the ship, Aidan gave Utta a flask of holy oil, with instructions to
pour the oil on the seas when the storm rose. When the prophesied storm
threatened to capsize the boat, Utta poured the holy oil on the water, and
the sea calmed down. Bede was at pains to point out, 'I heard the story
of this miracle from no dubious source, but from a most trustworthy
priest of our church named Cynemund, who declared that he had heard
it from the priest Utta.' In other words, Bede wrote the story within
the living memory of people who would have known Utta, Oswiu and
Eanflæd. The incidental detail of the story – that Aidan had access to oil,
that a priest would be commissioned to escort a royal princess and that
the long journey from Kent to Northumbria (a trip of some 700 miles
[1,127 kilometres] along the North Sea) would be undertaken by boat –
must have been true to the experience and expectation of the listeners;
otherwise, the story and its purported miracle could not have convinced
the audience. It is this kind of incidental detail, merely part of the
mechanism of the story for Bede, which provides us with valuable
insights into the daily lives of the Anglo-Saxons living during or before
the eighth century.

The same may be said for the many written *Lives* of Anglo-Saxon
saints which have survived, both in Latin and in Old English.
Hagiography, the writing of saints' lives, was a well-established literary
genre. Apart from educating the reader or listener in the ways of God,
this form of writing had to fulfil certain parameters: places associated
with the saints had to be recorded, because these became cult centres, and
churches that claimed an association with the saints gained in prestige
and wealth. The saints themselves needed to be placed in a recognisable
Anglo-Saxon context and landscape, but their behaviour and deeds had
to emulate those of Christ. In this form of literature, too, the incidental
detail describing the world inhabited by the saints gives us some valuable
snapshots of daily life. In the Old English *Life* of St. Cuthbert, for
example, the hagiographer wanted to describe the moment at which
a precocious young Cuthbert would have his divine calling revealed

to him. The literary aim was to contrast the wildness and wasteful frivolity of youth with the serious, purposeful life Cuthbert was to lead, and so we are given a rare and vibrant cameo of children at play in seventh-century Anglo-Saxon England: 'At that time, many youths were found gathered together one day on a piece of level ground…. They began thereupon to indulge in a variety of games and tricks: some stood naked, with their legs stretched out and pivoted skywards, and some did one thing and some another.'

From the eighth century onwards, a variety of Anglo-Saxon sources survive, some secular, some ecclesiastical, written by both men and women. The majority of the surviving written sources, however, were copied in their surviving form in the tenth century, and the greater number were written in the West Saxon dialect, which, after the depredations of the Vikings, the destruction of monastic houses in the north of England and the resurgence of literacy under the West Saxon King Alfred at the end of the ninth century, became the predominant literary form. One of the achievements of King Alfred's reign was the formalisation and drawing together of yearly records written in Old English: the *Anglo-Saxon Chronicles*. Originally kept by monastic houses as an aid to computing the date of Easter, these yearly accounts served as an annual summary of major events. Entries were largely concerned with the activities of the elite: battles, genealogies, deaths of kings and brief biographies of important ecclesiastical personages. Some entries also included extraordinary natural disasters which must have had an impact on the daily lives of poorer Anglo-Saxons: AD 740, 'This year York was on fire'; AD 671, 'This year many birds died of a disease'; AD 671, 'This year was the severe winter'.

Due to the variable nature of survival of the sources, information from Old English documents is patchy in terms of regional coverage, and in terms of population. All the surviving written texts were commissioned by, and written for, the wealthier section of the Anglo-Saxon population. However, surviving texts cover a wide range: poems, personal letters, law codes, wills, charters, chronicles, medical texts and even textbooks for schoolchildren, written in both Latin and Old English, have survived the vicissitudes of the last thousand years to provide a variety of insights into the intimacies of daily life in Anglo-Saxon England.

After the Norman Conquest of England, the new Norman king, William, set about the task of working out what his new kingdom was

worth, and how much he could exact from the population in terms
of swingeing taxes. To this end, William instigated a survey of his domain,
as recorded (in Old English) in the *Anglo-Saxon Chronicle* for 1085:

> he sent his men over all England and into every shire and had them
> find out how many hundred hides there were in the shire, or what
> dues he ought to have yearly from the shire. Also he had a record
> made of how much land his archbishops had, and his bishops
> and his abbots and his earls and, (though I relate it at too great
> a length) – what or how much everybody had who was occupying
> land in England, in land or cattle, and how much money it was
> worth. So very closely did he have it investigated, that there was
> no single hide nor virgate of land, nor indeed (it is a shame to relate
> but it seemed no shame to him to do) one ox, nor one cow, nor one
> pig which was there left out, and not put down in his record, and
> all these records were brought to him afterwards.

These records are collectively known as the *Domesday Book*, and they
form a unique record of the size and worth of a medieval population,
both before and after the Norman Conquest.

Chronology

There are a number of ways of dating events in the Anglo-Saxon period.
Documentary sources can go some way to providing a chronological
framework from the seventh century onwards, though it is often
difficult to link archaeology and documentary evidence. For example,
the high-status male who was buried in a richly furnished chamber
grave at Prittlewell, Essex, almost certainly belonged to a royal family,
but there are no surviving documentary records to tell us who he was
or when he died.

For the early Anglo-Saxon period, dating is based almost entirely
on comparative typology and stratigraphy. For example, where Anglo-
Saxon furnished graves do intercut, it is possible to say that the first grave
must be earlier than the second grave which cuts through it and disturbs
it. This means that the grave goods buried with the second grave must
be later in date than those buried with the first body. By comparing
relationships between graves and grave goods, and noting any changes

in the size, shape and decoration of specific artefacts, such as button brooches or shield-boss design, it has been possible to create relative chronologies which show that one brooch type is of an earlier date than another, or one spear type is later than another. This method of dating is not without problems. Some artefacts in the grave may have been heirlooms, for example. The main problem with dating based on types of artefacts is that it is a 'floating' chronology, not anchored by specific dates. Only when artefacts are found in conjunction with coins is it possible to assign anything like a date to an assemblage, and even then, early Anglo-Saxon England was not a monetary economy, so coins buried in graves may have been in circulation for many years before burial. The coins do, at least, give a *terminus post quem* – a date after which the objects must have been buried. By using available coin-dated assemblages, and by comparison with Continental artefacts where coin dates are more plentiful, it has been possible to build up quite closely dated chronologies for a range of early Anglo-Saxon artefact types. Similar methods have also been used to create typologies for later Anglo-Saxon artefacts, particularly pottery.

For the later Anglo-Saxon period, coins become much more useful as a source of dating evidence. As burials with grave goods decline, however, it becomes much more difficult to date burials. Often, radiocarbon dating has been the only resource for dating later Anglo-Saxon burials and rural settlement sites. Unfortunately, radiocarbon dating for the Anglo-Saxon period is notoriously difficult because of an Anglo-Saxon 'plateau' in the calibration of dates. Recent improvements in calibrating this period, plus an awareness by archaeologists that they need to provide a number of samples for dating, rather than single samples, to allow for Bayesian analysis, is improving and refining the results from radiocarbon dating.

Chapter 2
Society, Taxes and Administration

In the beginning, Anglo-Saxon England was divided into countless small territories, each controlled by local tribal leaders, whose names are recalled (if at all) in the names of small villages and towns. By a process of marriage, warfare, killing of potential contenders for the throne and cunning, the strongest kings gradually amalgamated and obliterated the weaker kingdoms, until, by the time of the Viking conquests, Anglo-Saxon England was divided into a number of powerful territories (often simplified as 'the heptarchy' of the kingdoms of Kent, Sussex, Wessex, Essex, East Anglia, Mercia and Northumbria), each with kings supported by the paraphernalia of kingship, including bishops, law codes, palaces, mints and flourishing international links. After the Viking depredations, England was split into two – the Danelaw, controlled by the Vikings, to the north, and the kingdom of the West Saxons, the last surviving Anglo-Saxon kingdom, to the south. In the end, these two kingdoms were amalgamated to form a united England.

By the middle Anglo-Saxon period, a complicated hierarchy of ranks was in place. Below the king were his ealdormen, with responsibility to act as his councillors and deputies. At a similar level were the highest ranking reeves and the wealthy *gesið* (a term applied to both men and women). *Thegn* (thane) came into general use as a term from the ninth century (when *gesið* was falling out of use). Like reeves, *thegns* were in service to a lord, and a *thegn* could hold different positions of superiority according to the man he served. A king's *thegn* could be a man of great wealth and power. Thegnly rank could be acquired through wealth as well as inheritance: a *ceorl* could rise to the rank of *thegn* if he could afford a sufficiently grand residence. A *ceorl* was the lowest rank of freeman, and the majority of them would have been independent farmers. *Ceorls* employed slaves and unfree labourers. Independent landholders were obliged to pay taxes and perform public duties and had the right to participate in local courts and to swear oaths in court. Less-successful farmers might become tenants or *geburas*, paying rent in labour or in kind.

By the end of the Anglo-Saxon period, the financial and legal affairs of England were closely controlled by kings through a powerful and

sophisticated bureaucracy. Kings were supported by powerful men
of rank, who were major landholders. The king had at his command
judges, administrators, ealdormen and reeves, all of whom could receive
grants from the king in return for services. 'Reeves' were men with
administrative responsibilities. The most powerful reeves worked directly
for the king; reeves were powerful at a local level, running shires (hence
'sheriff' – shire-reeve) and managing estates for local landowners. Reeves
also worked for bishops and looked after the affairs of local boroughs
and towns. The king's reeves were particularly active in local courts,
administering justice, overseeing trade and collecting taxes. The level
of obligations owed by those below the rank of king to a large extent
determined their status.

Allegiance

The family was the primary unit of social security in early medieval
society, and Anglo-Saxon England was no exception. Obligations
to family and kin traditionally overrode other social obligations. In the
early years of Anglo-Saxon settlement, it is very likely that the head
of the extended family was synonymous with the tribal leader, so there
was limited conflict of interest. With the emergence of an elite, and the
formation of kingdoms, local warlords bound warriors to them with
oaths of allegiance and the giving of gifts, in particular, *here-geatu*,
'heriot' or 'war-gear' (*here* means army). Inevitably, leadership based
on loyalty bought in this way was at the expense of family loyalty,
and this caused some problems. One of the reasons why the story
of Cynewulf and Cyneheard, recorded in the *Anglo-Saxon Chronicle*
in AD 757 was considered so important that it needed writing down
was that it provided a clear case of a conflict between family loyalty and
loyalty to the lord – because members of the same family were fighting
for two different lords. For the Chronicler, the key aspect of this story
was that it demonstrated that loyalty to the lord ought now to be placed
before kinship: the elite had established their authority. Briefly in this
story, the king, Cynewulf, was killed in a surprise attack on a private
house by Prince Cyneheard and his warriors. Cyneheard and Cynewulf
were related, but Cyneheard had a bloodfeud to settle, Cynewulf having
been responsible for depriving Cyneheard's brother Sigebryht of the
kingdom. This already complicated story of family and political fighting

becomes even more confusing because Cynewulf and Cyneheard's men were also drawn from related families. Cynewulf's men, who were nearby, rushed to the king's aid but were too late. Cyneheard's warriors, having killed the king, offered their kinsmen, who were supporters of the dead king, safe passage out of the house if they wanted to avoid bloodshed. Their kinsmen, loyal to Cynewulf, refused and, in the ensuing fight, were killed. More of Cynewulf's followers arrived at the barricaded gate of the fortified house in which Cynewulf's killers were waiting for them. Prince Cyneheard offered Cynewulf's followers their choice of wealth and land if they would offer him the kingdom and reminded them that some of their kinsmen were already supporting him. They refused saying that no kinsman was dearer to them than their lord and that they would not come to terms with his killer. They, in turn, offered their kinsmen within free passage out, but Cyneheard's followers would not take up the offer, 'any more than your own men, who were killed with the king'. Fierce fighting broke out and Cyneheard and all his men, except one, were killed. Even in King Alfred's day, it was recognised that the need for a kinsman to protect or avenge his family had to be legislated for, though it was placed below the obligation to a lord; 'We decree that a man be permitted to fight alongside his lord without becoming liable to a charge of homicide if someone attacks the lord ... in the same way, a man may fight alongside his kinsman by birth if someone attacks him wrongfully – except against his lord.'

Some idea of the nature of the heriot given to a man to bind him to a lord is given by some tenth- and eleventh-century wills. As part of his will, made between 1040 and 1045, a man called Thurstan bequeathed 'two marks of gold and two horse and their trappings and a helmet and a coat of mail and a sword and two shields and two spears' back to the royal lord who had given them to him as his heriot.

Weaponry and status

It is clear from both documentary and archaeological sources that conspicuous display and consumption of wealth was fundamental for an elite male to maintain power and position in society. The wills of wealthy males from the later Anglo-Saxon period make it clear how much effort and expenditure was invested in embellishing the male warrior costume. Swords were probably limited to the upper classes and were invested with particular significance and symbolic, as well as literal, value. This emphasis on valuable weaponry persisted throughout the Anglo-Saxon period. In the pre-Christian furnished graves, the highest-status males were buried with swords, which, rarer than other forms of offensive weapons, were a sign of high rank. Later documentary sources show that the link between swords, display and status continued and even became more exaggerated with the formation of kingdoms. The young Prince Æthelstan's will (dated to AD 1014) included several gifts of swords: 'the sword with the silver hilt which Wulfric made and the golden belt', 'the silver-hilted sword which Ulfcytel owned' and 'the inlaid sword which belonged to Wither' are mentioned, in addition to another eight individually listed swords. One of the swords which the prince left to his brother Edmund was an heirloom – it was described as having belonged to the famous King Offa, who died in AD 796. Ancient swords like these were highly prized, and it may well be that a sword acquired mystique and even sacred characteristics according to its history: in the poem *Beowulf*, the eponymous hero, returning to his uncle Hygelac, king of the Geats, presented him with a 'famous treasure sword' which had been given to him by King Hrothgar, having previously belonged to King Heorogar (Hrothgar's elder brother), and King Healfdene before that. The list of prestigious owners added to the allure and value of the treasure (Figure 7).

Swords were the pre-eminent weapons of the aristocrats, along with helmets and armour. Helmets are a significant warrior accoutrement in heroic poetry, but archaeological examples are relatively scarce. The first Anglo-Saxon helmet to be discovered was the Benty Grange, Derbyshire, helmet, found in 1848, dated to the mid-seventh century, and associated with a burial. This helmet, made of leather over a metal frame, had the image of a boar on its central ridge, but was also decorated with small crosses. The dramatic helmet from Sutton Hoo Mound 1, also deposited as part of a funerary assemblage, dates to the early seventh century. A helmet was also discovered with a high-status burial at Wollaston, Northamptonshire, in 1997. Another helmet was recovered from excavations at the urban site of Anglo-Saxon Coppergate, York. This helmet has a Latin inscription across the head piece which runs (in translation) 'In the name of our Lord Jesus, the Holy Spirit, God, and with all we pray. Amen. Oshere. Christ', but the panel of writing has been inserted incorrectly, so that the inscription is reversed. The same inscription also runs from ear to ear and is broken by the first, and with the two pieces transposed, such that the prayer no longer makes sense when read from ear to ear. Though the owner may have had literary pretensions, either the smith who fashioned it or the owner (Oshere?) or both were illiterate. This helmet dates to the second half of the eighth century. Not all helmets would have matched the expense of these known high-status examples; simpler helmets made of leather; rather than metal, (*letherhelm*) are mentioned in the documentary sources.

In addition to a helmet, a high-ranking aristocrat might have worn a tunic of chain mail. The chain mail is copiously illustrated in the Bayeux Tapestry and occurs in literature – *Beowulf*'s chain mail protects his life in his fight with Grendel's mother, for example – but archaeological examples are rare, though the pile of rusting iron found in Sutton Hoo Mound 1 was certainly a mail coat, carefully folded and placed in the chamber along with other weaponry.

Sword, helmet and chain mail were not common artefacts in Anglo-Saxon England, but for a free male, a spear at least, and sometimes a shield too, would have been part of his everyday personal equipment. In the early Anglo-Saxon cemeteries, spears are by far the most common weapons found in male graves.

Evidence that weapons were routinely carried as part of a male costume comes from law code 36 of Alfred, which legislates for accidental injury caused by a spear: 'if a man has a spear over his shoulder, and anyone is transfixed on it, he shall pay the wergild without the fine.' There was a recognisably 'non-combative' way of carrying the spear: 'if the point and the other end of the shaft are both on a level, the man with the spear shall not be regarded as responsible for causing the danger.' The implication of the law code is that the normal way of using the spear as an offensive weapon would be to raise the spearhead: if the spear was held horizontally at the time of the 'accident', no one could accuse the spear holder of having any intention of causing harm.

In addition to a spear, a shield might have been carried. Anglo-Saxons used round, flat shields made of wood and covered with leather, with a grip for the fist in the centre. Surviving archaeological examples have a metal boss in the centre, which served to protect the fist, deflect spear and sword thrusts and also to punch opponents in close-contact fighting. A detailed account of this sort of close-contact fighting is provided by the late-tenth-century poem 'The Battle of Maldon', which describes Earl Byrhtnoth's brave but doomed attempt to defeat Viking invaders: 'Then a Viking sent a southern spear, so that the lord of warriors was wounded.

Figure 7 Sword hilt with sword ring, Grave 204, Finglesham.

He then shoved with his shield so that the shaft burst and the spear sprang so that it sprang out. The warrior was enraged: he stabbed the proud Viking who had given him the wound with his spear…. Then he immediately shot another so that he was wounded in the chest through his chainmail.'

Later documentary sources show elite weaponry used in two different ways – to fight with and to demonstrate power and status. The sword which a four-year-old Alfred, future king of England, was presented (according to documentary sources) was entirely symbolic at the time it was given and could never have been intended for his personal use as a weapon. To what extent did the weapons buried with men in the earlier Anglo-Saxon period delineate social status, rather than active warriors? Archaeologists used to take it for granted that any male buried with a spear and shield must have been a 'warrior', actively engaged in fighting against the British or in protecting his Anglo-Saxon farmstead from marauders. There is some evidence to suggest that this picture offers an old-fashioned and fanciful view of early English society in general and early English males in particular. First, there is the problem that not everyone who was buried with weaponry has what might be termed a 'full kit'. Did ownership of a single spear and no other weaponry make you a warrior? What about those buried with a single shield, but without a spear? In practice, both could be offensive weapons. Furthermore, it has been suggested that not all those who were buried with weapons were necessarily capable of using them. It has been pointed out, for example, that a number of 'disabled' men were buried with weapons they apparently could not possibly have wielded. At Berinsfield, Oxfordshire, Burial 110 is of a male over forty-five years at the time of death. He was buried with a spear and shield, and in addition to a malunited left shoulder bone and slight to severe osteoarthritis in his spine and long bone joints, he also had evidence of spina bifida occulta. Although this sounds disabling, spina bifida occulta is a relatively minor genetic condition, which is very unlikely to have caused any inconvenience at all – it is possible to have spina bifida occulta without being aware of it. It should not be confused with the form of spina bifida which leads to severe impairment, and which an Anglo-Saxon, without access to modern medicine, could not have survived past early childhood. He would have been less physically powerful than younger men, his back would have ached from the osteoarthritis on the lower vertebrae, and perhaps his shoulder would have been causing him problems. Setting the spina bifida aside, the man's age and other physically disabling problems suggest that he was far from being the most fit or capable warrior in his community at the time of his death. Burial with weaponry, then, almost certainly said more about a male's social status or family status than about his fighting ability.

The case of Berinsfield Burial 110 requires further consideration. In Anglo-Saxon terms, he was old. Could he still have been a warrior? In the poem 'The Battle of Maldon', Byrthnoth is depicted as an active warrior and leader of a household troop, even though he is old. This may not have been the normal pattern. In the burial ritual, shields and spears become less common with age, and variations begin to occur within the ritual. At Great Chesterford, Essex, for example, a number of older men are buried with weaponry, as are a few children – a child aged eight to nine, another aged seven to eight (the teeth are missing from the surviving skeleton, so this age is open to a little variation, and the spearhead was in too poor a condition to measure) and an infant in a small grave.

It is noticeable that the length of the spearhead generally increases with age at this site, a finding replicated at other early Anglo-Saxon mortuary communities. Not so common is the presence of spearheads with inlaid decorative metalwork. Two of the three males over the age of forty-five (where age could be identified) had inlaid spears; the others were with two male adults and one male aged thirty-five to forty-five. The two older men also had the longest spears at the site, both over 1.3 feet (40 centimetres). In another part of England, at Worthy Park, Kingsworthy, Hampshire, the only two decorated spears in the cemetery were also buried with men aged over forty-five. It would appear that, at these sites, age brought with it a special status, symbolised by spears.

The presence of weaponry in the burials of children (where the age of maturity in Anglo-Saxon law codes is ten to twelve years) also suggests that weaponry was linked to status rather than active warriorship. This said, it should be noted that spears found in the graves of children are typically smaller than adult spears, and a period of practising with weapons must have preceded adulthood. The very young child buried with a spear at Great Chesterford is a rarity: secure examples in the Anglo-Saxon record of very small children buried with weapons are few and far between (Figure 8).

One further piece of evidence to support the idea that those who were buried with weapons in death, and perhaps therefore routinely carried weapons as part of their costume in life, held a different status in the community than other men is the fact that, at Great Chesterford as at other sites, those who show evidence of weapon injury are not necessarily the people who were buried with weapons. At Great Chesterford, a male buried with a single spear is the only weapon burial with a weapon injury – a healed head wound. By contrast, three of the sixteen men buried without weapons had injuries. An old man in Grave 125 had fractured ribs, another old man in Grave 75 had a head wound and the adult aged between twenty-five and thirty-five in Grave 93 had a fractured left clavicle and a depression fracture of the skull. Those who

Spear length and age at Great Chesterford

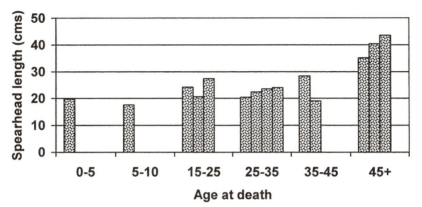

Figure 8 Spear length and age at Great Chesterford, Essex.

had experienced the most physical violence at this site were not the ones buried with weapons.

Royal and elite residences

The late seventh and early eighth centuries saw changes in the religious, social and political structure of England, and this is reflected in changes to the way settlements were laid out and in the development of a new kind of high-status or 'palace' site. The site of Cowdery's Down, Hampshire, with its timber-built halls in a range of sizes, fences, and boundary structures, appears to have been a high-status settlement site with a permanent population. A different category of site is the 'palace site', which appears in the archaeological record from the seventh century, the same time as Anglo-Saxon tribal areas were being consolidated into kingdoms, and the documentary record indicates emergent royal families. A number of palace sites have been identified by aerial photography (though underground, the outlines of walls and other features are sometimes visible from the air, particularly during dry seasons when the presence of archaeological features can affect the growth of overlying vegetation) and excavation. The best known of these is at Yeavering, Northumbria, which can be identified with confidence as the site documented by Bede as *Ad Gefrin*, the royal palace of King Edwin of Bernicia.

Yeavering was excavated over a long period by a team lead by Brian Hope-Taylor, whose findings had a huge impact on our understanding of royal power and prestige at this period. Hope-Taylor's plan of Yeavering revealed a series of aligned halls. There were some unique features, including a large enclosure, which has been tentatively identified as a corral for cattle, and an earth and timber construction thought to be an amphitheatre, a common feature of major Roman cities, but a unique structure in an Anglo-Saxon context. Like other palace sites of this period, however, it does not have any defensive ditches, embankments or palisades.

What is evident from the archaeological analysis of the site is that occupation at Yeavering was seasonal. It was almost certainly used as a place where the king could display his power at the appropriate times of the year, promulgate law, dispense justice and collect tribute in the form of cattle. Edwin and other kings like him almost certainly travelled around their kingdoms and would have had a number of other palace sites, including Bamburgh, documented as an important royal site by Bede, and Sprouston and Millfield, where palace complexes have been identified by aerial photography.

Documentary evidence shows that, by the tenth century in Anglo-Saxon England, houses could be a direct reflection of social status. In one Old English document, the *Gepyncðo*, it was stated that a *thegn* should possess, as a minimum, 'five hides of land, a bell and a *burh*-gate'. This list of requirements was enlarged in a twelfth-century document from Rochester, which also demanded that a *thegn* should have 'a church and a kitchen'; without these appurtenances, a man was not a *thegn*. A *burh* in Old English was a 'defended place', which might range from a reused prehistoric hillfort, such as Ramsbury, Berkshire (derived from the compound *hræfnesbyrig*, raven's fort), to a 'town', as in Bury St Edmunds, Suffolk (a settlement which grew up in the tenth century at the gates of a monastery), to 'defended manor house', such as Bibury, Gloucester, named after Beage, the daughter of Leppa, according to a document of 718–745, which recorded that the estate was leased out to the two women for their lives. At the time of the document, the estate was unnamed, described only as 'by the river called Coln': by the time of a charter in 899, it was recorded as being called *Beagan byrig* (Beaga's manor house).

One such manor house was excavated at Goltho, Lincolnshire, excavated in the early 1970s. Lying beneath a Norman motte-and-bailey castle, the manor consisted of a fortified earthwork enclosure, built in the

middle of the ninth century and enlarged around the millennium. It was
a high-status residence, as evidenced by the range of artefacts found
on the site and by the fact that it consisted of a number of buildings with
separate functions – the houses of the lower members of society tended
to be multi-functional. The ninth-century fortified enclosure held all
the appurtenances of an Anglo-Saxon of thegnly estate. There was
a substantial hall, as well as domestic offices which have been identified
as the kitchen, weaving sheds and 'bowers' arranged around three sides
of a courtyard, as well as garderobes. The ditch and rampart around
the enclosure were clearly intended to be defensive, but, although this
was a time of Viking incursions, the textual evidence suggests that these
private strongholds might have been intended to stand against local rival
power groups. The reference for the year AD 757 in the *Anglo-Saxon
Chronicle* (discussed above) gives some insight into both the functions
of the buildings inside the fortifications at Goltho and the usefulness
of the fortifications. The account describes a small stronghold enclosing
a hall, with separate sleeping quarters for the women (bowers) and for
the king and his mistress. Cyneheard entered the stronghold, catching the
king unawares, and killed him and his retinue – in spite of the fact that
some of the king's retinue were kinsmen of the prince's retinue. When
news of the atrocity reached the king's *thegns* in the morning, they rushed
to Meretun, where they found the gates of the stronghold locked against
them. Fighting took place outside the gates, before the king's *thegns*
managed to break in and kill the prince and his followers. Incidents
of this sort, where private fortified residences became a refuge for the
wealthy aristocrat, were sufficiently frequent for King Alfred to legislate
for these circumstances. In law code 42, Alfred ruled that

> a man who knows his opponent to be dwelling at home is not
> to fight before he asks justice for himself; if he has sufficient power
> to surround his opponent and besiege him there in his house, he
> is to keep him seven days inside and not fight against him, if he
> will remain inside; and then after seven days, if he will surrender
> and give up his weapons, he is to keep him unharmed for thirty
> days, and send notice about him to his kinsmen and his friends.

The layout of the excavated manor house at Goltho, Lincolnshire,
suggests that the entrance gate would have stood at the north side of the
enclosure, providing an impressive entrance to the courtyard. A visitor

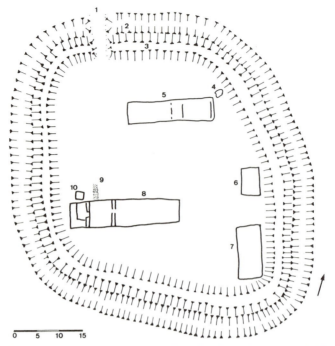

Figure 9 Plan of Goltho, late Anglo-Saxon fortified *thegn*'s residence: 1, probable site of gate; 2, probable location of ditch; 3, probable location of pallisaded embankment; 4, latrine; 5, weaving sheds; 6, kitchen; 7, bower/private sleeping quarters; 8, hall; 9, stone path; and 10, water pit.

would have had to cross the entire courtyard to reach the main door of the hall, which was approached by a stone pathway (Figure 9).

Another law of Alfred suggests that such fortified residences were not confined to the lay elite: bishops and archbishops also lived in fortified residences at this time, and commoners tried to emulate the fortified house. Fines ranged from 120 shillings for breaking into the fortified residence (*burh*) of a king to 90 for an archbishop, 60 for a bishop or ealdorman and between 30 and 15 for lower-ranking freemen, while the fine for breaking the fence around a *ceorl's* house was 5 shillings – the same amount of compensation that was to be paid to a *ceorl* if his slave was raped.

Taxes

One feature of the seventh-century palace at Yeavering is its large enclosure. Its purpose is not certain, but there has been speculation that

it was a corral for cattle, brought to the king as tribute. This idea
is corroborated by a number of cattle skulls found under the floor
of one of the buildings. Before the introduction of a monetary economy,
cattle offered a form of mobile wealth, and kings accumulated wealth,
amongst other ways, by demanding annual tributes from subjects.
In addition, however, it is almost certain that a king like Edwin could
have maintained his power over a large kingdom such as Bernicia only
through an efficient administrative system and the levy of taxes from his
people. Early documents hint at the existence of a tax or *gafol* by noting
land that was exempt from such dues.

One form of levy was the *feorm*, provisions of food or other goods
which would be sent by local landholders to the king and his entourage
to their royal residences or estates within the vicinity as they travelled
around the kingdom. The laws of Ine of Wessex suggest that, at least
by the early eighth century, the form of the levy had been standardised:
every ten hides of land were to give provisions of 10 vats of honey,
300 loaves, 12 casks of Welsh ale, 30 casks of clear ale, 2 full-grown
cows or 10 wethers, 10 geese, 20 hens, 10 cheeses, 1 cask full of butter,
5 salmon, 20 pounds (9.07 kilograms) of fodder and 100 eels. A hide
of land was not necessarily a fixed area. Traditionally, it was the amount
of land required to maintain a family, so the area of a hide would vary
according to the quality of the soil and other environmental factors.
Though the use of coins as currency had been introduced to Anglo-Saxon
England from the seventh century, surveys of large estates in the mid-
eleventh century indicate that, even at this late date, peasants were still
only paying a small part of their rent in coin.

By the time of the first Scandinavian raids on England, the people
of Anglo-Saxon England were used to an accepted system of taxation.
Money collection was well run. Local reeves or stewards were confident
in their roles and expected no difficulty in collecting revenue. In addition
to other taxes, all trade and markets were overseen by reeves and dues
were paid. The codes of Æthelred include a detailed list of taxes levied
on all imports into the country, as well as taxes on ships – a halfpenny
toll for a small ship coming into Billingsgate and a penny for a larger
ship with sails, but four pence for a larger merchant ship. Various foreign
traders were listed, along with the duties they were to pay. Men from
Rouen with wine or fish; men from Flanders, Ponthieu and Normandy;
men from Huy and Liege and Nivelles and even 'subjects of the Emperor'
who were entitled to particular privileges were obliged to pay tolls,

as well as seasonal taxes to enable them to continue their business:
3 lengths of cloth, 10 pounds (4.54 kilograms) of pepper, 5 pairs of gloves
and 2 casks of vinegar at Christmas and Easter. Furthermore, if the port
reeve or town reeve or any other official accused anyone of not paying
the toll, then the merchant had to find six witnesses, and all had to swear
that he had paid the toll and point out the person to whom he had paid it.
Under these circumstances, it is hardly surprising that the first person the
first Viking Scandinavian raiders in England met (and murdered) was
an unwitting tax collector, the reeve of Dorchester. In AD 787, he went
to meet a foreign ship that had landed at Portland in Dorset, expecting to
meet traders: 'three ships came, and the reeve rode to them … and he did
not know who they were, and they killed him. They were the first ships
of the Danish men to come to England.' The Vikings not only terrified
the population by attacking, killing and looting but they also demanded
ransoms for their captives and extorted large sums in return for 'peace'.
The burden of paying off the Vikings must have placed a tremendous
strain, not just on the wealthy but on the population as a whole. The sums
of money extracted by the Vikings were vast: under Æthelred, the Vikings
received £10,000 in AD 991, £16,000 in 994 and £24,000 in 1002. The
wave of Viking invasions in 1007 was temporarily averted by a massive
payment of £36,000, but, of course, the Viking army soon returned.
Evidence for the way in which money was haemorrhaging out of England
is provided by the sobering fact that the majority of known Anglo-Saxon
coins have been found in Scandinavian contexts. Almost 30,000 Anglo-
Saxon coins, mostly dating from the late tenth to the mid-eleventh
century, have been found in Sweden alone. Hoards found in Britain
are also instructive. The Cuerdale Hoard, buried in about AD 905,
and found by a river bank in Lancashire in 1840, probably represents
part of this Viking booty. A proportion of the hoard was looted before
it could be catalogued, but the remainder weighs about 105 pounds
(47.62 kilograms) of silver, including around 7,500 coins, of which over
1,000 were Anglo-Saxon, around 5,000 were newly minted coins from
the mints of Viking Northumbria and East Anglia and the rest were
of Continental origin, perhaps from Viking raids on France and Germany.

The Trewhiddle Hoard from Cornwall is another example
of Viking bullion, buried but never recovered. This hoard consists
of pieces of hacksilver (silver objects that were broken up for bullion)
and several items which clearly came from a church, including a silver
chalice and a silver whip. These items may have been stolen, but late

Anglo-Saxon sources also record churches being forced to sell estates and melt metalwork down to pay the Viking levies. For poorer people, the situation may have been even more desperate.

The tenth century saw the beginning of what could be called a proper monetary economy in Anglo-Saxon England. In about AD 973, King Edgar brought in sweeping reforms to the currency which were to last for the next 150 years. As a result of these reforms, and as a result of the authority and well-regulated efficiency of what was effectively an Anglo-Saxon civil service, currency was recalled and replaced every six years, and careful overseeing of markets by the king's reeves ensured that old currency did not circulate. To change currency from the old to the new, however, people had to pay a fee to a moneyer. In effect, it was what would be termed today a 'stealth tax' – a tax on the wealthy, but one which would have hit poorer members of society hard, making long-term saving a difficult prospect (Figure 10).

In addition to other taxes, landowners and those who held estates by royal charter were also required to support the military strength of the king through the 'three burdens' – maintenance of bridges (which also included fords or any other appropriate way for an army to cross a river), maintenance of town fortifications and providing men for military service. These three burdens were first formalised as a duty to the king in the time

Figure 10 Paying taxes to the reeve: from a manuscript illustration showing Joseph's brothers offering him payment in his capacity as Pharaoh's reeve.

of Offa of Mercia (d.796). The dyke which has his name, and stretches for 64 miles (103 kilometres) from Rushock Hill in Herefordshire to Mold in Clwyd, is still a formidable barrier and a testament to Offa's ability to command manpower and resources, and to the effectiveness of government. By the ninth century, the 'three burdens' had been established as a duty across Anglo-Saxon England. Although the responsibility for implementing the burdens lay with the aristocrats and landowners, in practice the majority of the labour would have been carried out by their unfree tenants and slaves.

A taxpayer, then, had to be a person of wealth and status to be able to bear the demands placed on their purse by the crown. Being a taxpayer brought with it some automatic status. A law of Ine stated that, if fighting broke out in a monastery, a compensation of 120 shillings had to be paid. If anyone fought in the house of an ealdorman or of 'any other distinguished councillor', then 60 shillings compensation was to be given to the householder, and 60 shillings fine to the crown. If a fight broke out in the house of a taxpayer (*gafolgeldan huse*), 6 shillings were to be given to the taxpayer and the crown would receive 120 shillings in compensation for the offence, in recognition of the king's role as protector of the taxpayer. Such privileges of status may not have been enough; some wealthy Anglo-Saxons may have chosen to remain unfree rather than incur the taxes laid on the free.

Church and state

The conversion of England to Christianity was spearheaded by the conversion of kings. The emergence of kingdoms and the conversion to Christianity were intricately connected in a way that makes it almost impossible to draw a line between secular and religious life in early medieval England. The leading churchmen were all of noble birth, often closely related to the local royal family. Land was given by kings to religious establishments, but the religious establishments were run by close kinsmen of the kings, and to a great extent, certainly in the first centuries of conversion, religious establishments were an integral aspect of royal power and status.

The close ties of loyalty, allegiance and blood between royal houses and religious establishments are evident in the careers of some of the leading Christians, as is the way in which religious houses were viewed as part of the family assets. Benedict Biscop, for example, a leading Northumbrian cleric, served in the *comitatus* (royal warband) of King Oswiu until he was aged around twenty-five, when he received an estate from Oswiu on which to build his monastic house. Benedict's presence in Oswiu's personal household guard indicates that he was at least of noble birth and may well have been related to the royal family. Similarly, the eighth-century King Æthelbert of the South Saxons transferred an estate at Wittering (West Sussex) to a nobleman of his household named Diozsa, to found a religious community. Later, Diozsa transferred the estate (and the job of running the community) to his sister. Religious land and buildings, like any other estate, tended to be kept in the family in this way. Benedict Biscop was at pains to prevent his unsuitable brother from 'inheriting' the monastic community at Wearmouth, but, following normal practice, he found another family member to take on the task, appointing his cousin Eosterwine as abbot to succeed him. The foundation and maintenance of religious houses was in many ways an extension of the careful deployment of resources around the family.

Just as the king drew in taxes, so did the church. The laws of Canute illustrate the welter of tithes due to the church in a year: plough alms fifteen days after Easter, the tithe of young animals at Pentecost, the tithe of the harvest at All Saints, Peter's Pence on St. Peter's Day, church dues by Martinmas and light dues of a halfpenny worth of wax from every hide at Easter eve, at the feast of All Saints and at the Feast of the Purification of St. Mary. Payments were also due to the church for each body buried (*soul scot*).

The extent of the blurring of lines between church and lay society, even at the highest levels, is exemplified by the late Anglo-Saxon will of Bishop Ælfwold of Crediton. His will makes it clear that he was an extremely rich man – his bequests of gold alone came to more than 200 *mancuses* or 25 pounds (11.34 kilograms) in weight. Some of his wealth consisted of artefacts he had already lent to his retainers, particularly religious material such as a cope, mass vestments and a chalice and patten worth nearly 20 *mancuses*. He also bequeathed eight religious books, two tapestries, three seat coverings, a slave, and bed clothes for his chamberlains. All these might seem reasonable wealth and belongings for a high-status ecclesiastic. In addition, however, his will revealed that he had lent horses to the men in his household (who were also to be given 5 pounds in money to divide amongst themselves according to their rank), which he allowed them to keep. He also owned wild horses, thirteen other horses (of which four were to be given to the king, two saddled and two unsaddled), three helmets, eight coats of mail, two tents and a sixty-four oared ship in the harbour.

The status of women

It is easy to miss women in the Anglo-Saxon documentary sources, because Old English writers used the words 'men' and 'he' in a gender-neutral way, though a woman might be specified as a *wifman*, while the male was a *waepman*. Translators of Old English sometimes use 'he' when the writer actually intended to include women as well. A notorious example comes from the medical texts, where the patient appears to be a 'he' right up to the point when 'he' gives birth. Personal names are not necessarily any more helpful. Women's names and men's names can be indistinguishable unless a hint is given by the context.

Elite women played an active role in Anglo-Saxon political and economic life. One aspect of women's independent status in Anglo-Saxon England is indicated by the fact that they were held legally responsible for their own actions, and a married woman was judged independently of her husband. A law of Ine asserted that: 'if anyone steals without the knowledge of his wife and children, he shall pay a fine of 60 shillings.' There is a codicil, however: if his wife and children do know about it, they will all go into slavery. The burden seems to be on the woman to ensure that the family remains honest and free.

Charters and other documents show women arguing for their rights in court. A high-profile case involved a lawsuit between a man called Leofwine and a woman called Wynflæd, who were in dispute over ownership of estates. Wynflæd called no less than twenty-four witnesses to swear oaths on her behalf, of whom thirteen were women, including the Abbess Eadgifu, the Abbess Leofrun, Æthelhild, another Eadgifu and her sister and her daughter and 'many other good thegns and women'. Wynflæd won her case, though she was obliged to give Leofwine back his father's gold and silver. A woman's oath had validity in a court of law. Another celebrated case was heard at a shire meeting at Herefordshire in the early eleventh century, at which both royal and ecclesiastical representatives were present. A man called Edwin brought a charge against his widowed mother for land he claimed was his. After a farcical start – none of those he had brought to represent him knew the details of the case – his mother was called to the meeting. She, the record says, asserted that she had no land that belonged to him, then became very angry, and in front of the assembled meeting, she announced that she willed all her land and goods to her kinswoman Leofflæd and nothing at all to her son, calling on all those present to witness her will. Leofflæd's husband, with the agreement of the meeting, had the will written down in a gospel book of St. Ethelbert's minster. This event illustrates the power of women to act for themselves in a public forum, to have complete charge of their personal affairs and to be able to make an oral will in front of witnesses which was considered to be binding.

Women of substance wrote (or had written for them, in the case of Edwin's mother) wills. The large number of women's wills could be indicative of their status and wealth, but it might also hint at an underlying insecurity in their position. By having their wills written down, they offered their inheritors some protection against avaricious male kinsmen. Surviving wills suggest that daughters inherited equally with sons, and, with few exceptions, there is no preference shown for male as opposed to female heirs. In his will, King Alfred (d.899) noted that his own grandfather had bequeathed money 'on the spear side rather than the spindle side', but he reminded his male relatives that he was free to name who he liked in his own will, male or female. He gave his male relatives the option of acquiring what he had bequeathed to women during their lifetimes, but only if they paid for it.

Women's names crop up with interesting and informative frequency as an element in place names. The Beaga who gave her name to Bibury is not an isolated example. For example, in the seventh century, Bamburgh was given to the Northumbrian queen Bebbe as her morning gift, and took her name. An Eadburg gave her name to Edburton, Sussex; a Deorlufu gave her name to Darlton, Nottinghamshire; a Wulfgifu gave her name to Wollaton, Devon; an Æthelflæd gave her name to Elton, Berkshire; and in AD 985, Wulfrun received the town which took her name and became Wolverhampton. Other women's names are linked to fords (Eadburg of Aberford), bridges and ways. Women also gave their names to churches. Some of these were known saintly women, such as Pega, the sister of St. Guthlac, whose name is commemorated in Peakirk, Cambridgeshire. Others may have been patrons or founders of churches, such as the Ælfgifu who gave her name to Alvechurch. What all these names demonstrate is that women of status in Anglo-Saxon England owned manors and played an active administrative role, just like their male counterparts, in local society. Perhaps, not all women carried out their civic responsibilities with equal ability: a late charter refers to a woman called Leoflæd, who lost estates in Warwickshire because of her incompetence. Marriage did not automatically result in a woman giving up her responsibilities, because a wealthy married woman would own her own estates and be responsible for the administration of them. Some husbands were also happy to hand decision making to their partners. A man called Osulf and his wife Leofrun wanted to give money to the church at Bury St Edmunds to allow four priests to sing twelve masses a week: Osulf left the choice of priest to his wife and the abbot.

Further down the social scale, women of *ceorl* ('churl') class and above were responsible for the management of their households. Law codes state that women had special boxes or cupboards in the house to which they alone had access. The will of Wulfwaru included a grant of a 'good chest, well decorated' to her women in common, perhaps for them to sell and share the profits, or perhaps the chest was valuable in its own right and was to be used to brighten up shared women's quarters? There is evidence of chests and other containers from Anglo-Saxon burial contexts, though both men and women were buried with boxes and containers of one sort or another. Sets of keys, however, were part of a wealthy woman's burial costume. Like male weaponry, keys may be symbolic of status, rather than functional, but locks are known from Anglo-Saxon settlements, and it is not unreasonable to suppose that the keys found in burial contexts locked the kinds of boxes described in law codes to which only their female owners, and not their husbands, were considered to have access (Figure 11).

The role of a queen in early medieval England was not always easy. 'Maxims I', from the *Exeter Book*, stated that the queen, like her husband, must be generous. His duty was to excel in warlike arts, and she must 'excel as one cherished among her people, and be buoyant of mood, keep confidences, be open-heartedly generous with horses and with treasures; in deliberation over the mead, in the presence of the troop of companions, she must always and everywhere greet first the chief of those princes and instantly offer the cup to her lord's hand, and she must know what is prudent for them both as rulers of the hall'. Except for participating in battle, what is striking here is the extent to which the queen and king shared duties and power. The queen was expected to have personal wealth, separate from that of the king, and to give gifts out of this treasure (with all the access to power that the gift of wealth

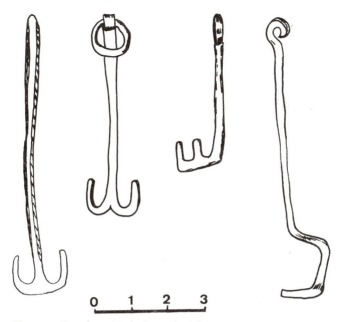

Figure 11 Keys from Anglo-Saxon burial contexts.

implied in the Anglo-Saxon world), and the comment that she was
to 'know what is prudent for them both' implies that she was expected
to have some input in terms of offering counsel and advice.

The literary picture of a queen is supported by a number of historical
figures. Pre-eminent amongst Anglo-Saxon queens must be the
late-eighth-century Cnyethryth, the wife of King Offa, and the only
Anglo-Saxon woman to have had a coinage issued in her name. Alcuin,
an internationally respected Anglo-Saxon scholar and cleric who acted
as advisor to King Charlemagne, described her as the 'controller of the
royal household', and often asked his greetings to be conveyed to her
in letters he sent to her husband and visitors. He also recommended that
Offa's son, Ecgfrith, learn piety from her. That her relationship with
her husband was an equal partnership is indicated by the fact that
Pope Hadrian I named both of them jointly in a privilege he granted.
Cynethryth's name also frequently appears as a witness on charters
issued by her husband.

Æthelflæd, 'Lady of the Mercians' (d.918) and daughter of King
Alfred, was a resourceful and active partner to her husband, Ethelred,
and when he died in AD 911, she continued to rule Mercia, though her
brother Edward managed to take London and Oxford from her. That she

continued to control Mercia with great effectiveness after her husband's death at a time of Viking threat and instability is evidence of her own ability, but also reflects the support she had as a leader from the Mercians and the respect of her brother. It was only after her death that Edward moved in and swiftly took control of Mercia. Though queens rarely ruled in their own names, and then only after the deaths of a ruling spouse, Æthelflæd is not the only Anglo-Saxon case. The *Anglo-Saxon Chronicle* remarks laconically for the year AD 672 that 'King Cenwalh passed away, and Seaxburg his queen reigned for one year after him.'

Some queens came to prominence only after the death of their husbands. Queen Eadgifu (d. c.966/967) does not have much presence in the documentary sources relating to the reigns of her husband, Edward the Elder, and her stepson, Æthelstan, but with the accession of her sons, first Edmund and then Eadred, she became more important. While her age, experience and relationship to Edmund and Eadred may have played a part in her rise to prominence, her economic status – she owned significant lands, especially in Kent, which she may have even ruled on behalf of her sons – also made her independently useful to the crown. Queens, like any other subject, could find their fortunes taken away from them by an aggressive king: following the death of Eadred in AD 955, there was a vicious struggle for power between Eadgifu's grandsons. The first to succeed was Eadwig, who removed all Eadgifu's lands, but they were later restored by the accession of another grandson, Edgar, to the throne of Wessex in 959. By this time, she was in her sixties and had almost retired to a monastery, but her political influence was still such that her appearance at the celebration of her great-grandson, Edgar's second son, in AD 966, helped to buttress the royal family at a time of potential division and further aggression.

There is no doubt that the literary picture of a royal daughter as a helpless and passive pawn, a prize to seal a contract between kingdoms, had a measure of truth. Eadgifu's life illustrates the way in which a queen's position was closely linked to the status of her male relatives, but her own personal wealth and behaviour could act as a buffer to give her a measure of independent power and choice. One woman who exemplified the ability of a clever and politically astute woman to use her resources to best advantage was Edith (also known as Eadgyth), born between 1020 and 1030 and died on 19 December 1075. She was the daughter of the powerful Godwine of Wessex. Her life could read as a tragedy worthy of *Beowulf*. Her father murdered her husband's brother. Her brothers,

Tostig and Harold, became implacable enemies, and it was Tostig's treachery in harassing England and siding with Harald Hardrada in an attempt on the throne of England which led to the Battle of Stamford Bridge. Tostig was killed in this battle; Edith's other brothers Harold, Leofwine and Gyrth were killed at the Battle of Hastings. Edith herself, however, managed her affairs with canniness and skill. Her marriage to King Edward the Confessor was arranged by her father and was almost certainly a matter of political expediency. It is unlikely that Edward cared much for her, and when Godwine and his sons were outlawed in 1051, Edward attempted to divorce her. She was brought back to court when Earl Godwine was reinstated. Their marriage was childless. All this could have been very difficult and dangerous, but Edith herself encouraged the idea that she and Edward had lived in saintly chastity in the *Life* of St. Edward, which she commissioned. When William the Conqueror took the throne of England, many of the leading Anglo-Saxon landholders quickly found themselves dispossessed, but not Edith. At the time of the Norman Conquest, she was the fourth largest landholder in the country, owning tracts of land in the north-east Midlands and the Welsh borders, and her patronage and compliance were vital to legitimise William's rule and ensure a united England.

It is clear from historical sources that royal women had to chart a difficult course. Their marriages were a matter of political importance: a marriage negotiated between royal families was often an extension of a political negotiation, either for peace or to re-establish overlordship and ties of allegiance and tribute between unequal powers. An unwise marriage could bring trouble or allow opposing groups an excuse to claim a throne: Anglian royal families were adept at using marriages between their princesses and neighbouring tribes, particularly the Picts, to argue for the rights of an Anglian claimant to a neighbouring throne. Given the possible threat to family resources and stability posed by the marriage of a woman, a safe alternative was to move royal princesses into religious houses, where they would be out of reach of any ambitious noble hoping to turn a royal liaison to their advantage. This may explain the burgeoning of nunneries in the years immediately following the conversion to Christianity. For example, over thirty royal nunneries were recorded before the death of Bede in 735.

Placing a royal princess in a nunnery, however, should not necessarily be viewed as detrimental to the woman. For many Anglo-Saxon royal princesses, monastic life gave them freedom from the often fatal consequences of being a political pawn, whilst allowing them security and significant levels of political power. The *Life* of St. Hilda (d.680) of Whitby offers an important case in point. She was the daughter of Hereric, a nephew of King Edwin. All Bede revealed about Hereric is that he was poisoned while in exile. Hilda's sister had married and her son Eadwulf became king of East Anglia before entering a Continental monastery. We know nothing of Hilda's life until the age of thirty-three, but at this age, some personal or political change saw her enter monastic life as well. She was persuaded to become founding abbess of a double monastery at Whitby – she was a woman in charge of a religious house of men and women, a house which became a centre of learning and influence. Hers was not an isolated case. Amongst the many senior female abbesses, Cuthburg of Wimborne and St. Æthelthryth of Ely also stand out as leading religious and political figures of their day. Ninth-century abbesses took their place in the religious hierarchy too. Abbess Cwenthryth, daughter of King Cenwulf of Mercia, for example, is known for her tenacious fight to hold her ecclesiastical lands against Archbishop Wulfred of Canterbury.

The attacks of the Vikings and the tenth-century monastic reforms, strongly influenced by Continental practice, both undermined the position of women in the church. By the tenth century, the days of the powerful abbesses were over, though women continued to play an important role as patrons of the church. In many ways, the Anglo-Saxon period was a halcyon period for women. Their economic independence from their husbands was guaranteed, they took their place in law courts and business and the aristocratic woman could wield tremendous power, both in secular and in religious life. It is symptomatic of the changing attitude towards women that Queen Cynethryth, who throughout her life was much respected, who was valued as a connection by Alcuin, who founded and supported a range of religious houses and who retired from secular life after her husband's death to run a monastery at Cookham, Berkshire, was known as the 'wicked Quendrida' to post-Conquest writers.

Chapter 3

Housing and Households

Archaeology provides the best insight into social organisation in the
early Anglo-Saxon period, and this chapter will start by looking at the
evidence for the earliest houses and farmsteads of the Anglo-Saxon
settlers, taking into account the use of buildings, the organisation
of domestic space, the location of boundaries and the way in which the
archaeological evidence shows the development of a more hierarchical
society in the seventh century. In the seventh century, *wics* or proto-
towns were built, followed by true 'urban' centres in the wake of the
Viking upheavals. Archaeological evidence also gives a dramatic
picture of social organisation in Anglo-Saxon towns, with planned
streets and building plots, centrally organised infrastructure, including
drains and metalled roads, and tightly packed buildings with spaces
for craft activities, sleeping and rubbish dumping. Documentary sources
round out this picture, illustrating the ways in which the development
of urbanisation challenged a kinship-based society, while sources such
as wills add detail to the minutiae of Anglo-Saxon material culture and
values, as well as providing insight into the way families were structured
and organised.

Early Anglo-Saxon rural settlement

The transition from the late Romano-British period to the Anglo-Saxon
period was marked by a clear change in the use of materials for buildings.
Tile, stone, brick and glass had been used in the fourth century, but
in late-fifth-century Anglo-Saxon England, these building materials
had been abandoned in favour of wood, thatch, earth and turf. These
construction materials do not survive well over the centuries, and
Anglo-Saxon buildings are relatively difficult to spot in archaeological
contexts. The first type of Anglo-Saxon building to be recognised
by archaeologists was the sunken-featured building (SFB) (also variously
termed *grübenhauser*, grubhut and sunken-floored building), a structure
consisting of a pit with two, four or six post holes at its periphery, which
supported a tent-shaped roof. There has been a debate over whether the

floor of the pit was the floor of the building, or whether a plank floor was suspended over the pit, and evidence for both uses has been found.

SFBs have played an important part in shaping a long-running misconception of Anglo-Saxon daily life. Early Anglo-Saxon people and artefacts in England had been identified through the cemetery archaeology by the seventeenth century, but the location of their associated settlements remained a mystery, even though an Anglo-Saxon hut was excavated (but not recognised as Anglo-Saxon) in Oxfordshire in 1857. At last, in the 1920s, the Oxford archaeologist Edward Thurlow Leeds, excavating at the site of Sutton Courtenay, then in the county of Berkshire, realised that the clay doughnut-shaped objects he was finding in his excavations (now known to be loom weights), belonged to early Anglo-Saxon culture, and that the pits in which he was finding them represented the floors of Anglo-Saxon huts. SFBs were relatively easy to identify on the ground by the excavation methods of the day, once Leeds had pointed out their characteristics and published his excavations, and for some time afterwards, SFBs were the only recognised sign of early Anglo-Saxon occupation. The soil filling the sunken floor of Anglo-Saxon huts could be rich in artefacts – not the brooches, swords and gold associated with the burials of this period, but domestic 'rubbish', such as animal bones, broken pottery, loom weights, fragments of bone combs and pins, slag from metalworking and other debris from domestic activities. Because archaeologists had failed to identify any other form of dwelling, it was assumed that these cramped, rubbish-strewn, semi-underground, windowless dwellings represented the living quarters of the pagan Anglo-Saxons – a stark contrast to the well-constructed villas that the Romano-British had lived in before the Anglo-Saxon invasion. The contrast between the elegant, civilised, native Britons and the uncouth foreigners who had supplanted them seemed to be particularly obvious at sites such as Eccles, Kent, where Anglo-Saxon SFBs were found in close proximity to a ruined Roman villa, while the villa was being used by the newcomers as a place to bury their dead.

Leeds described the dwellings he had found as 'cabins' and described their use in uncomplimentary terms: 'In such cabins, with bare headroom, amid a filthy litter of broken bones, of food and shattered pottery, with logs or planks raised on stones for their seats or couches lived the Anglo-Saxons.' As late as 1948, a survey of British monuments by the Council for British Archaeology described the early Anglo-Saxon 'invaders' as living 'in a culturally primitive condition – their habitations were so wretchedly flimsy – a rectangular scraping in the ground with wattle halls and thatched roof seems to have been the limit of their known architectural competence'. This uncomplimentary, but powerful, image of Anglo-Saxon daily domestic life is still embedded in much general writing about the period, though advances in archaeological understanding of settlement sites supply a very different picture. From the first discovery of SFBs, archaeologists were uneasy at the apparent disparity between the documentary evidence describing much grander residences, the wealth, splendour, technical expertise and the cultural sophistication evident in the contemporary burial archaeology, particularly from sites such as the seventh-century princely barrow burials at Taplow and Mound 1, Sutton Hoo, and the evidence for Anglo-Saxon settlement from the ground. Several Old English sources described great timber-framed halls, such as *Heorot*, described in *Beowulf*: 'the hall rose up high and wide between the gables'. Perhaps *Heorot* was described with poetic license, but the eighth-century historian Bede used an image of a hall to evoke the spiritual ignorance of the pagans. For a pagan, life was like the passage of a bird out of a storm, into the warmth of a hall, and then back out into the darkness again, not knowing where it had come from or where it was going to. This story had to conjure up a familiar scene to the book's listeners if it was going to offer an effective image, yet the SFBs found in archaeological records could not possibly match the description of Bede's hall.

The problem with Anglo-Saxon timber-built halls is that, substantial though the buildings may have been above ground, rising to two storeys in some cases, their archaeological footprint consisted of only ephemeral post holes or plank trenches, which were easily missed with the excavation techniques employed by Leeds. It was only when large areas of topsoil were cleared from a sizeable area ('open-area excavation') that it was possible to 'join the dots' and appreciate the scale and size of the timber-framed structures which seem to have been the main houses of the Anglo-Saxons. These substantial wooden buildings could be up to 82 feet (25 metres) in length, with opposing, centrally placed doors on the longest walls, and aisles created by structural supporting pillars.

A second reason why the earliest Anglo-Saxon settlements escaped observation was that Anglo-Saxon settlements of the fifth to the seventh century lacked any form of boundary or perimeter, rarely had fences

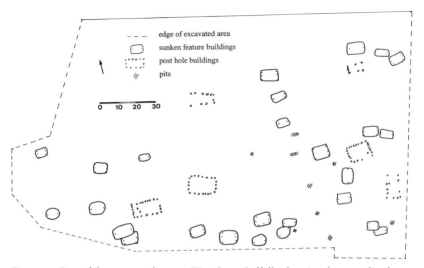

Figure 12 Part of the excavated area at West Stow, Suffolk, showing the sprawling layout of huts, buildings and halls.

separating the different buildings, and the buildings, when they fell into disrepair, were simply abandoned and a new one erected where there was space. The effect of this was that Anglo-Saxon settlements seem to 'wander' across the landscape. At Yarnton, Oxfordshire, for example, the earliest Anglo-Saxon settlement is a considerable distance away from the modern village that it evolved into. At Mucking, Essex, Professor Helena Hamerow's important analysis of pottery sherds from the site was able to demonstrate that the settlement had effectively relocated several times over the course of its use, with only eight to ten post-built buildings and fourteen SFBs standing at any one time. Mucking offers a very rare example of a site where both a settlement and its associated cemetery have been excavated, which allowed Professor Hamerow to calculate that each post-built house would have been home to about six individuals. In other words, though the total number of buildings on an excavated Anglo-Saxon site may be large, the settlement as a whole consisted of only two or three families living in a large farmstead made up of post-built buildings and some satellite SFBs. The picture at Mucking was corroborated by the evidence at West Stow, Suffolk, where, again, the chronological evidence offered by the pottery and metalwork suggested that, for the period of its use, the settlement consisted of three timber-framed buildings supported by about six SFBs each (Figure 12).

There still remains the problem of the purpose of the SFBs. Many of the excavated hollows are filled with what appears to be domestic waste. The four-post SFB 16 at West Stow contained two dog carcases as well as a spindle whorl, fragments of pottery, some glass beads and a comb. Several SFBs at West Stow contained hearths. Other huts at the site, however, add consolidating evidence to the growing picture that SFBs were 'workshops' for productive activities such as weaving, pottery making and smithing, rather than living quarters. SFB 15 at West Stow, for example, was filled with a row of loom weights which appeared to have fallen to the floor along with the shelf on which they were stacked when the hut wall collapsed, while SFB 36 contains a scattering of loom weights, spindle whorls and bone needles associated with textile manufacture. At other sites, such as Packenham, Norfolk, similar rows of loom weights have been found on the floor, where they had dropped from an abandoned vertical loom.

Though modern interpretations about Anglo-Saxon living conditions have had to be revised, placing daily life in large, comfortable, above-ground wooden houses, rather than in semi-subterranean squalor, the question of how so much debris – including animal carcasses – came to fill the pits of the SFBs is still open to debate. At West Stow, some of the SFBs showed evidence for floors, so it is possible that rubbish simply dropped through gaps in the timber flooring. According to this hypothesis, the pits beneath the floor served to prevent the floors from rotting by contact with the damp soil. Alternatively, it has been suggested that the pits served as useful cellars for storage. Again, it is possible that, when the SFBs became dilapidated and were abandoned, their pits provided a handy place to throw domestic rubbish. All these possibilities may have been true for different settlements at different times, but a very recent review of settlement debris has offered a further explanation, which will be discussed later in chapter 4.

Middle Anglo-Saxon rural settlement

Although SFBs and post-built buildings continued to be a feature of Anglo-Saxon settlement to the end of the Anglo-Saxon period, the seventh century saw a change in building style, settlement layout and organisation, probably linked to changes in Anglo-Saxon social structure, and reflecting a more hierarchical society, with the rise of a princely 'elite', the growth of Anglo-Saxon kingdoms, an expansion of communities and probable growth in population. This social change is reflected in sites such as Cowdery's Down, Hampshire, in use from the sixth to the eighth century. Here, excavations have provided evidence for complex timber buildings up to 28 feet (8.5 metres) wide and 72.2 feet (22 metres) long, some with external buttressing to support a high roof or even two storeys. At Cowdery's Down, too, there is evidence for more careful alignment of buildings and signs of fencing around some of the houses.

This period also saw the development of elite 'palace' sites, such as Yeavering, Northumbria, or Cheddar, Somerset, with substantial timber buildings providing space for ritual and royal activity. The most substantial structure at seventh-century Yeavering was a building measuring 82 feet (25 metres) by 39.37 feet (12 metres) made of enormous timbers set into foundation pits 6.6 feet (2 metres) deep.

Also associated with the rise of kingship was the development in the seventh century of *wic* settlements; proto-town sites with dense populations. The first of these to be recognised through excavation was the place recorded in Old English documents as 'Hamwic', south of the modern Southampton. It was laid out in about AD 700 on a new site as a planned settlement with a grid-like pattern of streets covering about 111.2 acres (45 hectares). Buildings on the site were timber framed with wattle-and-daub walls, and people living here were engaged in craft, trade and production.

Hamwic, like counterpart settlements at Gypeswic (Ipswich, Suffolk), Lundenwic (the Aldwych, London) and Eoferwic (York), was badly affected by the violent Viking incursions. The majority of *wic* sites declined into the ninth century: Hamwic was largely depopulated by AD 900, as trade and production moved behind the walls of *burhs* (planned towns).

Urban houses
Some time during the Viking settlement at York, in the early tenth century, the area of the city known as Coppergate was parcelled up into small tenements, marked by straight fences running at right angles to the street. The boundaries of these plots of land were retained for the next 1,000 years – it was only when some properties were amalgamated in the nineteenth century, and the site was cleared in the 1970s, that the Viking Age property boundaries were lost – though the outer boundaries still mark the edge of the modern development.

The new houses within these boundaries almost certainly fronted onto the street (the tenth-century street front lies under modern Coppergate Street and could not be excavated). They were constructed of vertical posts, round which withies (strong, flexible branches) had been woven to make walls. The buildings measured 14.46 feet (4.4 metres) in width and an estimated 22.31 feet (6.8 metres) in length. Though their construction was relatively strong, they were vulnerable to fire. The charred remains of posts bear witness to a number of devastating fires which swept through the tenements. Besides being rebuilt after fires, the tenements' walls were repaired regularly as they rotted and decayed. They had central hearths and earthen floors. Other internal features included large pits. When excavated, they were full of rubbish, but these deposits may belong to a period after the abandonment of the houses. When the houses were being used, these pits may have served as a store, with planks over, though there is no archaeological trace of such structures. The buildings also appear to have had benches running along either side of the long walls, a construction typical of Viking houses. The quantity of debris from manufacturing processes at this site, particularly iron working and smithing and leather working, is a caution that these buildings may not have been only, or even, dwellings. It is possible that they were used as shops fronting onto the street, with workshop areas to the rear of the properties, but the presence of quernstones for grinding grain and the range of broken cooking pots from the site suggests that domestic activities were also carried out in these spaces.

By the late tenth century, new buildings with semi-basements were constructed within the same plots at Coppergate. One of these had a planked floor, and another had a mat of fine brushwood and willow twigs spread between the walls – a form of wall insulation? There has been some discussion as to whether these structures were semi-subterranean or had cellars. In other urban contexts, such as Oxford, late Anglo-Saxon buildings with cellars have been excavated, showing that pressures on space familiar in later medieval urban contexts also existed in Anglo-Saxon towns. At the later phase of Coppergate's use, dwellings were associated with more high-status manufacturing industries than before: one of the plots was used by a jeweller, whose waste fragments of amber and jet were found in the excavations. The neighbouring house was used to produce wooden cups, and it is possible that this industry may have given the street its name, because the 'gate' element is derived from the Old Norse *gata*, meaning street, while the 'copper' element, rather than deriving from 'copper' as one might expect, actually derives from the Old Norse *coppr*, meaning 'a cup', according to place-name experts. Coppergate is 'cup-makers street'.

Late Anglo-Saxon rural settlement

Though the tenth century saw the rise of urbanism in Anglo-Saxon England, the majority of the population continued to live rural, agricultural lives. In the countryside, though, from the late Saxon period, settlement was clustered around nucleated sites – the forerunners of modern villages – in contrast to the dispersed settlement of the earlier period. The processes that led to the nucleation of villages in Anglo-Saxon England are still not fully understood, though they are linked to changes in agricultural practice and technology, changes in patterns of landholding amongst the elite, the rise of the manorial system and the growth of parishes. Excavations at sites such as Wharram Percy, Yorkshire, show the continuation of post-hole structures as the main dwellings, with household plots marked out and houses laid out according to a regular plan. At the other end of the social spectrum, excavations at Goltho, Lincolnshire, have revealed the plans of a defended late Saxon thegnly residence.

Construction materials

Throughout the Anglo-Saxon period, wood was the pre-eminent building material for domestic and secular buildings, as the Old English verb for building – *timbran* – implies. Wood surviving in waterlogged deposits indicates that the chief building material was oak. Stone seems to have been used for building only from the Christian Anglo-Saxon period, exclusively for churches, and even then, it would seem that Anglo-Saxon church builders were more familiar with carpentry techniques than with masonry. Apart from the surviving nave of the church of St Andrew's Greenstead, Essex, which is of stave construction, and whose timbers have been dated from AD 1063 to 1108 at the time of felling, we have no extant examples of Anglo-Saxon wooden buildings. The Anglo-Saxon tower of the church at Earl's Barton, Northamptonshire, was constructed to look like a timber-framed building and gives us some clue as to how ornate high-status, late Anglo-Saxon timber buildings may have been.

The earliest Anglo-Saxon stone buildings either reused existing Roman buildings, such as the churches of Reculver, Kent (AD 669), or Bradwell-on-Sea, Essex (AD 653–664), or incorporated some of the Roman building material (*spolia*) left lying in the landscape. The seventh-century Anglo-Saxon church at Hexham, Northumberland, used material robbed from the Roman town of *Coria* (Corbridge) some 4 miles (6.44 kilometres) away, and the imposing aisled church at Brixworth (probably dating to the mid- or late eighth century) drew on a wide range of sources, some a considerable distance away, for its Roman building material, including Roman Leicester.

Not until the tenth century, it would seem, did Anglo-Saxons start quarrying stone for building purposes. However, the workmanship at Anglo-Saxon churches suggests that Anglo-Saxon masons were skilled in stonework and that Roman buildings were not being robbed simply because they offered an easy and accessible source of building material. In the crypt at Hexham, for example, smaller, more manageable Roman building material was overlooked in favour of enormous building blocks, each weighing over a ton. Massive pieces of decorative stonework were also incorporated into the building plan, including altars, relief carvings and a massive tombstone. The intention here, as in other church buildings, may have been to deliberately associate the new Anglo-Saxon church with Rome and Rome's Christian past.

In addition to *timbriend*, a builder, other Old English words hint at other building-related crafts. A tile maker was a *tigelwyrhta*, but such a craftsman was likely to have worked within an ecclesiastical setting. Average Anglo-Saxon houses were more likely to have had turf or thatch roofs; walls would have been made of timber planking, earth or wattle and daub.

Lighting

Though there were apertures to let light in and smoke out, the majority of Anglo-Saxon houses did not have windows, and window glass was unknown until introduced into ecclesiastical buildings after the conversion to Christianity. The Bayeux Tapestry, made after the Norman Conquest, probably by Anglo-Saxon embroiderers, illustrates several different types of the late Anglo-Saxon house. The smallest – the ones looted by the invading Normans as the army foraged for food, and so possibly representing the dwellings of lower status farmers – are conspicuously lacking in windows, compared to the highest-status building with its tower, imposing door and staircase (Figure 13).

The art of glass window making seems to have been introduced to Anglo-Saxon England in the seventh century, when Benedict Biscop of Northumbria invited glaziers from Gaul to provide windows for his new monasteries at Monkwearmouth in AD 674 and Jarrow in AD 681. Even when churches had windows with glass, windows were almost certainly a rarity in normal domestic dwellings. A hint as to the rarity of windows is that the Old English word for them, *fenester*, is derived from Latin; they were not part of everyday life.

Artificial lighting, too, was generally restricted to the elite, though an iron tripod bowl, possibly part of a beeswax lamp, has been excavated at the early Anglo-Saxon site of West Stow, Suffolk. High-status, seventh-century burials from Sutton Hoo, Prittleswell, and Broomfield, Essex, had candle holders filled with beeswax, an expensive commodity, and

Figure 13 Anglo-Saxon houses in the Bayeux Tapestry.

a late Anglo-Saxon list of requirements for a church includes reference to *leohtfæt, blacern, cyllan* and *sapbox* [lanterns, lamps, censers and resin boxes]. The quantities of candles and beeswax consumed by a church cost so much that, by the late Anglo-Saxon period, the 'scot' or tax to a church included *leoht-gescot* [light tax].

The difficulty of bringing light into an Anglo-Saxon house may explain the general preference for buildings aligned on an east–west axis. Entrances were centrally placed on the south and north sides, allowing direct light to shine into the interiors for the longest possible stretch of the day.

Organisation of internal space

Perhaps the most fascinating aspect of early Anglo-Saxon settlements is that they were distinctively different, in terms of structure and organisation, from the settlements on the Continent which the earliest Anglo-Saxons migrated from. On the Continent, the typical *terpen* settlements of the North Atlantic seaboard show densely built longhouses with byres, carefully organised along pathways, with dividing boundary fences, and usually with one prestige building amongst the rest. These buildings had opposing entrances at the centre of the longest wall, with human habitation to one side of the entrance and byres at the other – humans and cattle were living under the same roof. But the number of byres associated with a building was not simply functional; it was also symbolic of status, for in many cases, scientific analysis of the soil in the byres has shown that no animals were ever stalled in there. Given the symbolic status of byres, then, it seems very odd that this building style, and the layouts of settlements, seems to have altered the moment the Germanic settlers came to England. However, the new Anglo-Saxon building style was equally not borrowed from the native Romano-British, although there is an argument that some Romano-British building techniques were adopted, or adapted, by the Anglo-Saxon migrants. The new layout of houses suggests that the Germanic migrants to the south coast of England lived a different kind of life than the inhabitants of the Continental *terpen*.

The lack of fences or boundary ditches associated with fifth- to early-seventh-century Anglo-Saxon settlements is a particular feature of settlement layout at this time across the country, as is the relative similarity of all the timber-built structures associated with the settlements. As far as the archaeological evidence goes, there appears to be no 'hierarchy' of settlements at this early phase of Anglo-Saxon culture. No fifth- to early-seventh-century settlements appear to be grander or have had more effort expended on them than others, and no single dwelling within any one settlement appears to be more important than the others. There is no fence marking out a 'special' building, and no controlling force organising the location of new buildings. This appears to be in direct contrast with the cemetery evidence, where the range of grave goods associated with different bodies, from the very rich weaponed male or jewelled female to the graves without any associated finds at all, suggests a much more hierarchical society. One explanation for the evidence may be that the settlements represent the farmsteads of one or two families, probably working closely together, almost certainly connected to each other by bonds of kinship, and probably with equal status, while the burial ritual reflects the status of the individual within the family or kin group. Some corroborative evidence for this explanation comes from cemetery sites where skeletal preservation has been good, and it has been possible to identify genetic anomalies, or distinct hereditary conditions, within the burial population. At Berinsfield, Oxfordshire, for example, a number of skeletons exhibited a small range of distinctive and relatively unusual genetic characteristics. It is possible to use this evidence to hypothesise family links between different graves in the cemetery, although this kind of study is in its infancy and more sophisticated analysis is required.

Anglo-Saxon SFBs were no more than unpartitioned, single-roomed spaces, but some of the larger post-built structures may have been partitioned into separate chambers. At Mucking, Essex, the largest post-built structure, measuring 41.34 feet (12.6 metres) by 22.31 feet (6.8 metres), had a partition across the eastern end, creating a separate chamber, with an eastern doorway for access, and a number of the smaller buildings also showed signs of an eastern chamber and third doorway.

Further discussion on the organisation of early Anglo-Saxon timber-framed buildings is exceptionally difficult; at Mucking, for example, none of the post-built structures provided evidence for a hearth or any other internal partitions or division of spaces beyond the eastern chambers mentioned above. SFBs offer barely more information; several had hearths, usually positioned in the centre of the building.

Late Old English documents suggest that, as well as using walls, people separated areas within houses with curtains. By the late Saxon period, separate areas for separate activities were more clearly defined, at least amongst the elite. The thegnly residence at Goltho, Lincolnshire, boasted a hall, bower, kitchen and weaving shed within a banked and ditched enclosure, with a probable gatehouse to control entry. This picture coincides with an entry in the Old English document called *Gethyncthu*, which stated that, to achieve the rank of *thegn*, a man's dwelling had to have a kitchen, a bell and a *burhgeat* or gate to his enclosed residence.

Household furniture and equipment

The household furniture and equipment, such as beds, which would have surrounded the early Anglo-Saxons in their lives is best known from their cemeteries, rather than from their settlements. Women have been found buried on their beds at the seventh-century sites of Swallowcliffe Down, Wiltshire, and Edix Hill, Cambridgeshire, for example; the beds consisted of wooden frames held together with cleats. Evidence from a complex wooden bed on which a seventh-century woman lay at Coddingham, Suffolk, suggests that her bed had an angled wooden headboard decorated with iron straps and carving. Elite beds would have been sumptuously dressed and decorated with linen and embroidered coverings; in the later Anglo-Saxon period, a rich woman called Wynflæd left property including 'a set of bed-clothes, all that is needed for one bed' to her grandson and 'her best bed curtain and linen cover and all the bed clothes which belong to it' to her granddaughter. Bed curtains were primarily for privacy, rather than to keep out draughts. One Old English word for bed curtain was *hopscyte*, the *hop* element means 'secret' or 'hidden' (as in the place names Hopwas [hidden place that floods] or Hope [Cove], Devon). Not all bedding was so luxurious or comfortable; in the eighth century, Boniface sent Hwætberht, abbot of Monkwearmouth–Jarrow, goat's hair bed clothes as a gift.

Wills of other wealthy women describe table linen, wall hangings and cushions or seat covers. At Prittlewell, Essex, the seventh-century elite-male burial included a type of folding chair often depicted in Continental and Anglo-Saxon manuscript illustrations, but never before found as an artefact. A stone carved chair in the church at Beverley gives some indication as to the shape of an ecclesiastical seat in the eighth century, but seating in the hall would normally have been on benches. *Beowulf* describes the way in which, after the feast, the benches were cleared to the sides of the hall to allow Beowulf and his companions to sleep, while King Hrothgar and his wife retired to a separate sleeping area.

Graves supply evidence for the boxes and chests in which household and personal goods would have been kept, as well as for the keys and barrel locks which would have secured personal possessions.

Family structure

Though it is possible to argue that each early Anglo-Saxon settlement consisted of an extended kin group, or, failing that, two or three families of equal status co-operating together in their use of the settlement area, this does not help us to work out the dynamics of the Anglo-Saxon family – was there a nuclear family or did families live together in extended kin groups? Did each timber-built house support one family or were dwellings divided according to gender or age groups? The archaeological evidence is too ephemeral to give any clear picture.

At one time, it was assumed that place names in which the suffix *-ingas* (the people of) was added to a personal name, giving rise to place names such as Reading, Berkshire (followers of Read), or Hastings, Sussex (followers of Haesta), represented the earliest Anglo-Saxon settlers in England, but this assumption has been categorically rejected by place-name experts since the 1960s, so the names of the earliest families who lived in the excavated settlements cannot be hypothesised from this evidence.

To reconstruct the Anglo-Saxon family and household structure, it is necessary to look at later documentary sources, which may also give partial insight into daily family life before the conversion to Christianity. What the documentary sources make clear is that the nuclear family – a mother, father and children – was the core unit of Anglo-Saxon society. Within the law codes, for example, a man's *hired* or household was synonymous with his wife and children, rather than including any wider kin group, and the 'kinless man' referred to in law codes and in poetry was one without close family, rather than one without any relatives at all. Parents held the prime responsibility for nurturing their children, and that this was perceived as being ordinarily a duty of love and affection is illustrated by the late Old English poem 'The Fates of Man', which insists that 'a man and a woman bring a child into the world, and dress him and train him and teach him', though the bitter point to the poem is that, after all their care to 'guide his footsteps and provide for him and clothe him', no parent can prepare for what will happen to their child when it has grown and leads an independent life. There is little doubt that Anglo-Saxon children were, normally, valued, loved and wanted by both their parents, not least by the literary assumption that parents would be devastated if their children pre-deceased them: 'what sight is more intolerable that the death of a child before its father's eyes?' asked King Alfred in his ninth-century translation of Gregory's *Pastoral Care*, as he sought to find an image of absolute misery. This poetic picture of loving and cherishing parents is illustrated elsewhere in other documentary sources. In the *Life* of St. Wilfred, a woman brought her dead baby to the saint, hoping to have it baptised, even though it was dead. The saint was not fooled, but, having noticed that the child was dead, baptised it anyway and brought it back to life, insisting that the child should be given to him when it reached five years of age. According to the story, the mother and father attempted to keep the child from the powerful bishop as it grew up, but to no avail; the bishop sent his men to forcibly reclaim the boy from the British community where the parents were hiding. Similar loving desperation was illustrated by the parents of Hwætred, a mad boy who had already killed several people before his mother and father took him to a saint hoping for a miracle. The expectation that parents would cherish and protect their children was so embedded in Anglo-Saxon culture that even monsters were expected to display strong maternal feelings. When the hero Beowulf killed the monster Grendel, his next opponent was Grendel's mother, seeking revenge for the loss of her only son. Nor is she the only parent in the poem for whom life became miserable after the death of a child; later, the poet notes that 'it is a sad thing for an old man to bear if his son should die on the gallows … he sees his son's room with sorrow, an empty hall…'. In reality, however, the normal relationships between family members could sour, as the public disinheritance of Edwin by his mother in favour of one of her kinswomen recorded in an eleventh-century charter illustrates.

At a time when life expectancy must have been relatively short, grandparents (*yldra fæder* and *eald modor*) did not play a prominent role in Anglo-Saxon accounts of family life, though specific words for great-grandparents (þridda fæder and þridde modor) emphasise the importance of genealogy, and being able to state your family lineage within Anglo-Saxon society. More important were the relatives of parents, and the relationship between a man and his sister's son was perceived as being particularly close. Specific Old English words for sisters, brothers, maternal and paternal aunts and uncles, and grandparents suggest the range of kin relationships of interest to an Anglo-Saxon family.

Cordial relationships between brothers and sisters are a particular feature of Anglo-Saxon documentary sources. The sources never draw any particular attention to this family link, perhaps because it seemed unremarkable, and often an underlying close bond between brother-and-sister pairings only emerges by chance, especially in religious contexts. When the nobleman Diozsa formed a religious community, his choice to inherit the community and the role of abbot was his sister. St. Willibald's wide-ranging travels on the Continent and to the holy land are known because they were recorded by his sister, Hugeburh. When the hermit St. Guthlac died, his body was cared for and his funeral arranged for him by his sister Pega, who was also instrumental in establishing his cult. Although Pega makes only the briefest of appearances in the Latin and Old English *Lives* of St. Guthlac, she was a significant religious figure in her own right, and though no documents survive to record her life, the place name Peakirk (Pega's church) indicates her local importance. These examples are all of religious men, whose relationship with their sisters may have been particularly strong because it represented a 'safe' link with a female (though a twelfth-century *Life* of St. Guthlac records that Pega lived with Guthlac on his island retreat until the devil took her form and tempted him, at which point he asked her to leave!). Close ties between brothers, their sisters and their sister's sons appear in references to secular society too. In AD 658, Penda of Mercia drove King Cenwalh of Mercia from his throne and into East Anglia for three years because he had 'forsaken Penda's sister', according to the *Anglo-Saxon Chronicle*. The *Anglo-Saxon Chronicle* also records, for AD 656, that Wulfhere, son of Penda, gave a massive public grant of land and money, free from all tax and rent, to the monastery at Medeshamsted, continuing the work of his deceased brother, Peada. The grant was witnessed, amongst others, by Æthelred, the king's brother, and Cyneburg and Cyneswith, his sisters.

Wealthier households encompassed a wider range of members than immediate family. Fosterage was built into Anglo-Saxon family life, as it was into many early medieval societies. When St. Guthlac's hagiographer wanted to describe the virtues of the saint when he was a boy, he noted that he 'was dutiful to his parents, obedient to his elders, and affectionate to his foster brothers and sisters': fostered children were a standard part of the household of the elite. Guthlac was an ideal child, of course, and the implication is that normal children were rude to their parents and elders and rotten to their foster siblings. Some relationships between foster children and their carers were warm and loving. St. Cuthbert, who was fostered as a child, stayed in touch with his foster mother when he grew up, and one of his first miracles was to save her house from fire. Prince Æthelstan left estates to his foster mother Ælswyth for her *myclon geearnungon* (great merit). Maltreatment of foster children was socially and legally unacceptable, of course, though no doubt it did happen. One law of King Alfred stated that, 'If anyone fosters out his dependants to another, and that person causes the death of the fosterling, then the one who fed it shall clear themselves if anyone accuses them.'

Documentary evidence suggests that children would be fostered at about seven years of age, though this was not fixed. Fosterage, like marriage, involved two kin groups in specific obligations and bonds of duty to each other. By taking in foster children, Guthlac's noble parents were ensuring that the families of the fostered children were tied to them in a bond of loyalty, but the bond was reciprocal. Foster parents were bound to protect and look out for their foster children as they would their own children. Although the act of sending their child away to be fostered might seem callous on the part of parents, in practice it was a way of widening the network of people who had obligations to protect their child in a society where the number of friends and relations who would stand up for them and swear oaths for them was crucial to their well-being and place in the social hierarchy. At a time when life expectancy was short, it also made sense for parents to ensure that, if their child was orphaned, another family cared for their offspring. Fosterage also allowed children to be trained and taught away from their own homes. In addition, the elite would accept the children (both girls and boys) of lower social groups into their homes as a method of ensuring the loyalty of their retainers.

Equally normal to wealthy households were slaves or bond servants. The distinction between slave and the lowest class of free person in Anglo-Saxon society was not particularly well drawn; when the eleventh-century slave woman Wulfflæd was mentioned in her owner's will, it was to say that she was to be freed on the death of her owner, with the proviso that she continued to serve Æthelflæd and Eadgifu. Servants and slaves were perceived as integral and necessary to an elite household in the later Anglo-Saxon period. One late law code attempted to limit the number of retainers a reeve took with him when he travelled; he was to take with him only his smith and his children's nurse. The motivation for this law code may have been to limit the number of mouths the reeve's hosts had to feed – the obligatory entertaining of the king's representative and his household may have been cripplingly expensive on occasions – but it also limited the opportunity for a reeve to travel with a large contingent of potentially threatening household warriors.

Personal names

Within elite households, personal names were usually formed by compounding two elements (such as 'æthel' [noble] and 'flæd' [overflowing, full] to make Æthelflæd, or 'ead' [riches] and 'gifu' [gift, sacrifice] to form Eadgifu) to form a diathemic name. Within elite genealogies, it is noticeable that alliterating diathemic names were created to link generations. Coenwulf (d.821) of Mercia's father was Cuthbert, his grandfather was Bassa and his great-grandfather was Cynreow. Coenwulf's brothers were Cuthred and Ceolwulf, and his children were called Cenelm, Cwenthryth and Burgenhild. This branch of the royal family had strong alliteration in 'C' names, with a secondary alliteration in 'B'. Ceolwulf of Mercia had a daughter, Elfleda, who married Wigmund, son of Wiglaf, and their children's names, Wistan and Eadburga, alliterated with their father's and their mother's names, respectively. The East Saxon dynasty, by contrast, was marked by 'S' alliterations (for example, Saewara, Saethryth and Sigeberht). The Anglo-Saxons did not use surnames, but family connections could be marked by alliterative elements in diathemic names.

It appears that not all the elite had diathemic names: Anna, king of the East Angles, Hild (Hilda) of Whitby and Bede are examples. It is likely, however, that these are abbreviated versions of their original names. Hild's father was Hereric and her sister Hereswith. Bede's name was recorded as 'Beadhere' (*baed* [prayer] and *here* [army]) in a ninth-century copy of the *Durham Confraternity Book*, which also included a copy of parts of Bede's *Life* of St. Cuthbert.

Sometimes a personal name was not enough to distinguish different individuals and by-names were added to, or even replaced, personal names. Bede recalled two Anglo-Saxon priests, both called Hewald, who were distinguished by the colour of their hair: Hewald the black and Hewald the white. He also recounted that Æthelburg, the seventh-century wife of King Edwin of Northumbria, was called 'Tate', meaning 'cheerful'. By the later period, and possibly with the influence of Scandinavian naming patterns, by-names became more common. Sometimes people were distinguished by their occupation, others by personal characteristics. Some were merely descriptive, labelling people as tall (*langa*) or small (*lytla*). Ælfweard Scirlocc ('bright hair') witnessed eleventh-century charters, while other by-names described characteristics, such as Æthelweard *stamera* and Godwine *drefla*, who were a stammerer and a driveller, respectively. The origin of some by-names is opaque, such as those of a late-tenth-century Ethelred Tredwude ('tread wood'), Æthelwine Muf (possibly 'stale') and the untranslatable Ælfhelm Polga. Still others were derogatory: amongst the printable names are the eleventh-century Godric *gupe* ['buttock'], Alestanus *braders* ['broad arse'] and Leofwine *bealluc* ['bollock'].

Chapter 4
Population Density and Life Expectancy

There is no clear way of calculating population density for Anglo-Saxon England. Neither archaeological nor documentary sources are sufficiently reliable. For the early Anglo-Saxon period, the population seems to have been relatively thinner on the ground than in the preceding centuries when England was under Roman rule. Environmental evidence from the Thames Valley, for example, suggests that, while there was continuity of farming practices from the late Roman to the early Anglo-Saxon period, with no dramatic changes in the types of pollen, insects or seeds retrieved from archaeological sampling, there was a reduced level of farming, and some areas formerly used for pasture and arable land returned to scrub, suggesting that the land was farmed less intensively, possibly because it was supporting a smaller population than before. Given that many modern English towns and villages have Anglo-Saxon place names, it seems that, at least by the end of the Anglo-Saxon period, there were small settlements scattered widely across England, but, as discussed in the previous chapter, the archaeological evidence suggests that most of the settlements were small villages or hamlets consisting of only one or two households.

The *Domesday Book*, compiled in the late eleventh century under the orders of William the Conqueror shortly after the Norman Conquest of England, provides a detailed account of the worth of lands before and after the Conquest, and slaves and estate dependants were included in that valuation. It is not a full census, however, and does not include information about religious establishments, nor about the children, wives and others who were not recorded. Estimates of population based on the *Domesday* survey vary between 1.5 million and 2.5 million.

There were a few densely populated centres. By the late Anglo-Saxon period, towns had been established across Anglo-Saxon England, with permanent urban populations at places like Wallingford, York, Oxford and Reading. By the eleventh century, Oxford's population may have numbered several thousands of permanent and seasonal residents, and there was such pressure on space in the thriving market town that the building plots along the town's main streets were narrow, with substantial cellars at the rear of the properties.

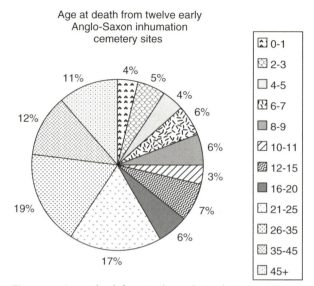

Figure 14 Age at death from twelve early Anglo-Saxon inhumation
cemeteries.

On the basis of the excavated skeletal remains, life expectancy
throughout the Anglo-Saxon period was short: the average Anglo-Saxon
life expectancy was twenty-five to thirty years, though this figure
is not based on complete population evidence. Infants, for example, are
notoriously under-represented in the archaeological record. Of the whole
mortuary population, nearly half the bodies died before their twenty-fifth
birthday. According to the evidence from the cemetery populations,
about 10 percent of those buried in Anglo-Saxon graveyards had
survived (and gained immunity to) childhood illnesses and the perils
of early adulthood – childbearing for women and violence for men –
and continued to live on into their fifties and beyond (Figure 14).

Childhood

There are a number of compound words in Old English which suggest
that 'childhood' was perceived as a special state, with its own attributes.
There were several words for being a child or behaving like a child:
cildhad [childhood]; *cildisc* [childish] and *cildsung* [childishness]; and
geoguðhad [youth] and *geoguðlic* [of youth], which usually referred
to slightly older children. Babies were distinguished from older children

by being referred to as *þa unsprecedlic cild* [the child that cannot speak]. Other words suggest characteristics of being young. Children experienced *geoguðmyrð* [the joy of youth] and were full of *geoguðlust* [youthful energy]. Children also had specific artefacts associated with them. Babies wore *cildcladas* [swaddling] and were rocked in their *cildcradol* or *cildatrog* [cradle], and children born into wealthier families were looked after by their *cildfostre* [nurse].

Late Anglo-Saxon prognostications, or predictions, about a child's future on the basis of its date of birth, show that Anglo-Saxon parents, like modern parents, wanted to know what lay ahead for their children. Law codes, *Lives* of the saints and evidence from the earlier Anglo-Saxon furnished inhumation cemeteries show that boys and girls would pass through several stages on their journey from birth to old age and that these stages were characterised by particular events and activities.

Birth

Pregnancy and childbirth were an inescapable part of most secular Anglo-Saxon women's lives. The dangers of childbirth are graphically illustrated by a number of women's graves which also contain foetal remains. Some of these burials may not represent deaths associated with childbirth, such as the burial of a woman in her fifties from Westgarth Gardens, Suffolk, an early Anglo-Saxon inhumation cemetery, whose grave goods included the poorly preserved remains of a foetus. In other cases, where women of childbearing age have been found with children, it is not possible to be certain that complications during childbirth led to the deaths of mother and baby. The strange early Anglo-Saxon burial of a mother and foetus from Worthy Park, Kingsworthy, Hampshire, however, is beyond dispute. Here, the articulated bones of a baby lie between the mother's legs, and its feet are still enclosed within the pelvic girdle. The buriers were aware of the infant, because they covered its small body with chalk, though they did not remove it from its position, still held by its legs within its mother.

Late Anglo-Saxon medical texts offer a number of remedies to mitigate the impact of childbirth. There are remedies for inability to conceive, for lack of menstruation or to stop menstruation, advice for the pregnant woman and remedies to prevent miscarriage, stillbirth and birth defects. On the whole, Anglo-Saxon medical remedies, particularly those contained within the tenth-century medical text compiled for an Anglo-Saxon doctor named Bald, are prosaic, offering a range of herbal treatments for a variety of ailments. As a rule of thumb, the more impossible it was for an Anglo-Saxon doctor to treat a problem, the more complicated the remedies become. Remedies that might be described as 'superstitious' are actually much less common in Old English medical texts than remedies based on plant medicine, though they have received a disproportionate amount of attention from scholars. It is noticeable that pregnancy and childbirth fall into the category of diseases for which there was no other resort but ritual and superstition. In one Old English text, *Lacnunga*, the pregnant woman is advised to

> go to the grave of a dead man, and step three times over the grave, and say three times: may this be my protection against loathsome late birth, may this be my protection against miserable still birth, may this be my protection against loathsome deformities at birth. Then let the woman go to her sleeping husband and say: up I go, over you I step with live child, not with dying one, with a full-term birth, not with a doomed one. And when the mother feels that her child is alive, let her go to a church and go before the altar and say: I said this chant to Christ.

Typically, a wealthy woman would be attended by a *byrðenu* [midwife] to help her through the birthing process, and the new baby would be washed and swaddled. Although illustrations of Anglo-Saxon babies show them swaddled, it is worth noting that adults wrapped up in bedclothes mirror the style of the swaddled infants, and it may be that the illustrators are merely trying to show a baby wrapped in a blanket, rather than implying the very tight and restrictive swaddling clothes known from the later medieval period.

Infancy

A late Anglo-Saxon text describing Mary looking after the newborn infant Jesus offers us an ideal of Anglo-Saxon mothering: '*heo hine baðode, and beðede, and smerede, and baer, and frefrede, and swaðede, and roccode*' (she bathed him, and cherished him, and put cream on him, and carried him, and swaddled him, and rocked him). In addition to nurturing her newborn child, an Anglo-Saxon mother needed to feed him. There is some evidence that, certainly among the upper classes, a wet nurse might be employed to feed new babies. One unusual artefact from an infant burial at Castledyke, Humberside, is a mammiform vessel with a pierced base. It may be that the infant in this grave was unable to breastfeed for some reason, and this artefact, unique in the Anglo-Saxon record, was made in a desperate attempt to keep the baby alive. Other archaeological evidence for care of sick babies comes from the skeletal evidence of adults who had congenital deformities. At Worthy Park, Hampshire, for example, the early Anglo-Saxon inhumation cemetery contains the skeletal remains of an adult male who was born without his left arm. The fact that he was nurtured as an infant, and survived into adulthood, speaks volumes about the ability of early Anglo-Saxon communities to value their babies and accommodate the disabled.

It is difficult to put a precise date on the age of weaning, though very recent archaeological analysis of chemicals in the bones suggests that full weaning from breast milk may have occurred relatively late, at the age of about two. The baker in Ælfric's tenth-century *Colloquy* was proud to note that an infant would be weaned from milk to his finest bread.

Child rearing is an intimate, familial business, less public and less regulated than many other activities, so that the child's experience of life may vary enormously from one family to another. In this sense, it is impossible to describe the lived experience of individual Anglo-Saxon children except in general terms of what was perceived to be socially acceptable, but documentary sources such as the description of Mary's parenting of the infant Jesus, at least, offer a standard of behaviour which was socially acceptable. Anglo-Saxon texts persistently assume that children should be treated kindly, gently and lovingly.

Play and education

Toys are almost entirely absent from the archaeological record, but documentary sources show Anglo-Saxons, adults and children alike, engaged in all sorts of play, from somersaulting and cartwheeling in the *plaistow* [playground] to gathering on a winter's evening in the communal hall to listen to the *scop* [storyteller] singing tales of monsters and heroes. Old English texts show that 'play' was embedded in Anglo-Saxon culture, not as something restricted to children's activities or special occasions, but as an integral part of daily life for adults and children alike. Already, the Old English word *plege* had all the connotations of the modern English word – it meant amusement for the sake of it (as in a 'play sword'), athletic prowess (as in 'swordplay') and theatrical imitation.

Evidence for physical games comes from a number of sources.
An anonymous Old English *Life* of St. Cuthbert offers the most evocative
account of boisterous children's games. In this story, the young Cuthbert
is depicted at play with other boys, each showing off their athletic skills
and playing a game of 'king of the hill' at which Cuthbert excelled above
all the other children. Of course, this is hagiography and the picture
of the rough and tumble of the playground is designed to serve a number
of purposes; it is there to show that Cuthbert was physically strong and
superior to the other boys. Cuthbert was no wimp, and the story intends
to show the reader that, had he remained in the secular world, Cuthbert
would have been a muscular hero and leader of men. It is also there
to contrast the idle folly of the secular world, where boys wasted their
energy on chaotic physical pursuits, with the aesthetic, rigorous spiritual
world of service to God. This said, the audience of the *Life* must have
readily recognised the boy's activities, else the point of the story would
have been lost.

Bede's *Ecclesiastical History* shows that wild, physical, competitive
games, which must have encouraged the development of the warrior
elite, were hard to repress amongst the young monks. In an evocative
passage on youthful folly, Bede described how two young companions
of Bishop John could not resist an opportunity to race their horses
on a beautiful day, leading to disaster and a hard lesson for one of them.

The type and range of education available to Anglo-Saxon children
varied through the period, and the types of training deemed appropriate
also varied according to age, gender and social status. Grave goods from
the early Anglo-Saxon inhumation cemeteries give an indication of the
way in which boys were expected to prepare for their adult lives. Some
boys, aged six or seven, were buried with small iron spears. Generally
speaking, the length of spearheads increased according to the age of the
male buried with them, suggesting that the small spears reflected the age,
strength and skill of the young boys, rather than being symbolic of family
or other ascribed warrior status.

For the adult elite, physical pursuits continued to be important. The
post-Conquest Bayeux Tapestry shows Earl Harold Godwinson, one
of the most powerful men in the country, and shortly to be crowned king,
setting off on a diplomatic mission to the Continent with a bird of prey on
his wrist, accompanied by fine horses and hunting dogs. Keeping hunting
birds was the occupation of the elite – the bones of a peregrine falcon
found in the archaeological deposits at Oxford underline the town's

Figure 15   Duke Harold rides out with his hunting dogs and birds.

importance as a place visited by royalty in the late Anglo-Saxon period.
In the late tenth century, a wealthy man called Brihtric wrote a will
in which he bequeathed 'an armlet of eighty *mancuses* of gold and a short
sword of the same weight and four horses, two with harness, and two
swords with sheaths and two hawks and all his staghounds' to his royal
lord. Eighty *mancuses* of gold was a considerable sum of wealth, and the
conjuction of the gold, the weaponry and the hunting animals emphasises
the extent to which, for high-status males, hunting was as fundamental
to their status as fighting. When the young prince Æthelstan made his will
in the early eleventh century, his passion for the elite sports of swordplay
and hunting were demonstrated by his list of possessions: eleven swords,
a coat of mail, two shields, a drinking horn and a string of horses. His will
also mentioned his sword polisher and staghuntsman (Figure 15).

Besides boisterous, outdoor, competitive games, there are many
records of more formal entertainments. The contents of the treasure
chamber in the Sutton Hoo Mound 1 burial, Suffolk, give an insight
into the entertainments offered by the early-seventh-century elite. The
man buried at Sutton Hoo, possibly King Redwald who was described
by Bede as overking of all England, was given equipment to keep royal
guests entertained, which included a lyre and playing counters for board
games. The majority of our evidence for board games to date comes from

similar high-status burials. The high-status princely burial from Prittlewell, Essex (almost certainly the burial of a Christian, given the gold foil crosses placed on the body), included a dice among the rich treasures, while the later Old English poet commented that 'an idle hand contents the gambler when he throws the dice'.

Board games would be supplemented by other entertainments: there are Old English words for jugglers, acrobats and musicians. There were also storytellers and poets. An illustration from the *Lindisfarne Gospels* of King David playing on his harp shows an instrument identical to the one excavated from Sutton Hoo. The beautiful lyre discovered in Sutton Hoo Mound 1 serves as a reminder that everybody, whatever their status, was expected to contribute to communal entertainment. The most well-known surviving lyres are associated with the very high-status male barrow burials at Sutton Hoo, Suffolk, and Taplow, Buckinghamshire, but other lyres have been identified from early Anglo-Saxon inhumation cemeteries at Morning Thorpe, Norfolk (Grave 97); at Bergh Apton, Norfolk (Grave 22); and Saxton Road, Abingdon, Oxfordshire (Grave B 42). All these are the burials of males (though the Morning Thorpe grave also contains the disturbed remains of a female). The young man at Abingdon also had a sword and fittings, while the young male at Morning Thorpe had a spear and shield. Another lyre has been recovered from excavations at eighth-century Anglo-Saxon York. Few other musical instruments from the period survive. Bone flutes have been found, and Anglo-Saxon texts mention female timbrel players (*timpestre*). The will of the young prince Æthelstan (d. 1014) mentioned a number of personal possessions, including a silver-coated trumpet.

In the *Ecclesiastical History*, Bede provides an explanation for the way in which the format of vernacular heroic poetry was adopted and adapted by the church for its own purposes. According to this story, the Abbess Hild of Whitby was presiding over the evening entertainments, at which all the monks were supposed to sing. One monk, Cadmon, a lowly cattle herder, was so ashamed of being unable to recite poetry or sing, that he retired to the cattle shed to avoid the humiliation. There, he was blessed with a vision, and was able to sing and compose religious songs in Old English, and Bede's account offers us what he claims to be the first ever religious song written in the English language.

The eighth-century *Life* of St. Guthlac, written by Felix, illustrates the kind of education available to a high-status boy in the middle Anglo-Saxon period. Although Guthlac was a member of elite society, with access to the full range of education on offer, and with Christian parents, his hagiographer, nonetheless, complained that the bulk of his education consisted of listening to heroic poetry in the halls, which inspired him to leave home when he reached adolescence and ride out as the leader of a war band. Learning to read and write was not part of an elite boy's education in the eighth century, though being able to recite the histories of his family was. Men were commended for being *leothcræftig* [skilled in song], and listeners would expect to hear *leothorun* [wise counsel given in song]. One surviving Old English poem, 'Widsith', is written from the point of view of an ageing professional poet struggling to keep the attention of his audience. His poem reveals his function. Not only was he supposed to amuse his audience, he was also supposed to teach; his poems stored a communal hoard of important memories about the origins of feuds, land rights, boundaries, obligations through marriage and other important political news. These songs were effective entertainments. Wulfstan, bishop of York, complained bitterly that his monks would rather listen to heroic poetry than listen to Biblical texts; but heroic poetry was more than an idle entertainment. Such lays contained political history and lessons to be learned from the past.

If a high-status man needed to have something read to him, he had priests to do the job. Even the famous story about the young King Alfred winning a richly decorated book from his mother did not involve learning to read. His mother said she would award the book to whichever of her children could *recite* the contents, and the child Alfred quickly took the text to the family priest, and learnt it by rote. Only later, through experience, did Alfred realise the need for anyone in a position of authority to be able to read. He himself did not become literate until he was an adult, and, in a controversial decree, he insisted that no one could serve as a reeve or thegn or ealdorman unless they could read. Fearful of losing their status, these grown men 'applied themselves in an amazing way to learning how to read'. In his account of Alfred's *Life*, his biographer Asser gave an amusing account of war-hardened veterans being forced into learning

if one of them – either because of his age or because of the unresponsive nature of his unpracticed intelligence – was unable to make progress in learning to read, the king commanded the man's son … to read out books in English to him day and night…. Sighing greatly from the bottom of their hearts, these men regretted that they had not applied themselves to such pursuits in their youth, and considered the youth of the present day to be fortunate, who had the luck to be given an education.

The Anglo-Saxon government traditionally relied heavily on oral communication, but Alfred's educational reforms ensured a new supply of literate royal officials. Not the least of his reforms was the establishment of a school within the royal household to educate not only his own children, but also children of aristocratic and lesser birth. In fact, because literacy was never perceived as part of the attributes of a leading member of society, a literary education was not seen as confined to, or exclusive to, the elite. Within a ranking household, reading was a skill, like any other, that could be taught to servants. When Alfred stipulated that reluctant thegns should be read to day and night, his first suggestion was that the son (no doubt a product of Alfred's own school) should be the reader, but, failing that, he recommended a relative, or someone in the thegn's household, 'whether freeman or slave'.

There exists an extensive Old English vocabulary for schooling. A school was a *leorninghus* or a *leoarnungscol*, while a pupil was a *leorningcild*. Education was not restricted to children. Adults too could be *leornungmenn*, where the *-menn* element referred to all people, both men and women. There are also surviving school books, of which the best known is by Abbot Ælfric of Eynsham (c.950–1010). He was one of the leading scholars in the tenth century and was himself educated at the monastic school at Winchester under Bishop Æthelwold. In addition to his many influential and scholarly writings, he produced a textbook to help schoolboys learn Latin. This book, Ælfric's *Colloquy*, is written in lively style as a dialogue between a teacher and boys carrying out a variety of trades and occupations. Ælfric's boys hope to avoid a beating at the beginning of the text and promise at the end to go to the cloister without any clowning around.

Elite girls, too, were taught to read and write, at least if they were brought up within the monastic system. The best early evidence for the education of women is preserved in the correspondence of five Anglo-Saxon women to the Anglo-Saxon missionary Boniface, including Leofgyth (also known as Leobgytha or Leoba), who was educated at the convent of Wimbourne in Dorset; she says that she was taught by the Abbess Eadburg, who also corresponded with Boniface. Her first surviving letter to Boniface was written when she was relatively young.

In it, she asks Boniface to pray for her parents, and she invites
him to correct her Latin. Later, Leofgyth became the abbess of
Tauberbischofsheim in Germany, and her writings influenced the
work of other monks. The surviving letters of his female correspondents
show elegance and style, and his relaxed and thoughtful responses
to them shows that Boniface regarded these women as his intellectual
equals.

As indicated by the schooling of Leofgyth, Boniface, Bede and others,
schooling was primarily the concern of the church until the educational
reforms of King Alfred, and the chief purpose of schools was to provide
the church with an educated clergy literate in Latin. The first English
school was established at Canterbury by Augustine and his missionaries
shortly after their arrival in England in AD 597, and the success of this
first school is attested by the fact that native Anglo-Saxons trained
at Canterbury were able to supply the teachers to a new school founded
by Sigeberht, king of East Anglia, in the 630s.

The majority of early schools trained oblates – children who were
given to the monastery at an early age and who were destined for a career
in the church. Bede, for example, was given to Benedict Biscop to
be trained at the age of seven, the same age that Beowulf was fostered
by his mother's father to be trained as a warrior. It may be that for
parents, giving a child to the church was socially equivalent to fosterage,
with all the bonds of responsibility that that system implied. Bede's
writings reflect his education in grammar, bible studies, chanting and
computus.

The end of childhood

Grave goods associated with the bodies in early Anglo-Saxon cemeteries
give us some clues as to the age at which children were perceived to have
begun to take on the characteristics of adults, at least within a ritual
context. No abrupt age of transition to adulthood can be identified in
the grave goods associated with children's bodies, but significant changes
in artefacts and clothing do begin to take place at around the age of ten
to twelve in both girls' and boys' graves. It is at this age that boys began
to be given more adult artefacts – shields appear in some boys' graves to
complement their spears, and girls begin to be buried with adult sets
of brooches, beads, girdle hangers and keys.

This burial evidence conforms with law codes. One of the earliest
written laws, of the kings Hlothhere and Eadric of Kent, who reigned

in the late seventh century, decreed that, 'if a man dies leaving a wife and child, it is right that the child should remain with the mother, and one of the father's relatives who is willing to act shall be given as its guardian to take care of its property, until it is ten years old.' A ten-year-old child was regarded as an accessory to theft in the laws of King Ine of Wessex. Ten seems young to be treated as an adult in legal and ritual terms, though, in the event of both parents dying, this low age of majority may have been the best way to protect a child's property from unscrupulous kinsmen. However, some Anglo-Saxon kings were uneasy at the idea of a ten-year-old being an accessory to theft. In the early tenth century, King Æthelstan raised the age to twelve, and then, in an unprecedented move, he decided that, 'he, and those with whom he has spoken, think that no one should be executed who is under fifteen years old, unless he tries to defend himself, or tries to run away and refuses to give himself up.'

Once a girl or boy had passed the age of ten or twelve, it was, in theory at least, possible for them to fully participate in adult life, but, as the concerns of King Æthelstan and his councillors indicated, a legal threshold did not necessarily reflect everyday life. Full 'adult' grave assemblages for males and females in the early Anglo-Saxon graves were more normally associated with bodies over the age of twenty at the time of death – swords for men, and the wealthiest sets of grave goods for women – are uncommon before the early twenties. This age does not necessarily reflect the optimum childbearing age for women or fighting age for men, rather it is more likely to reflect the age at which a son or daughter would have acquired, through inheritance, marriage or other means, enough wealth to have established themselves as heads of their own households. Certainly something of this sort can be identified in early medieval Ireland, where documentary sources refer to a class of men known as the *fer midboth* [men of the middle houses]. These were a group of single males who were too old to be living in their parents' house, but did not have the wealth to set up their own households. They were characterised as being warlike, feckless and a noisy nuisance. St. Guthlac may have belonged to a similarly irresponsible Anglo-Saxon group of lads when he was a teenager. At the age of twenty-four, c.698, he entered the double monastic house at Repton, run by the Abbess Ælfthryth, but prior to that he had spent nine years as the leader of a successful war band, fighting on the Mercian border.

Sex and marriage

Just as in modern England, a relationship between couples in the
Anglo-Saxon period could be romantic and full of love, or it could lead
to heartbreak, jealousy, deception and recrimination. The poet of the Old
English 'Maxims' from the *Exeter Book* provided an intimate vignette
of a faithful wife awaiting her travelling husband, 'cherished by his wife,
the yearned-for returning Frisian, when his ship docks … she leads him
in, washes his sea-stained clothes and gives him fresh garments – and
sails with him to a landfall as his love demands'. In contrast to this
faithful loving couple, the poet reminds the reader of less virtuous
women, 'there are many promiscuous ones, and they entertain strange
men when the other is travelling far away.'

When couples fell in love inappropriately, their unions could cause
widespread hurt and damage, not least because the duties of kinship drew
the families of a couple together in ties of responsibility and obligation,
which could be devastating for all involved. Because Anglo-Saxon society
was structured around social gifts and obligations, marriages could be
arranged between opposing families in an attempt to resolve old feuds, but
the results could be disastrous. The poet of *Beowulf* recalled the marriage
of the Danish princess Hildeburh to the Frisian king, Finn. Hildeburh was
supposed to act as a 'peace weaver' between the two nations, but fighting
soon broke out, leading to the violent deaths of her brother, her sons and
her husband. Hildeburh's grief at the death of her male relatives is echoed
in the grief of another famous Anglo-Saxon lover, the narrator of the
poem known as 'The Wife's Lament', which describes a woman(?) whose
husband has gone overseas on his lord's service and whose kinsmen are
trying to separate the couple. The poem ends with the cry, 'woe is to the
one who must wait for love to come out of longing.' This lament for lost
love is echoed in the poem 'Wulf and Eadwacer', a complicated riddle
of thwarted human passions, perhaps describing a love triangle: 'In hopes
I have endured the remoteness of the footsteps of my Wulf, when it was
rainy weather and I sat weeping, and when the intrepid warrior pinioned
me in his arms – there was pleasure for me in that, but it was loathsome
to me too.'

Both 'Wulf and Eadwacer' and 'The Wife's Lament' may be read
as metaphors for the relationship between Christ and the church, but
the ambivalent relationships suggested by the poems seem to have had
a place in everyday life too. Several Anglo-Saxon texts denounce bigamy,

including a late Anglo-Saxon case where one woman married two brothers. Other marriages induced disapproval. When King Alfred's widowed father Æthelwulf, with four grown sons, returned from a visit to Rome with a Frankish bride on his arm, this useful political alliance was not greeted with unalloyed enthusiasm by his people, much less his own sons. The reason for this was that Princess Judith was only twelve years of age: she was too young, and the age gap between the old warrior and his new wife was too great. After all, she was younger than his sons. As might be expected, the presence of a new child bride in the royal household was a cause for concern – any male children she had might challenge her stepsons for the throne. In the event, Judith's presence in Wessex gave rise to further scandal in the royal house when, after her husband's death two years later, she married one of his sons. The marriage was politically advantageous to both – although there may have also been mutual attraction between Judith and her stepson – ensuring that Judith maintained her status at court as the wife of the king, and, as daughter of Charles the Bald, she gave her husband important social and political status. Though this marriage was shocking in the context of ninth-century Christianity, it may have seemed less questionable within a secular context. St. Augustine, in a letter to Pope Gregory seeking advice on the conversion of the Anglo-Saxons, posed a question about degrees of marriage, specifically, if it was lawful to marry a stepmother or a sister-in-law. Gregory's response was an unequivocal 'no', but he did note that 'there are many of the English race who, while they were unbelievers, are said to have contracted these unlawful marriages'.

There is very little evidence for the form taken by marital ties or associated rituals before the introduction of Christianity. A few references in the texts, combined with comparative evidence, particularly from early medieval Irish sources, suggest that marriages, if they were to be recognised by the families of the couple, required agreement and negotiation of a contract between the bridegroom and the bride's family. Part of this negotiation concerned the 'bride-price', a sum of money to be given to the bride, and which would revert to the bride's family in the event of a separation. The 'bride-price' has been interpreted in terms of a 'sale' of the woman, but the weight of evidence indicates that married Anglo-Saxon women had an independent economic status from their husbands – the 'bride-price' is more sensibly interpreted as a guarantee of good faith and good behaviour on the part of the bridegroom. The morning after the consummation of the marriage, the new husband also had to provide his wife with her *morgengifu* [morning gift], a sum of money which was absolutely her property, and over which the husband had no further control. Amongst other things, the *morgengifu* gave the married Anglo-Saxon women an exceptional level of economic (and, in practice, social and political) independence compared to women in later stages of English history.

The laws of Æthelbert of Kent, dating to the seventh century, had several points to make about the marriage contract at this early period. They say, first, that once a man has agreed to 'buy a girl', the bargain shall stand (*ceapi geceapod sy*), provided there has been no dishonesty. The law does not say what 'dishonesty' is, in this case – it may concern the girl, but it is more likely, given the general interests of Anglo-Saxon law codes, to relate to financial matters, such as the failure of one side or the other to provide the contracted sums of money. If there is 'dishonesty', she is to return to her family, and he will have his money back.

The next law in the sequence discusses various outcomes if the couple have a (living) child together, suggesting that the birth of the child automatically changed the financial relationship between the two. After a child is born, the wife is entitled to half her husband's goods if he dies, or, more interestingly for the nature of early English marriage, 'if she wishes to depart with her children'. If, however, the husband wishes to keep the children, she is entitled only to the equivalent of a child's share – *swa an bearn*. If she dies childless, however, her *morgengifu* remains in her family, rather than reverting back to her husband.

These elliptic laws are open to interpretation and dispute, but they do suggest the social, contractual nature of early Anglo-Saxon marriage, and the importance of live children within the marriage contract. In the eyes of the lawmaker, the central issues in marriage related to money and the financial implications in terms of inheritance and maintenance involved in the making and breaking of a marriage contract. There is no expectation that a marriage ought to be for life.

There are interesting hints in this series of codes on marriage, however, that at times the envisaged wedding did not go according to plan and that it sometimes happened (often enough to require legislation, anyway) that a bride was snatched before she could be 'sold'; 'if a man forcibly carries off a girl, he shall pay fifty shillings to her owner, and afterwards buy from the owner his consent.' The word 'owner' (*agende*) has been interpreted here, too, to portray women as hapless chattels in the formation of marriage alliances. In legal practice, a woman did indeed belong to the one who had put up the money for her with her family's agreement, and he rightly needed to be compensated for his loss.

Codes issued by kings in the later Anglo-Saxon period suggest that the meaning of marriage was changing. Perhaps under the influence of the church, the legal system began interesting itself less with marriage as a contract between individuals and their families, and more as a Christian institution, with a consequent erosion of freedom and rights. King Canute's laws, for example, imposed harsh penalties for any sexual activity outside a monogamous marriage. A man committing adultery would be punished 'according to the nature of the offence'. Incest was punishable by the loss of all possessions, though there is a codicil that 'the cases are not alike if incest is committed with a sister or with a distant relation'. A woman who committed adultery would lose all her possessions and her nose and ears. If her husband died, she had to wait a year before remarrying, and her *morgengifu*, and all the property which she had from her first husband, had to be returned to his nearest relative.

One form of Anglo-Saxon communal entertainment was riddles. These verbal challenges were sometimes intellectual, and sometimes Christian in import, and their importance as intellectual exercises and as a method of articulating complex philosophical ideas is illustrated by their popularity in the surviving texts. There are over ninety-five riddles in the late Anglo-Saxon *Exeter Book*, but many of the surviving riddles, including this one from the *Exeter Book*, were overtly sexual in tone:

I am a wondrous creature: to women a thing of joyful expectancy, to close-lying companions serviceable. I harm no city-dweller except the one who kills me. My stem is erect and tall – I stand up in bed – and whiskery somewhere down below. Sometimes the pretty daughter of a countryman will dare, rude girl, to grip me. She attacks me, red as I am, and seizes my head and clenches me in a cramped place. She will soon feel the effect of her encounter with me, this curly-haired woman who squeezes me. Her eye will be wet.

The answer to this salacious poem is 'onion', but the ribald comedy inherent in its deliberate double entendre still thrives in British comedy.

It goes without saying that the riddles for 'dough', 'cock and hen', 'poker', 'shirt' and 'key' were equally suggestive. The popularity of riddles, whose entertainment was based on a listener foolishly accepting the sexual innuendo, implies that late Anglo-Saxon attitudes to sex included some of the same embarrassed responses that it does in modern English society.

Anglo-Saxon Christian writers were very happy to comment on sinful and virtuous heterosexual relationships, but, in the context of the penitential literature, in which all possible crimes are imagined and condemned, they have surprisingly little to say. Anglo-Saxon artwork is also relatively restrained in comparison with some other cultures. Occasional images of naked men are found. Images of the sexual act are notably absent from Anglo-Saxon art, with rare exceptions, including a depiction of an 'erotic act' on a seventh-century gold seal matrix of Queen Balthilda, now in the Norwich Castle Museum, Norfolk, which depicts a bearded male and a long-haired female surmounted by a cross. A small pendant in the shape of an anthropomorphised penis was found at Carlton Colville, Suffolk. The naked man in this figure is not priapic, nor is the man on the Finglesham Man buckle. Lewd acts are, however, depicted in the Bayeux Tapestry. As an example of the restraint, or prudery, evident at one level in Anglo-Saxon society, the Bayeux Tapestry's illustration of a contemporary scandalous liaison between 'a churchman and Ælfgyva' merely shows the churchman touching her cheek. A less subtle counterpoint runs along the bottom margin of the Tapestry, however – well-endowed naked men. The first few scenes of the Tapestry show Harold's ill-fated trip to Boulogne and his interception by William's men as he landed in Normandy; the lower margin of the Tapestry offers pictures of everyday life, hunting, ploughing and sowing. As Harold is taken in close procession to Duke William, the bucolic scenes underneath the main story change, broken by the image of a naked, lustful man reaching for a naked woman.

The Bayeux Tapestry was sewn by women, almost certainly Anglo-Saxon women, but the main panel of the Tapestry itself shows very few women. There are no women at all at William's court or in any of the scenes depicting events in Normandy (an ominous sign of the impact the Normans, with their insistence on male primogeniture, were to have on the status of women in Norman England), and there are only three women in scenes depicting events in Anglo-Saxon England. Apart from Ælfgyva, one woman, King Edward the Confessor's wife, is shown at the foot of the King's deathbed, covering her face, while his liegemen surround him, and the archbishop and aristocratic males lay out the corpse and conduct the funeral. The third is an unnamed Anglo-Saxon woman, clutching the hand of a child while the invading Normans burn her house. This could be taken as a paradigm of a woman's place after the Norman Conquest – the first is the object of (and morally dubious provoker of) desire, the second is a passive mourner and the last is a victim of male aggression. On the other hand, all three images reflect the importance of children to males at the aristocratic end of the scale. Ælfgyva is plausibly identified as the wife of King Canute. According to a later story, Canute was impotent, and his children were the product of a liaison between his wife and a cleric. This story cast doubt on the legitimacy of Canute's heirs to the throne of England and supported William's tenuous claim. Edward the Confessor famously failed to produce any heirs at all. Norman propaganda wished to portray Edward as a saintly king, so that his lack of children (and the consequent battle for the throne of England) could be seen as directed by God: his lack of children was the product of religiously inspired abstinence. Finally, William deliberately embarked on a campaign of laying waste to land around Hastings. Harold could have let his men rest after their battle at Stamford Bridge, but William provoked the hasty confrontation at Hastings by burning Harold's own family lands.

Old age

After Beowulf's triumph over the monsters Grendel and his mother, the old King Hrothgar provided a feast for the hero, but also offered words of advice from an old warrior to one still in his prime. Old and full of wisdom, Hrothgar warned that youth, strength and good fortune were no guarantee against the turns of fortune. Urging Beowulf to think about his immortal soul instead of earthly rewards, Hrothgar conjured up all the disappointments the world had in store – sickness, sword edge, fire, flood, spear – and, if all these should be avoided, there was still *atol yldo* (dreadful old age).

The *Beowulf* poet refers more than once to the horrors of old age – the sapping of strength, the passing of friends or, worse, the loss of loved children – and to some extent, this picture of lost strength and power in a warrior society is reflected in the earlier Anglo-Saxon mortuary ritual, where the oldest bodies of both males and females are buried with proportionately fewer grave goods than younger adults. For males, weapon burial becomes less frequent with age. At the cemetery of Great Chesterford, Essex, for example, no adult males over the age of forty-five were buried with both spears and shields. However, at Great Chesterford, the three longest spears – all over 1.15 feet (35 centimetres) in length – were buried with males over the age of forty-five, and of the five inlaid spears at the site, three belonged to older males; the bodies of the other two could not be aged. The picture at Great Chesterford, then, offers a slightly different reading of old age. Old age did not necessarily bring with it a loss of status, but a change in status. King Hrothgar may have lamented his youthful past and his inability to challenge the monster Grendel himself, but nonetheless he retained power and status as king and leader of his people.

Other documentary sources idealise old age. After Earl Byrhtnoth's defeat by the Viking army at Maldon in Essex in 998, a poem commissioned by his widow to commemorate her husband's bravery exemplified the battle spirit of his loyal followers, including one old retainer, whose death speech, 'Hearts shall be harder, courage shall be keener, spirits shall be the greater, the more our strength fades', is a model for heroic old age.

Documentary sources also reveal that the church provided a positive environment for the elderly. A number of saints whose lives can be reconstructed lived to considerable old age and retained an active role in ecclesiastical society. Aldhelm (whose own name means 'old protector', suggesting a culture which valued the old and trusted over the new and untried) must have been about seventy years old when he died in AD 709. When he was about sixty-six, he was pressed to take a bishopric, but refused. The council rejected his protest, saying that 'maturity brought with it greater wisdom and freedom from vices'. Youth was hot and unpredictable, in contrast to wise old age. St. Boniface was actively engaged in dangerous missionary work in Frisia while he was in his late seventies or early eighties, and even so, it was not old age or disease that killed him, but a band of murderous pagans.

Not all elderly Anglo-Saxons enjoyed an active old age. In early medieval Irish society, the task of caring for elderly parents and relatives was considered sufficiently honourable (and onerous) to bring with it special status and inheritance privileges. Something similar may have happened in Anglo-Saxon society, though we lack specific evidence. The

Life of St. Cuthman may hint at such filial obligations. The *Life* records that Cuthman used to transport his disabled old mother in a contraption similar to a wheelbarrow, with a wheel at the front and a strap over his shoulders. One day, divinely inspired, he launched his mother on this contraption down a hillside, and where she came to rest, there he established his church.

In the later Anglo-Saxon period, the church may have taken on some of the social responsibility for the care of the elderly. The mid-Anglo-Saxon cemetery at Nazeingbury, Essex, is unusual for the high age at death of its mortuary population, including the skeletons of people who were chronically disabled. The cemetery was associated with a small church, and it has been suggested that this was a small monastic community offering hospice care to the sick and elderly.

Chapter 5
Food and Drink

'Every mouth needs food: meals must come on time' wrote the poet
of the Old English *Maxims 1*. The getting of food and drink was the
most time-consuming activity for Anglo-Saxons, both at the basic level
of survival and at the level of everyday social interaction.

Landscape and resources

A detailed knowledge of the resources in the landscape, and an
understanding of how to exploit those resources, was crucial to the
survival of the early Anglo-Saxons. For a family to eat, it had to be able to
acquire food by growing it, trapping it or buying it at a market. Integral
to that process was the knowledge of how the landscape worked – where
the best soils were, where water could be found (and whether the source
of water was reliable), what the best crops to grow were, where the land
would not support farming and where the best hunting was.

Central to successful agriculture and life was access to a reliable
source of water, and this concern is exemplified in the large number
of early Anglo-Saxon place names which state the location and type
of local water supply. Such names are not limited to simply identifying
that water is present: they often show precisely the kind of water source
you would find, and where to find it. Hopwas in Shropshire, for example,
told an Anglo-Saxon that this was a hidden site that flooded periodically.
Winterbourne is the site of a seasonal stream; Chadwell is the site
of a cold spring; Bedwell marks a place where water from a spring needs
to be collected in a vessel or water butt (Old English *byden*); Chalfont,
Urchfont and Havant, all 'font' place names (**funta*) are linked with
Roman settlements with springs, while place names ending in -ey (Old
English *eg*) indicate places that were islands in the Anglo-Saxon period:
Thorney, Osney and Ely.

Place names show the kinds of agricultural activities that were
carried out at settlements such as Barton (barley growing) and Beeston
(bee-keeping). Still others show routeways for moving live produce –
oxen could cross the river Thames at Oxford, while further upstream

in the settlements of Shifford and Duxford were fords for sheep and for ducks. Still other names hint at specific locations good for trapping wild animals: the place name Ludgershall in Buckinghamshire, for example, means 'secret spear trap'.

The work of environmental archaeologists has helped to create a moderately detailed picture of the type of food resources available to the early Anglo-Saxon population and the type of farming activity carried out in the early settlements. Analysis of animal bones gives information on what type of animals were reared for eating and the age at which animals were slaughtered for their meat. Analysis of pollen, seeds and insects can give information about the types of plants present in the environment, and recent analyses of stable isotopes (carbon and nitrogen) in some human bones from the Anglo-Saxon period have provided further information on early diets.

Agricultural seasons

The Anglo-Saxon solar year, according to Bede's thesis on the calendar, began on 25 December (midwinter) and was normally divided into twelve lunar months with provision for a thirteenth. Originally, it is possible that there were only two seasons in the Anglo-Saxon year, namely winter and summer; the idea of four seasons, derived from Roman models, was introduced with Christianity. The duties of a reeve, described in the Old English text *Gerefa*, emphasised the seasonality of Anglo-Saxon agriculture. Spring tasks included supervising the setting of madder and sowing linseed and woad. Autumn was the harvest month, but it was also known as *weod monað* [weed month]. In autumn, the woad needed further attention. November was *blotmonað* [sacrifice month], a time to slaughter animals, perhaps as a thank offering, but also to cull animals that could not be fed through the winter. Threshing was carried out in winter (Figure 16).

Two late Anglo-Saxon manuscripts illustrate labours associated with the months. The first, British Library Cotton MS Julius A.vi, was written in the early eleventh century, whilst the second, British Library Cotton MS Tiberius B.v, written at about the same time, was either a copy of the first, or both manuscripts were derived from the same (lost) source. Interestingly, they vary slightly in their illustration of the monthly

Figure 16 Digging in March.

activities, perhaps as a result of scribal error or perhaps because
the agricultural labours of the months were not sufficiently relevant
to the experience of eleventh-century monks for them to care. Both agree
that January was for ploughing and sowing, February was for pruning
vines (vine pollen has been found in a few late Anglo-Saxon contexts,
suggesting that viticulture was practiced in England at the time, but this
entry betrays a continental source) and March was devoted to digging,
raking and sowing. April was a time for feasting, while May was for
tending sheep. The Tiberius manuscript assigns reaping somewhat
prematurely to June, while the Julius manuscript suggests that cutting
wood is the better June activity. Tiberius has woodcutting in July,
which is when the Julius manuscript suggests mowing. Tiberius puts
off mowing until August, when Julius is more realistically reaping. Both
agree that September is for feeding up the pigs on forest pannage (and
in preparation for the winter slaughter) and have October as a time
for hunting wild birds. November is for stacking firewood and making
fires, while December is for threshing.

   Seasonality affected what Anglo-Saxons could grow and also limited
what they ate. Most types of food were only available for short periods,
though meat and fish could be salted. One of the characters in Ælfric's
Colloquy was a salter. Asked why his occupation is important, he replies,
'who could fill his cellar or store without my skill?' Grains could be dried
and stored using drying kilns, which may be represented by the clay
ovens found associated with some settlement sites. The link between
seasonality, agriculture and food consumption is suggested by a comment
in a late Anglo-Saxon manuscript called *Rectitudines Singularum
Personarum*, which acknowledges that the lower social orders were
entitled to food rewards or feasts at winter; Easter; after harvest sheaf
binding; after ploughing, mowing, rick making, wood carting and corn
carting; and 'many other times I am not able to list'.

Anglo-Saxon farming

The climate in Anglo-Saxon England appears to have been milder and damper than it is today, and this is reflected in the crops that could be sown. For example, recent archaeological evidence has shown that vines were cultivated in Hampshire from the ninth century to the Norman Conquest. In the opening paragraphs of his *Ecclesiastical History*, Bede specifically remarks on the good climate, fertility and abundance of the country he knew: 'the island is rich in crops and trees, and has good pasturage for cattle and beasts of burden. It also produces vines in certain districts, and has plenty of both land-and waterfowl of various kinds. It is remarkable too for its rivers, which abound in fish, particularly salmon and eels, and for copious springs....' On the whole, the archaeological evidence supports this picture of variety and abundance (Figure 17).

The Anglo-Saxons arrived in a land which had long been farmed, and though the evidence is not as conclusive in all parts of the country, it would appear that, although the Anglo-Saxons farmed less intensively than their Romano-British predecessors, they largely maintained pre-existing cultivated areas. The cultivated landscape of Roman Britain did not return to scrubland or wilderness. Where there was tree cover, the woodlands were almost certainly a carefully managed resource.

The evidence for successful arable farming at West Stow sheds particular light on the knowledge and farming practices of the early Anglo-Saxons who lived here. The soils in this area are particularly difficult; this is an area of low rainfall, with nutrient poor, unstable, sandy soils which are poor at retaining moisture. Successful cultivation of cereal crops would have required careful ploughing of the soil to prevent it from breaking up and blowing away, combined with good manuring, which in turn required an adequate supply of stock

Figure 17 Stoning birds with a slingshot.

animals to supply the manure. The soil conditions also required careful planting to minimise loss of crops in the summer; winter crops would have been important, because they would have ripened before the summer drought, and autumn-sown cereals such as rye would have reduced the effects of the spring winds on the soil.

Early English land units (hides) probably reflected the area of land required to support one family (*hiwung*). The *Rectitudines Singularum Personarum* suggested that a peasant *cotsetle* required a minimum of 5 acres (2 hectares) of land for subsistence, but the number of families supported by a single hide increased in the late Anglo-Saxon period, perhaps as a result of more intensive farming practices, and the size of a hide differed according to the resources and value of the land.

Agricultural practice for the early period is difficult to reconstruct, though by the time the first laws were written down the evidence suggests that the land was carefully managed and exploited. The laws of King Ine of Wessex (688–726), for example, refer to the protection of fences, meadows and pastures, the regulation of tree felling and the responsibility for straying cattle that damage cornland.

Bone evidence from Wraysbury (Berkshire) in the late Anglo-Saxon period shows that there was mixed arable and pasture farming and managed woodland too, to provide timber and hunting. However, by the eighth century, there is evidence of increasing specialisation in food production in some settlements as small villages provided particular resources for estates controlled by lords and for a growing urban population. At Hurst Park, East Molesey, Surrey, the middle Anglo-Saxon settlement consisted of six or seven sunken-featured buildings (SFBs), laid out in a regular pattern at equal distances from each other. Two parallel ditches ran through the site, apparently marking a driveway or road. There was one larger SFB on the site, with a ramp leading up to it. The regular layout of the buildings suggests an organised, purpose-built community. This impression is backed up by the fact that the site was in use for a short period only before it was abandoned. The environmental evidence from the site suggests that it had a very specific function as an area for grain processing. There was an area for burning, which appeared to have been used for crop drying and processing; parts of rotary querns were found on the site, and a dump of soil contained charred cereal grains, chaff and cereal weed seeds such as corncockle. Was this a dedicated crop-processing and storage site for a big estate with the larger hut representing a supervisor's station?

Woodlands provided an important food resource. Timber was useful for building and for fuel, but woodlands also provided a habitat for the wild animals which supplemented the Anglo-Saxon diet, as well as providing pannage for pigs, which would forage for mast such as acorns, chestnuts and beechnuts. Recent carbon- and nitrogen-isotope analysis of early Anglo-Saxon human bones has indicated that pigs played a much more important part in the diet than surviving animal bone evidence from settlements would suggest (the analysis also suggests that chickens, almost absent from the archaeological record, also played an important part in the diet). The importance of woodland as a resource is indicated by a law of Ine (d.726) which declares that 'anyone who destroys a tree in a wood by fire … he shall pay 60 shillings, because fire is a thief'. Pannage was such an important resource that laws were required to protect use of woodlands. According to Ine, anyone who persistently found someone else's pigs in his mast was owed 6 shillings, though if the pigs had only been there once or twice the fine was only 1 or 2 shillings.

A proportion of Anglo-Saxon law codes are taken up with settling other disputes between neighbours over animals, lands and boundaries. The hazards of owning land in common are indicated by an early eighth-century law of Ine, which assigns responsibility for damage to crops in the cases where commoners share a meadow, but some shareholders have failed to fence their part of the meadow and cattle have wandered in and eaten the crops – then the ones who left the gaps had to pay compensation to the others. Equally, all commoners had to fence their property (in both summer and winter). If they failed to do this, and a neighbour's cattle strolled in, there could be no claim for damages. Cattle appear to have been allowed to roam freely, finding food where they could, and the onus was on the grower to protect his crops. Given this legislation, it is not surprising to find more enclosures appearing around settlements from the seventh century onwards – not to pen animals in, but to keep them out. The exception to this is the animal that breaks down a hedge to get into an enclosure. The owner of the enclosure had taken all reasonable measures, so, in this case, the responsibility for damage lay with the owner of the animal.

By the end of the Anglo-Saxon period, parts of the country, particularly the Midlands, used an 'open-field' system of agriculture where arable land was divided into strips, which together made up furlongs and these in turn were grouped into fields, one of which

was left fallow each year. Fallow fields were not useless. In addition
to being used to graze livestock, Old English vocabulary indicates that
a number of food and medicine plants grew wild in the fields: rosemary
(*feldmædere*), mint (*feldmint*), parsnip (*feldmore*), rue (*feldrude*),
plantain (*feldwop*) and gentian (*feldwyrt*). Areas of the country with
open fields and nucleated settlements belong to the middle or late
Anglo-Saxon period. By contrast, more dispersed settlement patterns
found in the south and east of the country were probably a continuation
of earlier Romano-British or Iron Age practice.

An increase in food production from the eighth century onwards
may have been a result of the growth of powerful estates, though it may
also be linked to technological improvements in drainage and ploughing.
Deep ploughing with teams of oxen using turnboards, associated with
strip furlongs, created characteristic 'ridge and furrow' fields with
headlands for turning the ploughteam. Although 'ridge and furrow'
is usually associated with post-Conquest agriculture, excavations have
uncovered evidence of late Anglo-Saxon use of this technique, preserved
under the Norman castle mounds, at Oxford and Hen Domen,
Montgomeryshire.

Farming tools

There has been some discussion over the existence of an Anglo-Saxon
plough; the current consensus is that there is no firm evidence for the
existence of a plough before the tenth century. Prior to this time, tilling
was probably by using a wooden ard of the sort preserved in the grave
of the Sutton Hoo 'ploughman' and illustrated in the Bayeux Tapestry.
The Tapestry shows a horse or donkey pulling a harrow, but law codes
from the seventh century on indicate that oxen were usually used for
ploughing (Figure 18).

A late-tenth- or early-eleventh-century document lists the tools
a wise reeve needed to give to his servants if they were to work: *tola
to tune tilian* [tools to work the farm] included axe, bil, adze or hatchet,
mattock, shears, coulter, gadiron, sickle, weedhook, spade, shovel, ladder
and horsecomb. Many of the finds from the pre-Conquest high-status
manor house at Goltho, Lincolnshire, match this list. Iron tools from
Goltho included hammers and adzes for woodworking, auger bits for
drilling holes in timber, claw hammers, teeth from woolcombs or heckles

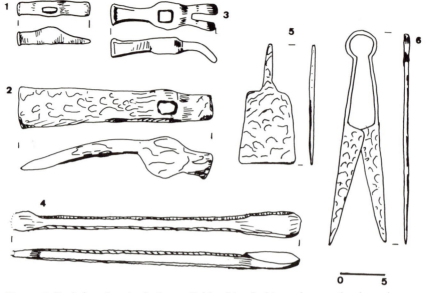

Figure 18 Tools from late Anglo-Saxon Goltho, Lincolnshire: 1, hammer head; 2, adze; 3, claw hammer; 4, auger bit; 5, tanged spud for weeding; and 6, shears.

to prepare wool and flax, shearboard hooks and shears for wool clipping, needles and awls for leatherworking, tanged spuds and weedhooks for weeding, a sickle and a double-ended pick for stoneworking.

Fish provided an important addition to Anglo-Saxon diets, and evidence for the exploitation of fish resources has been found in the archaeological record from the sixth century onwards. Place names such as Fiskerton (Northamptonshire) and Fishwick (Lancashire) indicate specialised fishing and fish-trading communities, and Bede refers to the skill of catching sea fish in a net. Net sinkers and line sinkers have been recovered from archaeological excavation. York has produced iron fish hooks, which suggests that the inhabitants may have been going out to sea to catch their own fish on long lines. The Vikings may have introduced the drift net; large volumes of sea fish were certainly being caught by the end of the Anglo-Saxon period, when the *Domesday Book* records a return of 68,000 herrings a year just from one town, Dunwich in Suffolk. Traps were also set in rivers and weirs to catch fish and eels. Bede thought that the island of Ely in Cambridgeshire was named for its copious catches of eels. Fish traps have been identified in archaeological contexts at Colwick (Nottinghamshire) and Wharram Percy (Yorkshire), but it appears that artificial fishponds were extremely rare before the Conquest.

Diet

The evidence suggests that the Anglo-Saxons had access to a large number of foods that are still grown and eaten in England today, and they also used some resources which are only rarely exploited today. Bread was almost certainly the staple of the Anglo-Saxon diet, to such an extent that the production of a loaf (Old English *hlaf*) of bread was singled out as the most important attribute of the male and female leaders of a community; the modern English 'lord' and 'lady' derive from the Old English *hlaford* and *hlafdig*. It is likely that bread was normally eaten with butter: Ælfric contrasted the normal bread and butter of the English with the Italian habit of eating bread with oil.

Evidence of small, hand-turned quern stones within settlement buildings suggests that part of a woman's daily routine would have been to grind grain and turn it into bread. Even when monastic houses and the owners of large estates had built water-powered mills, evidence from the relatively prosperous industrial tenements at York suggests that it was still common practice to grind grain in the home, though the comfortable citizens of York chose to grind their grain with costly Niedermendig lava from Germany, which gave a finer flour with less grit in it than local stones. Just because it was produced at home, though, did not mean that you knew what was in it – analysis of cesspits from tenth-century York included the presence of the poisonous weed corn cockle in sufficient concentrations to have given the consumers of the bread a stomach ache. In elite families, slaves might have been given the task of grinding corn by hand (the early seventh-century laws of Æthelbert of Kent refer to the king's female grinding slave), but by the late Anglo-Saxon period, large mills were more widespread. Some would have been powered by oxen, but the *Domesday Book* records more than 6,000 watermills operating on estates throughout the country, as well as a tide mill at the entrance to the port at Dover which was inconveniencing the shipping. The wooden remains of a mill at Old Windsor have been dated by dendrochronology to the late seventh century; this is the date at which the trees were felled, but it is likely that the beams were used to build the mill not long afterwards. While hand grinding was a female activity, the documentary evidence suggests that millers were male.

Salt was widely used to flavour sweet and savoury dishes. Honey was the only sweetener available in early medieval England. It was a valuable commodity, used to make the sweet alcoholic drink, mead, and regularly included in Anglo-Saxon medical recipes. Milk derived from cows, goats and sheep, as well as being used to make dairy products, was also a useful drink; one (fragmentary) late Anglo-Saxon will from Bury St. Edmunds provided for 4 pence for milk at a funeral feast. The main beverages at feasts were ale, beer (probably derived from fermented fruits, like cider), mead and wine. Though water was certainly drunk, other beverages were preferred. 'What do you drink?' the novice monk is asked in Ælfric's *Colloquy*. 'Ale, if I have it, otherwise water if I don't have ale,' comes the reply. Asked why he does not drink wine, the monk replies, 'I am not so lucky that I can have wine, and wine is not drunk by children and foolish people, only by adults and wise ones.' The novice also tells us about his diet: he is allowed to eat meat, vegetables and eggs, fish and cheese, butter and beans and all foods that are not taboo for a monk. In addition to their dairy products, Anglo-Saxons relied heavily on cattle, sheep and pigs for meat, though some types of domestic animal meat – horse and dog, for example – seem to have been taboo.

Analysis of plant material at the early Anglo-Saxon settlement at West Stow, Suffolk, showed that spelt, wheat, rye, barley and oats were all present. Spelt was cultivated in the Roman period and seems to have persisted as a crop in early Anglo-Saxon Suffolk, but by the middle Anglo-Saxon period, it no longer appears in the archaeobotanical record, suggesting that spelt had been replaced as a crop by other grain crops with higher yields. Rye, which was found in some quantities in pits at West Stow, was well suited to the free-draining sandy soils of the area, and wheat and barley were certainly cultivated. Evidence for oats was sparse, however, and it is unlikely that it was deliberately cultivated.

The inhabitants of West Stow were practising mixed animal husbandry. The bones from their domestic animals – cattle, sheep or goats (the two are not easy to distinguish in archaeological contexts) and pigs – were all relatively large and certainly no smaller than animals from late Anglo-Saxon sites. In terms of the quantity of bones, sheep or goat is the predominant species, followed by cattle and pigs, but cattle would have been the most important source of meat, and the bird bones found on the site are a reminder that domestic birds – chicken and geese – were also a significant source of protein.

It has been suggested that, to some extent, Anglo-Saxon diet was determined by wealth and gender. It has been noted that males buried with weapons are generally taller than males buried without weaponry, suggesting a better diet for those of higher status. Initial stable isotope analysis of early Anglo-Saxon skeletons also indicated that males, females and children might have had different diets, with males having better access to cattle protein. However, the most recent stable-isotope analyses have not provided positive corroboration of a single dietary pattern across the country.

Bone deposits of non-domesticated animals found associated with the late Anglo-Saxon settlement at Wraysbury, in the Middle Thames Valley, give an evocative picture of the kind of environment surrounding the typical late Anglo-Saxon rural settlement, and the kind of animal, bird and fish life surrounding the settlement. Animal bones from the site include mole; shrew; red and roe deer; beaver; field and water vole; field, harvest and house mice; and black rat. Water in the local rivers was clean, providing the settlement with eel, trout, salmon, pike, chubb, rudd, bream, barbell, gudgeon, burbot, perch and flat fish. Bird life associated with the settlement and its surrounding environment included mallard, buzzard, goshawk, partridge, woodcock, golden plover, lapwing, corncrake, woodpigeon, crow, robin, blackbird, thrush and house sparrow. Not all of these animals were present in the bone assemblage as sources of food, but they were all local; the only outsider in the bone assemblage was herring, which must have been caught at sea and transported to this inland site.

Excavations at Oxford, a thriving town in the late tenth century, have provided us with some detailed insights into the diet of richer townspeople at the close of the Anglo-Saxon period. Animal bones found in association with some of Oxford's higher status buildings show that the wealthier merchants and visitors were eating venison, hare, pike and oysters. Documentary sources suggest that some of the urban and suburban population had productive gardens, and bone remains suggest that the townspeople were keeping hens and pigeons for food and eggs, and raising pigs in their yards. Other environmental remains suggest that the inhabitants had access to a variety of fresh produce: evidence for broad beans, peas, hazelnuts, cherries, sloes, blackberries, apples, pears and plums has been found within the town ditches and pits.

Families in tenth-century Anglo-Scandinavian York may have been responsible for their own bread production, from grain to loaf, and they certainly had more to do with putting meat on the table than a modern urbanite could stomach. Bone evidence from York shows that the citizens were eating a typical diet of cattle, sheep, goats and pigs. As in late Anglo-Saxon Oxford, some pigs and goats may have been reared within tenement yards at York, but the cattle and sheep were reared in the surrounding countryside and brought in on the hoof to market. Skeletal evidence from within the tenements, such as animal skulls showing marks of violent blows to the head, indicates that cattle and sheep were purchased live from the market, then brought home on the hoof to be butchered in the backyard. Like the citizens of Oxford, people living in York were eating a wide range of birds, fruit and vegetables, and also had access to dill, coriander and linseed oil.

Unlike inland Oxford, late Viking York had access to the sea, and the diet of its inhabitants reflected this. Huge numbers of oysters were consumed, as well as lesser quantities of cockles, mussels and winkles. Sea-caught fish such as cod, smelt, eels and salmon, herring, haddock, flat fish, ling and mackerel were consumed by the occupants of the Coppergate houses, as well as river fish such as pike, roach, rudd, bream and perch.

Exotic foods

In addition to the wide range of home-grown and produced foods and drinks available to early English communities, some people also had access to spices, herbs, wine, oils, fruits and nuts from abroad. At different times from at least the end of the sixth century, Anglo-Saxon kingdoms had access to trade routes which stretched from the Baltic to the Indian Ocean, though these routes were sometimes disrupted by the vicissitudes of warfare and climate. It is unlikely that imported foods were readily available to everyone, yet they would have been used on special occasions and were sufficiently well known and accessible for various items – coriander seed, pepper and oil, for example – to be included as ingredients in remedies in the late Anglo-Saxon *Leechbooks*. The rarity of items may have contributed to their use in medicinal texts, and there is no doubt that some exotic commodities had great value. The Rhenish flagon of wine included in the lavish burial at Sutton Hoo Mound 1 was there to emphasise the extravagance of the burial. A record of the imported herbs and spices available to a monk who never left his Northumbrian home is preserved in the will of Bede, who is recorded as having bequeathed lavender, aniseed, cinnamon, cloves, cumin, coriander, cardamom, galingale, ginger, liquorice, sugar and pepper to his fellow monks.

It is clear from ecclesiastical correspondence that there was a lively exchange of exotic spices as part of the gift-giving amongst Anglo-Saxon church men and women, many of whom travelled widely, to Rome and beyond. How far other social groups had access to such exotic flavours is not known.

Mealtimes

Most of our information on mealtimes comes from an ecclesiastical context. Within monastic houses, meals were taken at set times through the day according to the rules of the house and the time of the year. In general, there were two main meals of the day, at noon and in the evening. On special days, other rules might apply, particularly during times of fasting or on holy days. On Sundays, for example, when the day was devoted to prayer, mealtimes were pushed to the very beginning and end of the day.

How much Anglo-Saxons ate probably related to how much food was available according to their status and the time of year, but there is some documentary evidence to suggest that Anglo-Saxon ideas of gluttony related not just to eating too much, but to eating in between set mealtimes. In a letter of Ælfric's to a Brother Edward, written at the beginning of the eleventh century, Ælfric condemned the gluttony of rural peasant women (though men were also implicated) who took food from the feast and ate it in communal privies. This is a difficult text to interpret. Ælfric may be condemning the gluttony of the women, who cannot even pause in their eating when they go to the toilet. Other parts of the letter deal with the Jewish taboo on eating blood, and there is also a section condemning the wearing of Danish (i.e. pagan viking) clothing. The whole letter is a condemnation of non-Christian, defiling behaviour. Whatever Ælfric's purpose in describing the 'outrageous scandal' (*husclic bismor*), he is echoing the implication of other Old English writers that secret eating, away from the communal table was inappropriate. The making, processing and cooking of food required communal effort, and the proper place to eat the communal food was in public.

Famine

In spite of the skills and knowledge of Anglo-Saxon farmers, the documentary sources make it clear that there were intermittent periods of famine, sometimes as a result of animal or human disease, sometimes as a result of unpredictable weather and sometimes as a result of warfare. Bede recorded that, by AD 681, 'no rain had fallen [in Sussex] and consequently a most severe famine afflicted the people and they were struck down by a cruel death.' So desperate were the survivors that (according to Bede) whole families held hands and threw themselves off cliffs into the sea to avoid slow death by starvation (though there may be an echo here of ritual sacrifice to the gods to bring about good harvests). In all, the *Anglo-Saxon Chronicles* recorded over fifty serious famine years from the fifth to the eleventh century. A late-tenth-century will from Durham indicates the social upheaval and misery behind the fact of famine. In this will, a woman freed all those 'whose heads she took for their food in the evil days'; in other words, those who had voluntarily become her slaves in return for the sustenance which the law guaranteed slave owners would give their slaves. It is possible to perceive the lady's act of taking on slaves as generous – free, they would have been left to starve. By contrast, the act of freeing them took away from her inheritors the expense and responsibility of providing for these extra mouths, while also throwing back on her freed slaves the burden of finding their own food and shelter. It has to be hoped for their sakes that the times were no longer evil.

Cooking

Bald's *Leechbook* provides evidence for the array of cooking vessels and implements available to an Anglo-Saxon cook, as well as offering hints as to how these vessels were used. Medical preparations might be boiled in a pot, a copper vessel or a jug with a lid, a pan or a kettle. Ingredients might also be simmered in a brass vessel. A mortar could be used for pounding, while sieves made out of cloth, linen if fine sieving were required, could be used to strain ingredients. The Anglo-Saxon doctor had access to a grater for grating, a wide pan for heating fat and a large kettle for boiling, as well as a saucer – for catching worms as they fell out in a remedy to relieve earache caused by 'worms in the ear'. Spoons, bowls, handfuls, cups, jugs, ounces and pennies were all used for measuring dry and wet ingredients. Though all these artefacts were used in a medical context for Bald's preparations, the wide Anglo-Saxon vocabulary for pots, pans, jugs and kettles, indicating different sizes and different uses, suggests that Anglo-Saxon doctors were simply making use of everyday cooking equipment or, at least, the range of equipment available to the elite.

Bread was cooked on a pan over a fire or by placing the loaf in the ashes of a fire or by placing it in an oven. Examples of Anglo-Saxon ovens are known from the archaeological evidence from the sixth century onwards, though it is difficult to prove that they were used for baking bread, but early documentary sources record bread ovens, such as that described in the early-eighth-century *Life of Ceolfrith*, where the oven is cleaned out before the loaves were put in it for baking.

The mainstay of Anglo-Saxon cooking was the stew, made in a cauldron or kettle suspended over a fire. In elite households, a metal vessel would be used, but the earthenware crocks found in lower status sites could also be used for stewing food and creating broths. Stewing was an economical way of preparing foods, particularly where the meat might have been dried, cured or derived from an older animal.

Roasting, by contrast, was a more luxurious way of preparing food. Illustrations from the Tapestry show food being brought to the table on spits. Butchery remains from the palace site at Yeavering also indicate that meat was roasted. Food might also have been fried: a tenth-century frying pan has been recovered from the excavations at York. It may have been used for frying griddle cakes, though there is a recipe in Bald's *Leechbook* for making an herb omelette in a frying pan.

Meat might also be mashed or ground finely to make a mince. The Old English word *mearg* meant marrow, and *mearghæccel* described a kind of meat pudding or sausage. Late Anglo-Saxon manuscripts and the Tapestry show small cut pieces of meat skewered and cooked over a fire.

On the whole, the range of meals available to an Anglo-Saxon was dependent on the seasons and fairly repetitive. As the cook in Ælfric's *Colloquy* is reminded, everyone could cook stewed and roasted food. The cook defends his skills by talking about his special dishes, in particular, a rich broth.

Tableware and feasting

In addition to symbols of warrior status and royal status, the grave goods associated with the princely burial in Mound 1, Sutton Hoo,

in the early seventh century, included a collection of objects symbolic
of the role of the tribal leader as host and feast giver. These items range
from relatively prosaic local productions to valuable exotic imports.
Feasting equipment associated with this single burial include a large
cauldron with a chain link to hang it from a roof beam, maple-wood
drinking cups, silver bowls from Byzantium, decorated drinking horns,
a pottery bottle containing wine imported from the Continent, wooden
buckets including an iron-bound, yew-wood vat which has been
estimated to have a capacity of about 178 pints (101.15 litres) and
two spoons. The presence of feasting equipment within the grave of the
rich, high-status East Anglian prince or ruler who was buried in Mound 1
in the early seventh century underlines how important food and feasting
was within the Anglo-Saxon community. A meal was not simply a matter
of taking in calories, it could also be an important communal act,
conferring obligations on the guests, reinforcing social bonds and
providing an occasion for the discussion and dissemination of important
information. Food was used to convey messages about ethnic identity,
status, religious affiliation, gender and occupation, as well as being
used to reward followers, cement political and kinship relationships
and create and strengthen social bonds at feasts, marriages, funerals
and other events.

The grave goods from the burial at Sutton Hoo offer some
important information about how meal times were conducted, how
meals were cooked and how they were consumed. Drinking clearly
formed an important part of the feast. It is noticeable that the Sutton
Hoo vessels, in common with other known Anglo-Saxon drinking
vessels, are not designed to be used by one individual throughout
a meal, in that they cannot easily be put down without their contents
spilling. Elite Anglo-Saxon drinking vessels are typically horn shaped,
like drinking horns, or the vulgar – there is no other word for it – glass
claw beakers, or they have rounded bottoms, like the glass palm
cups that have been found in some graves or the round maple-wood
cup/bottles from Sutton Hoo Mound 1. What the shape of these
vessels suggests is that either it was expected that the contents of the
vessel was to be drunk in one go, as might be the case with the small
palm cups, or vessels were to be passed from guest to guest around the
table, as seems likely with the larger drinking horns, and as happens
even today at ceremonial occasions, as at The Queen's College, Oxford,
for example, when the Boar's Head Feast, a relic of the medieval period,

sees an antique auroch's horn, full of an ale-based drink, passed from guest to guest.

The will of a rich woman called Wynflæd, which dates to around AD 950, shows the range of tableware such a woman might possess – 'a cup with a lid' (*ane hlidfæsþe cuppan*), ornamented cups, which she describes as 'her own' (*ieredan cuppan*), two silver cups (*sylerenan cuppan*) and a gold-adorned wooden cup (*goldfagan treowenan cuppan*).

Small, versatile, single-bladed iron knives are amongst the most common dress items found in association with Anglo-Saxon burials, and apart from fingers and the occasional spoon, they were the sole eating utensil. At Westgarth Gardens, twenty-nine burials, of men and women, included knives as grave goods. At mealtimes, it is likely that diners used their own knives to cut, spear and transport their food to their mouths, and perhaps to pick their teeth, too, though Bald's *Leechbook* does refer to a *toth gare*, which translates literally as 'tooth spear' or tooth pick.

Some of our best evidence for tableware comes from the *Leechbooks*. Bald's *Leechbook* required the use of spoons, large and small bowls, jugs, vats and large and small kettles for measuring out the ingredients. The picture of a plentiful variety of pottery, wooden, leather and metal tableware provided by Bald's *Leechbook* is corroborated by archaeological finds. Rare preservation conditions at Viking Age York have led to the discovery of a number of wooden bowls and cups made on site, and a range of wooden vessels have been recovered from early Anglo-Saxon inhumation sites. At Castledyke, Humberside, twelve graves contained turned wooden bowls decorated with metal fittings. Besides having metal decorations, the bowls at Castledyke were made from a variety of woods, and at Sewerby, Yorkshire, bowls found in graves were made from wild cherry, ash, chestnut, maple and beech, suggesting that the appearance of bowls as decorative items was as important as their functional use.

Finds of glass on Anglo-Saxon settlement sites are rare. Excavations at the early Anglo-Saxon cemetery at Morning Thorpe, Norfolk, recovered the remains of about 365 inhumations and 9 cremation burials. Of these, only one burial included a glass vessel. The occupant of Grave 148 was a male, whose disturbed grave included a spearhead and a pot. Inside the pot was a pale green glass cone beaker. At Westgarth Gardens, Suffolk, the small early Anglo-Saxon cemetery produced two glass vessels, both in male burials. One was a small, flat-bottomed green glass beaker with lugs on the rim for some kind of handle, found in Grave 62, which also contained a spear and shield, and the other was a cone beaker in Grave 51, which also contained a sword, scabbard, glass sword bead, shield and spear. The excavations at the early Anglo-Saxon settlement of West Stow, Suffolk, produced four fragments of brown glass, two of which certainly belonged to the same claw beaker. The scarcity of glass vessels, or of fragments of glass, in an early Anglo-Saxon context, suggests that precious few examples of imported glassware might be found in each community, though most people would have seen a glass vessel at some point in their lives.

Other forms of food containers occur. At Westgarth Gardens, for example, in addition to fragmentary sherds of pottery found in the grave backfill, the sixty-eight graves produced two wooden bowls with a rounded bottom, one of which had a bronze mount decorated with heads and stars and associated with the rich female adult in Grave 36; one wooden bucket with iron mounts and handle in a badly disturbed grave; an iron-bound bucket in Grave 66, accompanying a male with a sword, shield boss and sword harness; six decorated pots (four with weaponed males and two with richly buried female adults); and seven plain pots (one with a weapon burial; one with a disturbed weapon burial; two with wealthy females with chatelaines, brooches and a long string of beads; one with a poorly equipped burial, sex and age unknown; one with a juvenile; and one with an infant). It might be possible to give a value to different types and materials of vessels according to the number of occurrences and the age and gender of the associated burial. Meals were not just a matter of eating; they were also an opportunity to display and reinforce social ranking.

Chapter 6
Clothing and Appearance

Archaeological evidence and documentary evidence, including pictorial
representations in sculpture and manuscripts, make it possible
to reconstruct aspects of Anglo-Saxon appearance, including dress
and hairstyles, and provide evidence for the process of cloth production,
a gendered activity which must have dominated the daily life of women.

Early Anglo-Saxon clothing

The majority of early Anglo-Saxon burials seem to have been placed in
the ground wearing some kind of costume. Surviving clothing fasteners
and fittings such as buckles, brooches, lace tags and toggles mean that it
is possible to make fairly accurate reconstructions of early female Anglo-
Saxon clothing, though male dress is harder to reconstruct. Surviving
textile fragments, usually preserved in mineralised form through contact
with corroding metal items such as brooches, also help us to understand
the quality, patterning and colour of the garments worn in the fifth to the
seventh century. It must be stressed, however, that these costumes may
have been special, ritual costumes appropriate for funerals, rather than
daily wear.

Women's dress

Anglo-Saxon women, before the conversion to Christianity, wore a long
sleeved undergarment, over which was worn a long tubular sleeveless
dress, which was fastened at the shoulders by two brooches and gathered
at the waist by a belt. Long strings of beads might be suspended between
the two brooches, and knives, bags and chatelaines (sets of keys, rods
or other items) might be suspended from the belt. In the Anglian areas
of England, the sleeves on the undergarment might be held together
by a set of wristclasps – pairs of metal interlocking clasps reflecting the
Scandinavian links of the Anglian migrants. Meanwhile, dress in Kent
reflected stronger Continental, Frankish links – a Kentish Anglo-Saxon

woman might be buried with a long cloak held at the chest by a further large brooch. Shoes for men and women would have been made of leather, but without the metal hobnails which characterise late Romano-British burials.

Textile evidence suggests that the undergarment would have been made from fine flax, while the over garments were made from stronger wool twills. Cloths would have been self-coloured or dyed with vegetable dyes and were woven to create attractive chevron or checked patterns. Excavations at the extensive early Anglo-Saxon inhumation and cremation cemetery at Morning Thorpe, Norfolk, produced some relatively well-preserved textile remains, which showed that red (probably produced by madder), purple and blue dyes had been used. Hems and edges might be finished with tablet-woven braiding, commonly found sewn on as cuffs to strengthen the wrist of undergarments but also found in association with brooches at the chest, suggesting that tablet-woven braids were used to finish the borders of the over garment. Very fine tabby weaves found at sites such as Great Chesterford, Essex, also suggest the presence of veils or scarves, tucked under the brooches.

Jewellery in the fifth to the sixth century had a strong regional, tribal character and had a prominent role in the display of the body in the funeral ritual, so that it is possible to identify the general part of Britain to which a woman belonged on the basis of her brooches and other jewellery. A woman from the Thames Valley area typically wore a pair of applied or cast-saucer brooches, sometimes, with a third brooch for display – perhaps an equal-arm or small cruciform brooch, showing her northern Germanic tribal affiliations. Women in this area also wore elaborately chip-carved quoit brooches in silver, which give their name to a characteristic zoomorphic design (quoit-brooch style) found on other artefacts of the period. Further north, in Anglian areas of the country, wrist clasps, annular, penannular and cruciform brooches were more popular. Anglian women were not as concerned to have pairs of matching brooches as Thames Valley women and might add one or two more display brooches to their costume – perhaps a swastika brooch, a small–long brooch or, to display real wealth, a great square-headed brooch. While women in all areas might have had impressive festoons of beads and additional jewellery, Anglian women in particular favoured gold and silver bracteates (discs imitative of coins) and shield-shaped pendants and might also be found wearing silver bracelets and finger rings. In 'Saxon' areas of the country south of the Thames Valley, women preferred to dress with pairs of disc, button or decorated saucer brooches, although other brooch types – small–long, annular, cruciform and occasionally great square-headed – do occur. Meanwhile in Kent, the early Germanic repertoire of brooches was quickly replaced by gold- and silver-decorated Frankish-style brooches – pairs of silver square-headed brooches and button brooches, as well as Continental imports. From the mid-sixth century, pairs of disc brooches inlaid with garnet begin to appear.

Gold and garnet became more plentiful in England in the seventh century, especially in Kent, and this coincided with a change in burial ritual (the 'Final Phase' of furnished inhumation), which also saw a significant change in women's burial costume. In Kent, large composite disc brooches decorated in gold, garnet and other semi-precious material appear, often with a cruciform design. These large display brooches probably fastened a cloak, and replaced the Germanic large square-headed brooch. The whole burial costume of the richer women became less Germanic and more Byzantine: Germanic brooches disappear, bead festoons became much shorter and delicate metal pins – often linked by fine chains in pairs or sets of three – were used to fasten fine veils. This change in costume is replicated in other parts of England. Fewer women were buried in costume, and those who were, were buried with similar expensive jewellery, reflecting their affiliations with a rising Anglo-Saxon elite class, rather than proclaiming any local, tribal identity.

Bags and belt hangings

One characteristic of female dress in the furnished-burial ritual are bags or pouches, which, when worn, appear to have been suspended from the waist by a belt. The presence of some bags can only be inferred from a collection of artefacts in the appropriate area, but in the case of others, surviving fittings show that bags could be expensive accoutrements. One form of hanging bag was made by suspending a pouch from a ring. The ring was sometimes made from walrus ivory, but examples made from elephant ivory are known. Extraordinarily, it would appear that the material forming the pouch habitually covered these exotic materials. Other pouches were suspended from a metal bar. Some pouches were decorated, suggesting that they were intended to be visible. The wealthy woman buried in the barrow at Swallowcliffe Down, Wiltshire, had sheets of silver covered with repoussé decoration on the front of her bag: the metal had once belonged on another artefact and had been shaped to fit the pouch.

The contents of the bags pose a problem of interpretation. Commonly, bags contained collections of beads, latchlifters, Roman coins, brooches and other pieces associated with necklaces and dress fittings. Their purpose is not clear, but since the artefacts were hidden within the bags at the time of burial, it would seem that they were not part of the costume 'display'. Artefacts found within bags were often also fragmentary, worn or otherwise incomplete.

Whilst some women were buried with no grave goods at all, it is worth emphasising that some of the mortuary costumes were canvases on which personal, family or tribal wealth (in the form of ornate jewelled metalwork and other grave goods) was deliberately displayed before the objects were removed from the community forever by burial. At Worthy Park, Grave 30 contained one such adult female. Her grave goods included a gilt-bronze button brooch decorated with a human, moustached face at her throat (possibly holding a cloak) and pin fragments by her skull, perhaps associated with a headdress or hairstyle. She had two strings of beads which reached down from her shoulders to her waist. The bead strings were made up of forty-seven blue, red-purple, white, red, green-yellow and blue-green glass beads; thirty amber beads; two copper-alloy rings; a Roman coin, pierced for suspension; a copper-alloy pendant; and fragments of leather and textile. At her waist, the woman had an iron knife; her belt was fastened by a tinned copper-alloy buckle and had additional tinned copper-alloy rivets and a belt plate. She had a bag containing a glass fragment, a copper-alloy loop, nine Roman coins, several of which were pierced for suspension and a tinned copper-alloy disc. In addition, she had a chatelaine, consisting of metal fragments, copper-alloy finger rings, other rings and ring fragments, and some amber beads.

Dress from c. AD 700

For the late Anglo-Saxon period, there is less evidence for dress from the burials, but more from texts and illustrations. As might be expected, higher-status women wore the finest clothes. Bede related that Queen Æthelthryth, daughter of the powerful East Anglian king, Anna, would never wear linen, but only woollen clothes, would only take a hot bath before the three key feasts in the Christian calendar (that Bede specifies 'hot' indicates that the rest of the time she washed in cold water, as opposed to not washing at all) and ate only once a day. Her self-control and self-abnegation contrast with the life of luxury a normal high-status woman might demand, but Queen Æthelthryth was no ordinary woman. She entered the monastic life after successfully preserving her virginity through more than twelve years of marriage; her first husband died shortly after their marriage, and her second, Ecgfrith, made fruitless attempts to bribe the influential Bishop Wilfred to persuade her to consummate the marriage, before eventually agreeing that she could enter a monastery. Æthelthryth became a saint, later known as St. Audrey. In the later medieval period, a market was held on her feast day in Cambridge, and so poor was the quality of goods sold at this market, that they became known as 'St. Audrey's goods', giving us the modern English word 'tawdry'.

By contrast, the late-tenth-century St. Edith of Wilton, when chastised by Bishop Æthelwold of Winchester for wearing so much finery when Christ was interested only in the heart, smartly replied, 'Quite so, Father, and I have given my heart.'

Bishop Aldhelm criticised ecclesiastical men and women who decorated themselves, and particularly women who wore

> fine linen shirts, in scarlet or blue tunics, in necklines and sleeves embroidered with silk; their shoes are trimmed with red-dyed leather; the hair of their forelocks and the curls at their temples are crimped with a curling iron; dark-grey veils for the head give way to bright and coloured head-dresses which are sewn with interlaces of ribbons and hang down as far as the ankles. Fingernails are sharpened after the manner of falcons or hawks.

These complaints about ecclesiastical women give a hint as to the finery and costumes worn by rich women in the later Anglo-Saxon period.

The archaeological evidence gives some support to the ecclesiastical complaints about women's enthusiasm for fine dress. Some opulent 'Final Phase' jewellery has overt Christian symbolism, such as the beautifully crafted gold and garnet necklace buried with a female at Desborough, Northamptonshire: the central element of this necklace is a gold cross with a central garnet. The new, Byzantine-inspired fashion for veils might be thought to usher in more modest dress, but the gold and garnet triple pin-set-veil fastener found with a woman buried in a barrow at Roundway Down, Wiltshire, was purely decorative.

Men's costume

Men's clothing for the early Anglo-Saxon period is much more difficult to reconstruct than women's clothing, since dress finds are limited to evidence for a belt (a buckle or a knife at the waist) or occasional pins. While clothing exhibited women's status and identity, men's social identity was bound up in the weaponry they carried, rather than in the clothes they wore (Figure 19).

More revealing evidence for clothing comes from a few unusually rich burials, particularly the barrow burials at Taplow, Buckinghamshire; Sutton Hoo, Suffolk; and Prittlewell, Essex. What is interesting about these burials is that, although they have much in common, not least in their extravagance and opulence, they each show a different mortuary costume, and these costumes are not necessarily representative of everyday Anglo-Saxon male wear, but may more plausibly be an expression of new-found power and royal aspirations. This argument carries particular weight with the burial of the Sutton Hoo male, whose costume has a number of unique characteristics. At his shoulders were two gold shoulder clasps, decorated in garnet and millefiori with intricate animal designs. The pieces were made in a local workshop, and the craftsmanship they exhibit is breathtaking. The shoulder clasps are without any parallel in the Anglo-Saxon archaeological record. Equally unusual and well crafted is the beautiful gold and garnet purse, which did not actually contain the coins also included in this burial hoard: elsewhere in Anglo-Saxon burial costume of this period, bags are more usually associated with women. The great gold buckle with which the man is buried provides further evidence that his funerary costume was not designed for practicality. The gold buckle, decorated with an intricately woven animal interlace design, weighed over 14.1 ounces (400 grams). It is actually a hollow box: it is cast in two parts, opens on a hinge and has an ingenious locking mechanism. It could have been threaded onto a belt, but it never functioned as a buckle. One explanation for the costume (and some of the other 'props' in this grave) is that the owner was attempting to dress

Illustrations

1. Burgh castle, Suffolk; one of the shore forts built by the Romans to protect the coast from Saxons.

2. Dyke Hills, Dorchester-on-Thames: site of two early Anglo-Saxon burials.

3. The Anglo-Saxon church at Bradford-on-Avon.

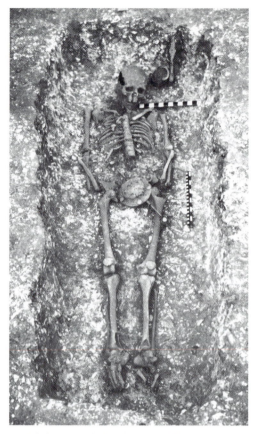

4. Male burial with shield, spear and bucket, Grave 49, Kingsworthy.

5. Reconstructed early Anglo-Saxon buildings at West Stow, Suffolk.

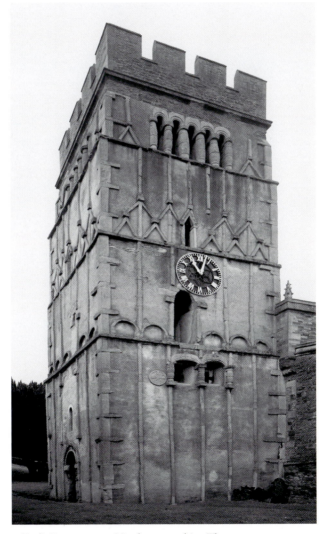

6. Earl's Barton tower, Northamptonshire. The stone masonry imitates a wooden building.

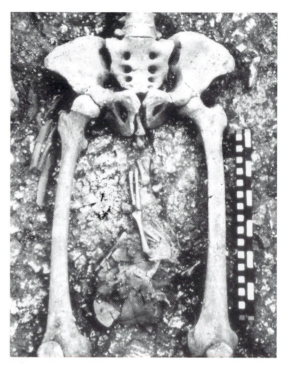

7. Childbirth mortality: Grave 26, Kingsworthy, female died in childbirth and buried with foetus.

8. Mammiform pot with pierced end associated with an infant burial photographed shortly after excavation at Castledyke, Beverley.

9. Glass claw beaker,
Grave 203, Finglesham.

10. Textiles preserved on the back
of a brooch, Grave 203, Finglesham.

11. Female burial with quoit brooch at left shoulder and beads and pouch-complex at right side, Grave 77, Kingsworthy.

12. The Anglo-Saxon church at Escomb, Northumberland, which includes Roman spolia in its construction.

13. Part of the Old English poem 'The Dream of the Rood' inscribed in runic writing on the Ruthwell Cross, Dumfriesshire.

14. Bead strings from grave 203, Finglesham, Kent.

15. Eighth century sculpture from Breedon-on-the-Hill, Leicestershire. The Anglo-Saxon church is built on the site of an Iron Age Hill fort.

16. Infant mortality: Grave 17A, aged 15–18 months, with pot and bead, Kingsworthy.

17. Disabling events: right forearm with healed fracture leading to disablement, Grave 14, Kingsworthy.

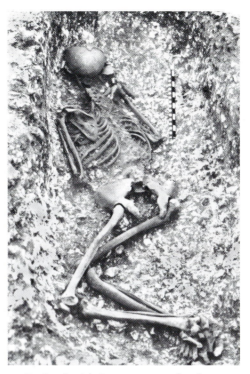

18. Deviant burial: Grave 43, young female, buried prone, Kingsworthy.

19. Stone fragment of an Anglo-Saxon animal head from excavations at Worcester Cathedral Chapter House.

20. The Norman motte and bailey castle, Oxford, which blocked the main western approach to the town, forcing a deviation still called 'New Road'.

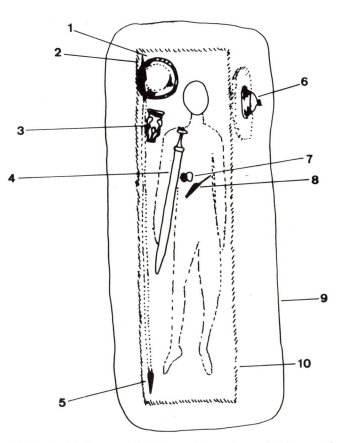

Figure 19 Weapon burial, Grave 204, Finglesham, Kent: 1, bronze bowl; 2, spearhead; 3, glass claw beaker; 4, sword; 5, spear ferrule; 6, shield (on edge); 7, silver and garnet buckle; 8, iron knife; 9, grave edge; and 10, coffin.

as a Roman war leader or emperor. The shoulder clasps represent Roman military epaulettes, and the buckle is modelled on the large military belt buckles of high-ranking Romans.

Belt buckles were always an important aspect of the Anglo-Saxon male costume. Evidence for the earliest Anglo-Saxon presence in England comes from the quoit-brooch–style buckles and fittings associated with male burials from Mucking, Essex, and Dyke Hills, Dorchester, Oxfordshire. The Dyke Hills burial has been interpreted as one of the early Anglo-Saxon mercenary warriors or *foederati* who, according to legend, were invited in to Britain by the British tyrant Vortigern. The inspiration for these early belts is thought to have been the belt equipment of the late Roman army. In certain ritual circumstances, a belt may have been the only item of clothing. An enigmatic gilt-bronze buckle from the cemetery at Finglesham, Kent, lay at the waist of a man. Though his burial also included shoe buckles and lace tags, a spear, knife, wooden box and bucket and pottery bottle, he was by no means the richest burial at this site. The buckle is particularly interesting because it shows in relief the form of a male figure, holding two spears and wearing nothing apart from a belt with a display buckle and a helmet (Figure 20).

Illustrations from later Anglo-Saxon manuscripts suggest that there are two later forms of male costume. One, more often associated with lower-status males, consisted of a short, belted tunic worn over leggings. Higher-status males might wear an additional long cloak, held at the

Figure 20 Finglesham man.

shoulder by a single brooch, such as is seen worn by King Harold in the Bayeux Tapestry as he set off on his ill-fated journey to the Continent. Inscriptions on later artefacts show that high-status males also wore personal jewellery. A massive ring of gold was found by accident in 1780, squashed into a cart rut. It bears the legend +ETHELVVLF REX and has been attributed to King Æthelwulf (839–858), father of King Alfred the Great.

Higher-status men wore cloaks fastened at the shoulder with a single circular brooch. In the Bayeux Tapestry, for example, King Harold and his nobles are portrayed wearing cloaks sweeping down below their knees. Peasants and labourers, by contrast, wear short tunics ending above the knees, belted at the middle. At a time when cloth production was expensive and time consuming, only the wealthy could afford to flaunt long cloaks.

Footwear is difficult to reconstruct for the whole Anglo-Saxon period. Lace tags and the occasional buckles in the area of the foot from the early Anglo-Saxon burials suggests that shoes were worn, but there is no evidence for the hob nails which characterise late Romano-British burials. A few examples of late Anglo-Saxon shoes survived from the excavations at York. These tenth-century examples of footwear were made of leather, constructed out of a single flat sole without a heel, which was sewn onto a shoe or boot also made of leather. When the soles wore out, they could be discarded, and a new one stitched into place. Manuscript illustrations indicate that the majority of ordinary people were habitually barefoot or wore ankle-high turnshoes.

Strap or hook tags make an appearance as an item of clothing fastener in the seventh to the eleventh century, but it is not absolutely clear what their purpose was. They may have helped to secure leggings.

Children's clothing

The majority of the grave goods found in early Anglo-Saxon graves are associated with the costume worn by the deceased at the time of burial, and the examination of the position of clothing fixtures, and the impressions of textiles sometimes preserved by the action of the corroding metalwork, has allowed archaeologists to reconstruct men and women's costumes from the early Anglo-Saxon period. It is noticeable, however, that children (that is, juveniles under the age of about ten to twelve, the customary age of maturity in Anglo-Saxon society) were buried with far fewer costume-related artefacts than adults. At the cemetery of Polhill, West Kent, for example, children's burials contained only iron knives (eight examples), iron buckles (two examples), beads (three examples) and a latchlifter which might be deemed part of their costume. No child was buried with a brooch, or shoe fittings, or any great strings of necklaces. The implication of the graves at Polhill and other sites is that children's clothes were different from those of adults, either because they required fewer fasteners than adult clothes or because fasteners on children's clothes were made of perishable materials such as wood, leather or cloth. It is even possible that children were allowed to go around without any clothes on at all in the pre-Christian period: the anonymous writer of the *Life* of St. Cuthbert recorded that some boys at play 'stood naked, with their legs stretched out and pivoted skywards', though this detail was removed from other versions of the *Life*. Rather than imagining naked children, it may be that the writer was pointing out the unseemliness of children doing handstands so that their clothing fell around their ears, leaving their bodies exposed. In the late Anglo-Saxon *Harley Psalter*, however, children are depicted as either naked or wearing a short, loose tunic reaching to the hips.

Winter clothing

'The Seafarer' poet evoked the bitter pains of a world at winter, describing feet so pinched by cold that they felt shackled by chains of ice. The ploughman of Ælfric's *Colloquy* was bitterly aware of the difference between his outdoor work and the comfort experienced by his lord and commented on the poor lad who worked with him, whose voice was hoarse from the cold and shouting as he urged on the plough oxen. Though there is some evidence that winters in Anglo-Saxon England were comparatively mild, the vivid and painful descriptions of bad weather in the surviving texts leave no doubt that Anglo-Saxons could not always shelter from their environment. In addition to the woollen and linen clothing they wore to keep themselves warm, they needed clothes to keep out the wet of rain and snow. The main material for wet-weather wear appears to have been leather. The Anglo-Saxon leather worker in Ælfric's *Colloquy* boasted of the range of garments he could create – boots, ankle leathers, shoes and leather trousers – and insisted that 'no-one is willing to go through winter without my craft'.

Hairstyles

Appearance was coded in Anglo-Saxon England – what you looked like, in terms of size, bodily afflictions, hairstyle, clothing and jewellery, gave the viewer personal information about your age, your status, your parentage, your work, your marital status, your ethnic affiliations and even whether you had ever been found guilty of criminal behaviour. At the time of the Anglo-Saxon migrations to England, male hairstyles were certainly linked to social status and, perhaps, to ethnic identity, too. So key were hairstyles to personal identity that some of the migrating tribes in Europe were described by them: the Longobards, who gave their name to Lombardy, in Italy, were 'the long beards'. In early medieval France, Merovingian Frankish kings were known as 'the long-haired kings'. Any male pretender to the throne had to have long hair, and one way of preventing an aspiring prince from staging a coup was to have his hair cut off: he could not be eligible for leadership until it had grown again. Similar attitudes towards hair probably prevailed in Anglo-Saxon England, though the evidence is scanty. When Gildas wanted to describe the four peoples who populated the British Isles – the Irish, the British, the Picts and the Anglo-Saxons – he identified hairstyles as differentiating them. He noted, for example, that the Picts were 'readier to cover their villainous faces with hair than their private parts … with clothes'. One of the most heated and divisive debates in the early Anglo-Saxon church revolved around hairstyles – should churchmen be tonsured at the front of their heads, as was the style in the Celtic church, or should they be tonsured on the crown, in the Roman fashion? (Figure 21).

Early images of male Anglo-Saxon faces place an emphasis on neatly trimmed facial hair. Moustaches are common, as in the Finglesham button brooch mentioned above. At Sutton Hoo, the striking helmet forms a moustached face, while the whetstone from the burial mound features enigmatic faces with neat triangular beards – a style mirrored on the Finglesham buckle discussed above. To touch or grab a man's hair was considered a gross insult: the law code of King Æthelbert of Kent has a fine of fifty sceattas for the crime of *feaxfang* (seizing someone's hair) – not a huge fine in the scheme of things, but greater

Figure 21 Hairstyles from Anglo-Saxon coins.

than the compensation fixed for the loss of a toenail or for a bruise hidden by clothing.

Ælfric, in a letter to Brother Edward, castigated those who wore their hair in the style of the pagan Danes, with *ableredum hneccan and ablendum eagum* – with their necks bare and their eyes blinded (by a long fringe falling across their faces). The Bayeux Tapestry suggests that Anglo-Saxons and Normans were differentiated by their hairstyles: King Harold and his Anglo-Saxon warriors wore long flowing locks, with long thin moustaches, while William and his men had their hair short, and shaved at the back, with longer hair at the front. Though the Tapestry was created some time later than Ælfric's letter, the Normans, grandchildren and great grandchildren of the Vikings (North men) who settled in northern France, seem to have had hairstyles matching the 'bare necks and blinded eyes' of the Danes Ælfric disliked so heartily.

The moustaches seen on Harold and his Anglo-Saxon warriors may have been more than a fashion statement, as suggested by an entry for 1056 in one manuscript of the *Anglo-Saxon Chronicle*: 'and Leofgar was appointed bishop, he who was Earl Harold's mass-priest and who in his priesthood kept his moustaches until he became a bishop'. Since the chronicler feels it necessary to comment on Leofgar's moustaches, their presence on his face was obviously considered inappropriate for a priest – perhaps moustaches were associated with warrior status, which Leofgar was reluctant to abandon. In the event, Leofgar was unable to live the priestly life, as he 'gave up his chrism and his cross and his spiritual weapons and grasped his spear and sword and so went campaigning against Griffin the Welsh king and [Leofgar] was killed there and his priests with him and Ælfnoth the sheriff and many other good men'.

Law 35 of King Alfred legislated for anyone laying hands on an innocent commoner (*unsynnigne ceorl*), and compensation was rated according to the level of injury done to the commoner through assault. If the commoner was scourged or placed in the stocks, then compensation of 20 and 30 shillings, respectively, had to be paid. To place a man in the stocks or to scourge him placed him in the category of slave – according to the Anglo-Saxon law codes, only the unfree could be treated in this way. Interestingly, in this context, the only other indignities envisaged as being inflicted on the 'innocent free commoner' in this law code had to do with cutting the man's hair:

> If he cuts his hair to insult him, in such a way as to spoil his appearance, he shall pay 10 shillings compensation; if he cuts his hair after the fashion of a priest's without binding him, he shall pay 30 shillings compensation; if he cuts off his beard '*gif he thone beard ofascire*', he shall pay 20 shillings compensation; if he lays bonds on him, and then cuts his hair after the fashion of a priest's, he shall pay 60 shillings compensation.

The purpose of the law code appears to be to legislate against lords who tried to force a churl (the poorest of the 'free' classes of man) to bond status, either by making him a priest (slaves worked as priests) or by taking away that which signified his free status. Key to reducing the status of a man was to cut his hair and beard, which acted as a visible mark of rank. With short hair and no beard, a man could not pass as a free commoner, hence the apparently disproportionate compensation.

There is some indication that hairstyles were used to differentiate between children and adults: late tenth- and eleventh-century manuscripts such as the *Harley Psalter* consistently show children with short, bobbed hair. There may also have been some links between hairstyles and female status, though this is not absolutely clear. The Old English law codes refer to *locboren* women – this may mean women who had loose hair, or it may mean women who carried keys to locks, i.e. held property and status.

Combs are a feature of the early Anglo-Saxon burial ritual, particularly cremations. At Worthy Park, Hampshire, miniature bone combs were placed in the burial urn with the cremated remains. Larger bone combs are sometimes found in association with female burials: a sixth-century female burial from Cassington, Oxfordshire, included

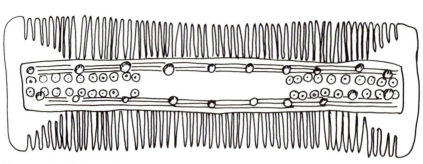

Figure 22 Anglo-Saxon bone comb.

a fine composite carved comb, complete with its own carrying case, emphasising the importance of hair and hairdressing as a statement of status – though no mirrors are found (Figure 22).

High-status men also treasured their combs. One was included with the burial of St. Cuthbert, a man noted for his ascetic lifestyle. Perhaps combs found in ecclesiastical contexts had a purpose in ritual cleansing, rather than reflecting personal vanity. Combs were not just for knots – they were also for nits, especially in the urban context of Anglo-Scandinavian York. Combs from York still have nits and lice adhering to their tines.

Textile production

Clothing had to be made, and the majority of Anglo-Saxon women would have spent a considerable amount of their working life engaged in producing cloth, because, at least until the tenth century, spinning, weaving and sewing were almost exclusively female activities. Textile production was always an important factor in Anglo-Saxon life, and the majority of a household's textile needs would have been provided by the women of the household, even into the later Anglo-Saxon period; the 'wise reeve' from the late Anglo-Saxon manuscript who needed to provide his servants with tools for working the farm was also cautioned to provide everything necessary for the household servants too: woolcomb, needle and awl were included in the list, indicating that a household would be involved in producing its own textiles, from carding the wool to sewing the cloth.

Environmental evidence from the earliest settlements in the Thames Valley, shows that flax was grown, perhaps for its oil, but also certainly to be turned into linen. The presence of a variety of cloth-making equipment in women's graves from the early Anglo-Saxon period – woolcombs, weaving battens, pin beaters, spindle whorls and wool shears – attest to the social importance of cloth making and also show the extent to which it was a gendered activity. Bone finds from the settlement site at Lechlade show that, although sheep were present, they were not particularly numerous; wool was not the only cloth being produced, but there is a lot of environmental evidence for flax, suggesting that linen cloth was being produced.

The majority of Anglo-Saxon garments were made of wool. Animal bone evidence shows that, by the later Anglo-Saxon period, there were three varieties of sheep producing black, white and brown wool. Once wool had been gathered, the first stage of preparing it for weaving was to comb the impurities from the wool. Wool combs were made of bone or wood and had iron teeth.

Gathering wool from sheep was a relatively simple process compared to the transformation of the flax plant into material. The flax had to be planted, tended, weeded and harvested, and the tough fibres of the plant needed to be prepared by rotting them and creating fibres.

Once the wool or flax fibres had been prepared, the fibres were spun on a hand-held spindle, weighted by perforated spindle whorls, to create a thread. This activity was ubiquitous throughout the Anglo-Saxon period. Spindle whorls are amongst the commonest finds on settlement sites, and their presence in female graves suggests that a hand-held spindle was part of a woman's daily costume and that spinning, like breadmaking, was part of the routine of daily life. Spindle whorls might be made of animal bone, pottery or stone, or from more exotic material such as glass, jet and amber (Figure 23).

The cemetery site at Lechlade, Gloucestershire, includes a number of females with weaving items in their graves. As well as weaving equipment, the associated settlement also includes finds of the characteristic Anglo-Saxon doughnut-shaped clay loom weights. Weaving was the next process in textile production. Anglo-Saxon women used upright, warp-weighted looms. Threads were suspended from the wooden top beam of the loom and held in position by doughnut-shaped fired-clay weights. Unlike other artefacts associated with textile production, loom weights, a common find in settlement excavations, are almost never found as part of a female grave assemblage. Technological change came in the mid-ninth century – finds

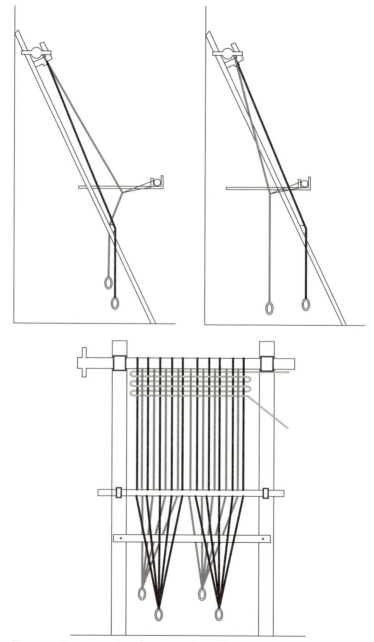

Figure 23 Reconstruction of a warp-weighted loom.

of loom weights decrease on settlement sites, probably indicating
a change to a two-beam loom. The end of the tenth century saw
the introduction of the horizontal treadle loom, and with it, the
'industrialisation' of cloth making. From the tenth century, textiles
were being produced in unprecedented quantities by dedicated cloth
makers in towns, and with this mass production came a new change –
males began to be involved in cloth production, beginning a process
that would lead to the formation of powerful guilds in the post-Conquest
period.

During the Anglo-Saxon period, ecclesiastical women gained
a reputation for the quality of their textile work. Finds from the seventh-
to eighth-century site of the nunnery at Barking, Essex, give considerable
evidence for cloth production, including gold-strip fragments from
woven braids. These are the very nuns to whom Aldhelm dedicated his
work *De virginitate*, in which he complains of women in religious orders
wearing coloured veils attached by costly headbands.

Silk was imported into England from an early period: there is
a surviving scrap of silk sealed into a metal cylindrical box in a seventh
century child's grave from Updown, Kent, for example. A ninth-century
braid fragment from the tomb of St. Cuthbert is made of imported cream
or dark red silk thread. Silk caps are also known from Viking York,
though such headgear is not shown in any manuscript illustrations
from the period.

There is no evidence for Anglo-Saxon knitting, though a single
woollen sock from Viking York survives which was made using the
Scandinavian technique called *nålebinding*, using fingers and a needle
to create the textile.

In addition to wool, the pelts of both wild and domestic animals were
undoubtedly used to make clothing, though evidence for furs is scarce.
Some clothing, many belts and most shoes were made from leather. The
bones from the early Anglo-Saxon settlement site at Lechlade include
a high proportion of cattle, and a leather worker's awl was found in
male Grave 57, suggesting that leather was also an important community
product. The striking number of calf bones in the archaeological deposits
from the settlement at Lechlade suggests that the community was
producing surplus cattle, which were being used to produce beef and
leather and, perhaps, also vellum – it has been estimated that the
production of a book like the *Lindisfarne Gospels*, for example, would
have used enough vellum to have required 1,500 calf skins. Perhaps

places like Lechlade were beginning to specialise in the production of leather or vellum to supply an increasingly literate elite, as well as producing surplus cloth. Such trade might explain the wealth of the community, demonstrated in the high-status, exotic artefacts found in some of the graves, including high-status weaponry, gold and garnet jewellery, cowrie shells and amethysts.

Chapter 7
Trade and Travel

The occupant of the early seventh-century ship burial at Sutton Hoo Mound 1, Suffolk, was buried with an array of artefacts breathtaking for the picture they give, both of insular craftsmanship and artistry and of the scale of international contacts available to the elite members of seventh-century Anglo-Saxon society. Even more difficult to grasp is the overt message of wealth the artefacts in the burial ground offer; they speak of a controlling group within Anglo-Saxon society who not only had the resources and contacts to accumulate the wealth deposited in the burial chamber, but also had a sufficient excess of such material to be able to consider the artefacts essentially disposable by placing them in the mound burial with the dead man. In this chapter, not just the making and distribution of artefacts of the Anglo-Saxons – rich and poor – will be considered, but also the kind of industry, trade, economy and network of transport routes which underpinned the massive gathering and producing of the material wealth of Anglo-Saxon England.

Woodworking

Wood was one of the most important resources for Anglo-Saxon production, used for constructing all domestic buildings throughout the period, for heating and for making furniture, carts and ships. Large quantities of timber were required to produce the charcoal needed to smelt metal ores and fire pottery kilns. To this end, woodlands were valued and carefully managed resources. The worth of good timber is illustrated by late Anglo-Saxon wills. The will of a wealthy woman called Siflæd, for example, reveals that woodlands formed a valuable part of her estate, and the value of a wood supply is indicated in the fact that she left 'to each of my brothers ... a wagonload of wood'. The importance of timber and logging has also left its mark in the place-name evidence. A late-tenth-century charter for Witney, Oxfordshire, records a *spon leage* and a *spon weg* to the north of the estate, which lay in the wooded clay lands on the edge of the Cotswolds. *Spon* means 'wood chipping', and the name suggests the place where timber from the woods was cut up, ready to be transported along the 'way' to the estate.

Wood was perhaps the most important raw material for the construction of everyday items, including housing, furniture, tableware, containers, decorative pieces, buttons, toggles and coffins, but, due to conditions of preservation, very little evidence for the manufacture of wooden artefacts survives. Evidence from waste cores found during the excavations of Viking Age Coppergate Street, York, show that carpenters there were using pole lathes to turn out cups and bowls. It is these craftspeople – the coopers – who gave the street its name. Woodwork on a larger scale was carried out using an axe to shape and carve the wood, as illustrated in the Bayeux Tapestry, which depicts the process of constructing of ships, from cutting down the trees, to making planks and building the vessels.

Stonemasonry and sculpture

Surviving walls from Romano-British towns and villas could have been a useful source of raw material with which to construct buildings, though this material was actually rarely incorporated in anything but ecclesiastical buildings. Stone quarries were also exploited in the later Anglo-Saxon period. A number of place names suggest stone quarrying activities, such as Quarrendon (Buckinghamshire); quarries are named in charters and other documents, such as the stone quarry (*stangedelf*) mentioned in 1002 at Standhill, Oxfordshire. Analysis of Anglo-Saxon church buildings indicates the source of their materials, some of which travelled significant distances from their original quarries. Quarries in the Cotswolds and the Isle of Wight, for example, supplied the raw materials for building churches in Hampshire. Few people lived in stone houses, but many would have had the experience of worshipping in churches built of stone, and a significant number were engaged in quarrying, transporting, building and sculpting in stone.

Other resources

Clay for potting is available widely in England, and iron ore for making metal could be found as bog iron or in surface deposits as haematite or carbonate iron ores, which were exploited at a variety of locations, such as the Weald, Lincolnshire, the Forest of Dean and Northamptonshire. Gold and silver occur in Britain, but the Anglo-Saxons were dependent on supplies from the Continent or on reused material from Romano-British sites.

A certain amount of craft activity certainly took place within each settlement, where raw resources for production were available locally. Early Anglo-Saxon settlements and later rural settlements were probably self-sufficient in textile production, as was discussed in the previous chapter. Each settlement probably produced its own pottery too, although even in the early Anglo-Saxon period, some pottery was being widely distributed. Early Anglo-Saxon pots were handmade, without a wheel, from local clays. These pots used to be described by archaeologists as 'grass tempered', though they also incorporated other forms of material to strengthen the clay matrix and are now more correctly termed 'organic tempered'. Organic tempered pottery was thought to be limited in production to early Anglo-Saxon settlements, though recent radiocarbon dates from the site at Yarnton in Oxfordshire now suggests that production of this type may have extended into the eighth or ninth century. Handmade pottery was fired in pits or in bonfires at relatively low temperatures (Figure 24).

In the eighth century, pottery began to be mass produced at industrial centres, fired in more sophisticated kilns. This pottery was coilmade on a slow wheel. The most important of these centres was Ipswich, the *wic* site supporting the kingdom of East Anglia. Pottery kilns have been excavated at Ipswich, and the huge output of the kilns is illustrated by the distribution of the pottery, which has been found at sites as far afield

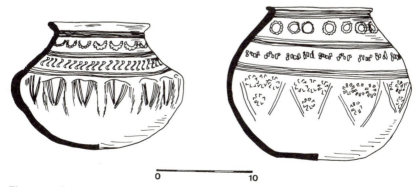

0   10

Figure 24 Cremation urns, Worthy Park, Kingsworthy.

as Oxfordshire to the west, Kent to the south and Yorkshire to the
north. Away from East Anglia, this characteristic pottery is only found
in association with high-status sites, showing how much this product
was valued. The pottery kilns at Ipswich are located in a small area
to the north-east of the middle Anglo-Saxon settlement, and it has
been suggested that this industry was set up by immigrants from the
Continent, who may well have established an enclave from which
to exploit their knowledge and technological ability.

During the ninth century, a form of the potter's wheel (though there
is not enough evidence yet to say what type) was introduced into
England. The East Anglian potters maintained their edge over other
regional pottery industries by quickly adopting new technology and
producing a type of ware known as 'Thetford ware', though pottery
production centres at Torksey, Lincolnshire, and Whitby, Yorkshire,
for example, were quick to follow suit. New, more efficient kilns
which supported the pots on clay arches or raised floors over the fires
were also introduced, and collapsed versions of such kilns excavated
at Torksey show that between twenty-five and fifty pots could be fired
as a single load.

In the late Anglo-Saxon period, lead-based glazes, which produced
orange, brown or yellow colours, were introduced. Stamford,
Lincolnshire, and Winchester, Hampshire, were particularly known
for their lead-glazed ware, and the value of this high-quality pottery
is revealed by its distribution. Stamford ware has been found in Ireland
and Scandinavia.

Bone and horn

Some boneworking would also have taken place within rural settlements.
Few Anglo-Saxon settlement sites are without evidence of some form
of boneworking. Animal bones and deer antler were essential materials
used to create a variety of artefacts, ranging from the ornate, complex
decorated combs found in graves, to boxes, knife handles, strap ends,
clothing toggles, gaming pieces, pins, needles, keys and pottery stamps.
Some of these artefacts – pottery stamps, for example – required only
limited effort to create, but the skill and abilities of Anglo-Saxon bone
workmen are exhibited in objects like the Franks Casket, carved from
whalebone. However, some Anglo-Saxon bonework debris from the

settlement sites show that highly skilled work was not restricted to the elite. At the early Anglo-Saxon settlement of West Stow, Suffolk, for example, delicate bone combs were recovered which would have required fine saws, drills, hammers and tools for incising the patterns. Horn cores and wasters from middle Anglo-Saxon *wic* settlements indicate that boneworking was one of the specialised industries of these production centres.

Metalwork

England is relatively well provided with accessible sources of metal. Gold, silver, tin, lead and iron ore were all found within Britain, and there is evidence of mining and quarrying. The lead deposits at Wirksworth, Derbyshire, for example, were mined and transported around the country – a render of produce from AD 835 shows that lead was transported from Wirksworth as far as Canterbury, Kent. Iron ore, however, was the most plentiful commodity, and numerous sites were worked across the country. A few early Anglo-Saxon settlements, such as Mucking, Essex, have produced evidence of slag, suggesting some iron smelting took place within settlements, though nothing to match the scale of iron smelting in contemporary Scandinavia, for example. The iron ore was smelted into iron by heating it to a high temperature in a shaft over a pit, for which huge amounts of charcoal would have been required. The end product was a mix of iron and slag, known as bloom, which required further heating and hammering before it produced iron. Much more common in early Anglo-Saxon settlement sites is evidence of hammer scale, the by-product of hammer-welding hot iron, suggesting domestic working of iron bloom (and the concomitant distribution of iron bars), perhaps to make the ubiquitous iron knives. Analysis of early Anglo-Saxon weaponry, however, suggests that much of the smithing showed considerable expertise and might have been the work of a specialist smith. Spearheads are the most common weapons found in graves. Usually, they were forged from a single piece of metal, with the socket flattened and folded to form an open tube into which the shaft could be inserted. Some spearheads were more complex, however: one seventh-century example from Broom Hill Quarry, Sandy, Bedfordshire, analysed by Dr Brian Gilmour, was made out of four pieces of iron with different properties, welded together to create a decorative pattern on the socketed blade.

Pattern welding was a technique particularly exploited by specialist Anglo-Saxon smiths to create highly prized pattern-welded swords. The technique involved repeatedly folding and hammer-welding a bar of iron to build up a tough layered structure. Strips of this steel were then twisted and hammered together, so that, when polished, they created a pattern of twisted lines along the length of the blade, an appearance memorably described by the *Beowulf* poet as *atertanum fah* (made with poisoned stripes).

A seventh-century cemetery find from Tattershall Thorpe, Lincolnshire, has provided us with information about the tools associated with smithing. During the excavation of the cemetery, a grave, located at a distance from any other burials, contained two deposits of metal-working tools and other materials. The iron tools included an anvil, hammers, tongs, a file, shears and punches. The hoard also contained copper alloy and other metals, glass and organic remains. The hoard may be associated with a foreign (Frankish) artisan.

Once metalwork had been turned into an end product, there were further specialised, high-status careers associated with metal craft. High-status males needed their weaponry to be kept in good order, probably more for display purposes than for any functional role the weapons might have. Swords, in particular, required special attention, judging from the royal bequest made by the young Prince Æthelstan (d. c.1015) to 'Ælfnoth my sword-polisher', and by-references in the *Laws of Alfred* and *Beowulf* to sword polishers and 'the polishers whose duty it was to burnish the warmasks'.

Owners, patrons and makers

From the beginning, some makers and owners placed inscriptions on their artefacts, and from this, we know the personal names of a number of craftsmen and their patrons. Often, these inscriptions were placed on high-status artefacts. The most famous is the enigmatic Alfred Jewel, now in the Ashmolean Museum, which may well be one of the *aestels* (perhaps a book pointer to help with reading) which King Alfred, in a surviving letter, said that he was sending out to all his bishops. The Alfred Jewel is set in a gold border, in which the legend '*Aelfred mec heht gewyrcan*' (Alfred ordered me to be made) has been placed. The late-seventh-century *Lindisfarne Gospels*, the most outstanding surviving manuscript of its era, records not only the name of the patron but also several other names of those involved in its construction over a period of years. This masterpiece was commissioned by the monastic house at Lindisfarne. The scribe was Eadfrith, who later became bishop of Lindisfarne. The book was bound by Æthilwold (who succeeded Eadfrith as bishop), and the cover was later ornamented with precious gems and metals by one Billfrith, the Anchorite. Finally, an additional note was written to tell the reader that Aldred the priest had added his own interlinear translation of the Latin text into English, thus producing the earliest surviving translation of the Gospels into the English language.

The *Lindisfarne Gospels*, the apex of manuscript art and illumination, represents the concerted product of skilled ecclesiastical craftsmen belonging to rich ecclesiastical houses, but it was not only the very wealthy and privileged who placed their names on their prized artefacts. Sometime in the seventh century, a woman was buried in a grave at Harford Farm, near Caister St Edmund, Norfolk. Due to the soil conditions, nothing of the woman's body survived in the ground, but her body was buried with a range of grave goods, including a beautiful gold and garnet composite brooch, set with ivory and glass to create a cruciform design. The brooch was possibly placed in a bag by her head, rather than being part of her costume. It was also an old piece, having been damaged and repaired, and the repairer had left his mark on the back in the form of a runic inscription which reads in translation 'Luda repaired the brooch'; there is also an inscribed animal decoration of twisted, biting snakes which may pre-date the repair. Craftsmen took other opportunities to advertise their names. A runic inscription on a stone shaft at Great Urswick, Cumbria, told the reader that one Tunwini had set up the monument as a 'beacon' for Torhtred in memory of his child, and asks the reader to pray for his soul. Meanwhile, on the lower part of the shaft, cut across two figures, the sculptor had added 'Lyl made this'. Bone workers, too, were proud of their skills – a bone comb case from Lincoln bears a runic inscription announcing 'Thorfastr made a good comb'.

Craftsmen may have been proud of their work, but some craftsmen, most notably smiths, were not necessarily credited with good character. In Ælfric's *Colloquy*, the smith tried to make a good case for the value of his profession – 'where would the ploughman be without his metal coulter, or the fisherman without his hook?' – but his work was belittled for creating showers of sparks and noise. One monk's debauched lifestyle so annoyed the Venerable Bede that he refused to name him, even though he was a good smith. One notorious ecclesiastical goldsmith was Abbot Spearhafoc (c.1047/1048–1051), a monk from Bury, whose work was so famous that he was commissioned to make pieces for royalty. In the end, the temptations of his craft proved too much for him; given the task of making a crown, he fled abroad with the gold and gems.

Amongst the most socially important metalworkers in the later Anglo-Saxon world were moneyers, who had responsibility for producing coins. Many of their coins carry their names, and so the identity of several thousand moneyers are known from the period. Moneyers' names are predominantly English, though in the Danelaw, more names have a Scandinavian origin, and there is also a sprinkling of Frankish names – perhaps Continental moneyers were brought in to help establish mints in Anglo-Scandinavian England. They seem to have worked independently of politics and not as a part of the personal retinue or household of kings, in that the same moneyers minted coins in the name of different kings – a change in kings did not affect a moneyer's right to mint coins. Moneyers represent an elusive, non-religious, wealthy burgess class in later Anglo-Saxon society, only rarely glimpsed in the documentary sources. They seem to have had sufficient social status and respectability in urban society to act as witnesses and lawyers and to sign charters.

Trade and markets

Early Anglo-Saxon England

As we have seen in earlier chapters, Anglo-Saxon England after the end of the Roman Empire may be characterised as rural, agricultural and local. The large villa estates, supported by slave labour, the bureaucracy and system of taxation, and the urban markets which characterised late Roman Britain had disappeared in Anglo-Saxon England. It is tempting to contrast Romano-British 'civilisation', with its systems, rules and monetary economy, with the more basic subsistence lives of the later fifth- and sixth-century inhabitants of Anglo-Saxon England. It is true that, once the supply of coins from the Roman Empire had dried up, late Roman Britain and early Anglo-Saxon England were no longer able to mint and use coins, and systems of trade inevitably became more fragmented. This is not to say, however, that the daily life of early Anglo-Saxons was based on a hand-to-mouth existence. The quantity and quality of artefacts removed from circulation and placed in cremation and inhumation graves testifies to the fact that early Anglo-Saxons had a sufficient surplus of wealth to bury some of their dead with it, and that, even though trade routes may have been more local and restricted than under the empire, Anglo-Saxon society produced surpluses, supported significant trading networks and had skilled craftsmen.

Metal artefacts from early graves suggest that economies were more than local. Women's brooches, for example, have a regional distribution, with regional concentrations of particular types. Finds of the so-called small-long brooches are typical of this phenomenon; they are concentrated in Anglian areas of sixth century, with a focus on Cambridgeshire, which suggests the possibility of either a dedicated smiths' workshop centred near Cambridge whose products were distributed by itinerant traders or an itinerant craftsman going from settlement to settlement with his moulds and scrap metal. Both methods of production and distribution may have operated at the same time.

Sixth-century graves contained artefacts from far afield. Long necklaces are a case in point. At Sewerby, Yorkshire, nineteen graves contained 679 beads made out of clay, amber, jet, crystal and glass. The clay was modelled out of Roman fired pottery or tile and could have been retrieved locally from an abandoned villa, and the amber and jet could have been collected from the local beaches, but the crystal and glass imply access to overseas resources. Anglo-Saxons at this time may well have been working in glass – one type of glass claw beaker is found more commonly in southern England than on the Continent, suggesting a workshop in Kent – but glass itself was not made in England. The main source for glass on the Continent at this time was Ravenna in northern Italy. Cubes, known as *tessarae*, of this material were traded across Europe for reworking into vessels or beads. The majority of the glass beads worn by the women at Sewerby, however, were imported from the Continent, some having their closest parallels in Frankia and others being matched by beads from Alemannic graves in Schretzheim in Germany.

Beads are relatively small artefacts, and it is not difficult to imagine parcels of beads being transported to England from the Continent, but a range of other imported artefacts, both bulky and fragile, found their way into early Anglo-Saxon graves and settlements, including glass vessels imported from France and the Rhineland and lava quernstones from Niedermendig in Germany. Elephant ivory, whose origins lay

in East Africa or India, and perhaps was introduced into western Europe
through Byzantium, was a surprisingly common artefact in early Anglo-
Saxon England, particularly used in the making of bags and pouches,
and found frequently as an incinerated artefact in cremation urns. It has
been suggested that some of the degraded or fragmented pieces of ivory
identified in cremation pots may have come from walrus tusks, and
it has also been suggested that some of the ivory found in England
in the fifth and sixth centuries came from locally found fossilised
mammoth tusks, but the coincidence of ivory becoming rare in
England in the seventh century, at the time of the Arab expansion into
the eastern Mediterranean, leading to a loss of western access to Africa
and India, suggests an eastern source for the majority of early Anglo-
Saxon ivory.

It is extremely difficult to work out how the farming people whose
bodies were found in the fifth- and sixth-century graves of Anglo-Saxon
England came by their exotic imports. This was a society without
a monetary economy, but it obviously had material wealth to trade and
exchange. The Romans came to Britain to exploit its resources, including
hunting dogs, metal (especially tin, silver and gold) and slaves, and it may
be that at least two of these commodities – slaves and dogs – continued to
be supplied to the Continent from Anglo-Saxon England. Analysis of the
distribution of types of artefacts shows that rivers and old Roman roads
were key to the regional transportation and distribution of artefacts.
As for the mechanisms by which artefacts changed hands, it is difficult to
be certain. Even at this early date, there may have been people who made
a living by carrying and exchanging goods from settlement to settlement,
and there may have been local markets or fairs, though this must remain
conjectural. A woman buried in a seventh-century grave at Lechlade,
Gloucestershire, had with her a collection of nearly 200 uncut,
unpolished garnets. The uncut stones underpin the evidence that Anglo-
Saxon jewellers were cutting and shaping their own stones, rather than
fitting pre-cut gems imported from Continental workshops. The presence
of these stones in a woman's grave is a reminder that there is reason
to suppose she was trading in these artefacts herself – women in Anglo-
Saxon England, married or otherwise, had a measure of economic
independence not seen again in England until the early twentieth century.
A male burial at the cemetery site at Watchfield, Oxfordshire, contained
a set of scales, and Chris Scull, the excavator, has suggested that the
presence of weights and scales in this and other burials indicates that they

were used to weigh precious metals and bullion for trade and exchange. The majority of the known sixth- and seventh-century burials with scales and weights belong to men, but a set found with a rich female burial at Castledyke, Humberside, is a further reminder that both women and men may have been involved in early Anglo-Saxon trading networks. Some artefacts may have been transferred through coastal piracy, raiding, battle booty and tribute. Gift giving and acts of reciprocation to enhance social bonds between communities, leaders and their followers may also have played a significant part in the distribution of goods and surpluses in early Anglo-Saxon England.

Middle Anglo-Saxon England

By the seventh century, it is clear that access to resources and production were being channelled into the hands of fewer and fewer members of Anglo-Saxon society, as a social and political elite established themselves in conjunction with the emergence of early kingdoms. It is clear from archaeological and textual evidence that monasteries and other ecclesiastical centres were major places of craft production and played a prominent role in acquiring raw materials, controlling resources and producing artefacts. They were also vital in bringing new skills and technologies into England. When Benedict Biscop returned from his extensive travels in Gaul and Italy and began the building of his monastic houses at Monkwearmouth and Jarrow, he famously brought in masons and glaziers from the Continent to do the work and to train Anglo-Saxons in these new crafts. Excavated examples of Continentally inspired sculpture and coloured window glass survive. Ælfric's *Colloquy* noted that a late Anglo-Saxon monastery had access to a range of metalworking specialists: goldsmiths, silversmiths, ironsmiths and coppersmiths.

Alongside the ecclesiastical centres, emerging royal houses sought to secure and control trade with increasing levels of success. The man in the Sutton Hoo Mound 1 burial, possibly to be equated with King Redwald of East Anglia, epitomises the new elite. A map showing the origins of the artefacts found in his early seventh-century burial would include the bronze bowl from Coptic (Christian) Egypt; silver bowls and spoons from Byzantium; wine from the Rhineland; artefacts made from imported gold, millefiori and garnet (the latter almost certainly coming from India); and a collection of coins, each from a different mint in Merovingian France.

The fact that the coins in the Sutton Hoo ship burial were all from different mints is instructive; the resources at the command of the family who created the mound monument still did not include a monetary economy. The coins in the burial were artefacts, rather than representative of currency values, but the idea of using of coins for trade was beginning to infiltrate Anglo-Saxon society, at the same time as the emergence of settlements devoted to production and trade, the emporia known as *wics*. *Wics* are undefended, planned settlements which probably had permanent inhabitants who were craftsmen and traders, and where international trade took place. Whether trade in these emporia was under the royal control or not and whether they functioned as places of general trade or as places where only elite goods were exchanged are still matters for debate.

Prior to the introduction of coinage, wealth seems to have been estimated in terms of cattle, a unit of currency also used in early Medieval Ireland. The Old English word for cattle was *feoh*, which came to be synonymous with 'riches', 'treasure' and 'moveable property'. *Feoh* was compounded with a number of other words in Old English, showing that everyday attitudes to wealth have not changed over millennia. Anglo-Saxons would promise wealth, *feohbehat*; demand money in compensation, *feohbot*; take illegal bribes, *feohfang*; refuse to take illegal bribes, *feohleas* (which also had the meaning of being poor); be greedy for money, *feohgeorn*; be miserly, *feohgifre*; be generous, *feohgift*; be well off, *feohstrang*; and waste money, *feohspilling*.

With the emergence of *wics* came the first Anglo-Saxon coinage, modelled on the coins of Merovingian France. Gold coins (called *thrymsas* by numismatists), probably the 'shillings' of the earliest English law codes, were being issued from a mint in London by around 640, and archaeological evidence from the *wic* associated with London (called *Lundenwic* in the documentary sources) shows a busy coastal trade, in the form of pottery produced by the large pottery kilns at Ipswich (*Gypeswic*), as well as international trade in the form of glass and other artefacts. Slaves were a product we know was being exported from London, because Bede records the sale of Imma, a nobleman captured in battle and taken to London to be sold to a Frisian trader.

The best known of the *wic* sites is Hamwic, to the south of modern Southampton, on the banks of the river Itchen, which has been the focus

Figure 25 Manpower for haulage: men pulling a loaded wagon with a harness.

of a series of excavations and publications from the 1960s to the
present. The settlement was established on a previously unoccupied site
c.700. Coin finds from Hamwic include examples of a new type, the
silver *sceatta* or penny, which was introduced c.670, and which was,
in various forms, to remain in use as the most common form of currency
in England until the fourteenth century. The introduction of this silver
coinage allowed items of smaller value to be exchanged for coins
(Figure 25).

It used to be thought that *wic* sites were the main centres of trade
and production in Anglo-Saxon England, but recent archaeological
discoveries, aided by an increasing number of finds by metal detectorists,
suggest that a second type of site may have been equally, or even more,
important in everyday market transactions. These sites, controversially
termed 'productive sites', are characterised by large quantities of coins
and metal objects. They appear to have been transient places where
seasonal gatherings took place for the purposes of trade and exchange.
The recently excavated site at Lake End, Dorney, near Windsor,
Berkshire, is a good example of this archaeologically ephemeral, but
significant, site. No evidence of timber-framed buildings or permanent
settlement was found at the site, but sunken-featured buildings and
refuse pits suggested intensive use of the site, even if only on a periodic
basis. What was remarkable about this site was the range of imported

artefacts found here, including tin-foil–decorated Tating ware from Germany, Ipswich ware from the potteries in Suffolk and wheel-thrown pottery from Northern France. Glass from the site was probably imported into Britain through Kent. There was also evidence for manufacturing taking place – 92.6 pounds (42 kilograms) of slag were recovered from the pits at Dorney – and for spinning, weaving, bone and antler working and some woodworking.

From the eighth century at least, much of rural England coalesced into large, productive estates. At Higham Ferrars, Northamptonshire, archaeological excavation has demonstrated the existence of such an estate, with a complex of buildings and enclosures, and a large malting oven, suggesting significant quantities of grain were being brought into the site. The complex also apparently had some judicial function, based on the executed bodies found in association with the site. It has been suggested that Higham Ferrars operated as a tribute centre, amassing goods for the regional landowner or lord. The political and social mechanisms by which these large estates were brought together are still not clear. Towards the end of the Anglo-Saxon period, however, many of these large estates (with the notable exception of ecclesiastical lands) had fragmented into smaller units, controlled by local leaders, who established their houses with a church nearby, creating the classic medieval manorial estate before the Conquest.

Late Anglo-Saxon England

The Viking impact on Anglo-Saxon England cannot be underestimated. To some extent, the Viking influence may be read as negative, leading to the destruction of monastic houses, the abandonment of Anglo-Saxon *wic* settlements and the decline of learning. On the other hand, the Viking presence was a catalyst for important and lasting change in England. The Danish Vikings were traders and merchants as well as raiders, and their settlement in England was rapidly followed by urbanisation, which in turn fostered what has been described as the 'first English industrial revolution'. Excavations at Anglian and Viking Age York have revealed the extent of manufacturing and production which took place when the Danes settled in York, which they held from 866. Between c.850 and 900, a glass-making furnace was established. Fragments of glass at this site were Roman, suggesting that the furnace was constructed to recycle glass collected from the surrounding area – York had been an important Roman city in the Romano-British period. It is possible that the tenement buildings found at Viking Age Coppergate were shops with workshops to the rear. Pottery and crucibles for metalworking were found in association with the central hearths. A range of other crafts were carried out in the tenements at York, including woodworking, stone sculpture, leatherworking and boneworking. Evidence includes waste from products, such as cores from turning wooden bowls, discarded artefacts and trial pieces, such as a late-ninth-century animal jawbone which was used by a craftsman to try out incised decoration in an art style known as *Trewhiddle* (after a hoard of silver objects decorated in this style found at Trewhiddle, St Austel, Cornwall).

The Vikings also appear to be responsible for the development of the Anglo-Saxon fortified town or *burh*. A document called the 'Burghal Hidage' listed all the *burhs* which formed a defensive network across the country in the early tenth century. The first *burhs* – Hereford, Tamworth and Winchcombe, for example – were initiated in Mercia, the first archaeologically recognised examples not appearing in Wessex until the reign of Æthelwulf (839–858). By the time of the 'Burghal Hidage', however, there were thirty-one places, almost all established by King Alfred or Edward the Elder. *Burhs* were not all identical. Some were small, with a primarily defensive purpose, such as 'Sashes' on an island in the Thames in Berkshire, the site of which has never been satisfactorily identified, and which was probably short-lived and which never had an urban status. Others, such as Winchester or London, were already important thriving market towns. With their defensive walls, metalled streets, houses with shops fronting the main roads, mints and markets, these were the first settlements in Anglo-Saxon England which can really be described as 'towns'.

The increasing power of the government to administer and intervene in daily life, illustrated by the new settlement hierarchy exemplified by the creation of late Anglo-Saxon towns, is also reflected in the mints of the period. Towards the end of the ninth century, there were only a few mints located in the most secure royal centres: London, Canterbury, Rochester and Ipswich. King Alfred, however, initiated a network of new mints. By the time of Æthelstan, thirty-five different mints are named on his coins, and coin evidence from the time of Edgar indicates that there were between sixty and seventy mints operating at any one time, all carefully controlled by legislation.

Even at the end of the first millennium in southern England, the smallest denomination of coinage was worth the equivalent of 25 pounds today, though coins might be halved or quartered to give slightly smaller denominations. Even so, everyday transactions for the daily necessities of life must have been based on barter and exchange, rather than coinage. In the northern area of Viking influence, coin production was more prolific. Excavations at Viking York have produced dies for hammering coins, and a hoard found in 1840 contained 10,000 *stycas*, small silver coins circulating in large quantities in the eighth and early ninth centuries.

Excavations of the late Anglo-Saxon town at Oxford reveal the range of occupations of the urban inhabitants. Evidence for fishmongers, wine merchants, moneyers and smiths have been found (the latter occupation indicated by a silver ingot mould found in a late Anglo-Saxon well). In addition, there is archaeological evidence for leatherworking, shoemaking, butchery, horn working and cloth making – evidence for retting flax and even hemp has been found just outside Anglo-Saxon Oxford on the river floodplain. Excavations at late Anglo-Saxon towns such as Oxford show the range of luxury items available to both the prosperous townspeople and the wealthy landowners who came to do business in the towns. The wealthier inhabitants of Viking Age York could buy Rhenish wine and lava quernstones from Niedermendig, Germany; sharpening stones of Norwegian schist, amber and soapstone from Scandinavia; and silk from Byzantium. One fragment of a silk cap from Coppergate, York, had an unusual weaving fault shared by a piece of silk from Lincoln, which suggests that the same bale of cloth was responsible for both finds.

A curiosity from York is a tenth-century forgery of an Arabic coin. It is not clear where the forgery was made, but its presence at York implies contact with the Near East and raises the possibility that perfumes, oils and spices were also to be found for sale in the bigger towns. Bald's *Leechbook* contains a number of remedies requiring exotic spices, including cumin, pepper and coriander. Such items might be present in the remedies because they were included in the Mediterranean texts which Bald copied, but Bald, or his scribe Cild, was quite happy to substitute a local herb for an inaccessible foreign one, and it is entirely possible that all the exotic ingredients included in Bald's recipes could be found in the markets of London or York.

The merchant in Ælfric's *Colloquy* provided a simple insight into the consumer markets of Anglo-Saxon England and Europe. He knows his customers well: he is useful to the king, the ealdormen, the wealthy – and all people. He explained how he made his money by filling his ship with English goods which he sold on the Continent, then returning to England with Continental luxuries such as precious metals and clothing, purple cloth and silks, elephant ivory and tin, sulphur and glass, which he then sold on the English market. Asked if he sold for the same price as he brought, the merchant retorted that then he would have no profit, to provide for his son and wife. Kings were keen to promote the trade: late Anglo-Saxon laws rewarded a merchant who crossed the sea three times at his own expense with the status of a 'thegn'. That such an incentive was required indicates the personal and financial risks taken by merchants, and the extent to which the crown profited from their activities. Towns in the late period were the most profitable markets: the townspeople were the only consumers of the fisherman's labour, according to Ælfric's *Colloquy*, whose fisherman claims they bought all he could catch. This picture of a man working at a single trade and selling his entire produce in the town exemplifies urban Anglo-Saxon life: both the fisherman and the town dwellers are completely separated from the self-sufficient lives of the early, rural Anglo-Saxons. The vignette of the fisherman working to supply a town market exemplifies the growth of mercantile urban centres. The fisherman is asked where he intends to sell his wares: the Old English word for selling was *cypan*, which gives us our modern word 'cheap'; the surname Chapman; and a number of place names, such as Cheapside (London), Chipping Norton (Oxfordshire) and Chipping Sudbury (Gloucestershire).

Women participated in urban trade in the late Anglo-Saxon period too, though they are less obvious in the documentary sources. Æthelred mentioned 'women who deal in dairy produce' in his list of those who had to pay market tolls. They were to pay a penny in each of the two weeks preceding Christmas.

The layout, function and development of smaller towns in later Anglo-Saxon England are still relatively unknown, perhaps because the majority lie under modern English towns. It is likely that small towns with their markets developed under aristocratic or ecclesiastical control. Work at Bampton, Oxfordshire, by Professor John Blair has illustrated that the important minster at Bampton was at the centre of the town's development, and he has drawn attention to a significant number of other towns which appear to have a minster as their nucleus. It was almost certainly the minster community who ensured the navigability of the Thames at this point by cutting a canal.

Travel and transport

The majority of journeys undertaken in Anglo-Saxon England were
certainly local and were carried out on foot; it is no surprise that a recipe
in Bald's *Leechbook* offers a cure for tired feet. A large proportion of the
population was tied to the land, and their access to travel was restricted.
A law of Wihtred of Kent noted that a servant travelling on his own
on Sundays was to pay his lord compensation: travel should only have
occurred on the lord's business. Moving away from your own locality
made you a stranger, and that, as will be explored in Chapter 9, was
a dangerous thing to be. Some seasonal travel was inevitable, as animals
were moved for pasturing. In Kent, for example, a series of old
droveways have been identified which connected manor estates to the
forests of the Weald to facilitate a transhumance system.

However, some long-distance travel did take place, for trade, and
also for pilgrimage, both within and beyond Britain. The Anglo-Saxons
inherited a network of land routes across the country, some of which
certainly remained in use through the period, including ancient routes
such as the ridgeway paths which pre-dated the Romans. For travel
across the country, the old Roman roads remained the major routeways.
The location of important settlements close to old Roman roads, often
identified by the place-name element *straet* (street), such as Stratford-
upon-Avon (Warwickshire) or Streatley (Oxfordshire), indicate the
persistent use of Roman roads such as the Fosse Way and Watling Street,
as do a number of burial sites. Roads and paths through the Anglo-Saxon
landscape were a focus for burials in the early period. Roads also acted
as boundary markers and were, at least in the later Anglo-Saxon period,
a locus for meetings of the 'hundred', where administrative and legal
matters for the local area were discussed. Roads, then, as well as being
a corridor for movement, also had a ritual and social dimension, because
the major highways through the country represented an aspect of a king's
power. Roads were places where kings showed and displayed their
control of society. To travel off the road was prohibited and restricted
by law; to travel on the road was to acknowledge the right of the king
to control his people's travel. Later Anglo-Saxon law enshrined the king's
right to call on his men to carry out a number of duties necessary to the
smooth running of the country, and maintenance of bridges was one
of those duties. Where bridges could not be built, there were ferries – four
are recorded at different points along the banks of the river Humber, for

example. Well-maintained roads supported trade and communication across the country and also enabled armies to travel at good speeds, as King Harold's famous march demonstrated. By contrast, the chronicler recorded with satisfaction the fate of King Svein's Viking army when they advanced on London in 1013, 'many of his host were drowned because they did not trouble to find a bridge'. The Old English word for army is *here*. The word survives in the place name Hereford, which marks an important crossing close to the Welsh border, and the number of *herepaths* mentioned in Old English charters reveals the importance placed on overland routes for the defence and protection of Anglo-Saxon kingdoms.

Accounts of battles suggest that men of fighting age would be expected to walk long distances to fight battles and that battles were habitually fought on foot. One of the most famous marches in Anglo-Saxon history was that undertaken by King Harold's heroic, but ultimately doomed, supporters in the year 1066. Based in southern England, King Harold heard that Harald Hardrada of Denmark had come to England with a conquering force. Mustering his men, King Harold and his troops marched up the Roman roads from southern England to Stamford Bridge, Yorkshire. The Battle of Stamford Bridge was fought, with Harold and his troops the victors, but they had barely had time to recover from the effects of battle when the weary men learnt that William had finally launched his attack on Anglo-Saxon England. There was nothing to do but turn around and march back from Yorkshire to the south coast, and Hastings, a journey of 275 miles (442 kilometres) which, remarkably, took only a fortnight. It is a testament to the stamina and courage of Harold's men, as well as to Harold's leadership, that, so the story goes, Harold and his exhausted army came so close to defeating William and his troops. Though the achievements of Harold and his men were impressive, this journey was not unique to the Anglo-Saxon world. King Æthelstan and his entire court took only eight days to travel from Winchester to Nottingham (a distance of 154 miles or 248 kilometres), and the body of St. Æthelwold (d.984), it is recorded, took only two days to be transported 69 miles (111 kilometres) from his place of death at Beddington, Surrey, to Winchester, his place of burial.

Documentary records focus on the overseas travels of the elite, most of which contained an element of pilgrimage and had Rome as their destination. Kings who abandoned their thrones to go on a one-way journey to Rome included the East Saxon Offa and Cædwalla of Essex.

Church men also travelled, often in large groups. Ceolfrith, for example, travelled with eighty companions – a serious endeavour in terms of logistics, expense and food supply. Though the records concentrate on the elite, there are hints that travel to Rome had popular appeal. Anglo-Saxon women, in particular, were warned of the threat to their moral welfare if they were not sufficiently cautious in Italy. There were pilgrim routes across England, too. Glastonbury Abbey in Somerset was wealthy partly as a result of pilgrims travelling to see its saintly relics.

Horse riding was an elite activity. When the teenage St. Wilfred (AD 634–709) approached the boundary of Lindisfarne monastery, he was riding on a horse and carrying a spear. The combination of horse and spear was enough to convince the monks that he was a warrior, and they refused to let him in until he had convinced them that he was not a threat. Finds of horse trappings in early Anglo-Saxon burials show that horses of the elite had highly decorated harnesses with tinned or silvered metal spangles. A rare find of a highly decorated wooden saddle bow fragment, studded with silver rivets and decorated with strips of inlaid horn, came from late-ninth-century York. Examples of stirrups have been found in Viking contexts, for example the silver-decorated stirrups found by the river Cherwell, Oxford, which may have originated in a Viking grave.

Even at the close of the Anglo-Saxon period, the majority of the English army moved around and fought on foot. This point is emphasised in the late Old English poem 'The Battle of Maldon', in which a fight on foot between the Anglo-Saxons, led by the veteran warrior Earl Byrhtnoth, and a marauding band of Vikings was being won by the Anglo-Saxons until an Anglo-Saxon traitor rode away on Byrhtnoth's horse. The horse, and not its rider, was recognised by some of Byrhtnoth's soldiers, who, believing that their leader had deserted them, also fled the scene. Only Byrhtnoth's own loyal household warriors, knowing the truth, stayed on to fight to the bitter (and fatal) end. Carts and wagons were used to carry people and goods, and sometimes these vehicles were pulled by hand, rather than by animals, as illustrations and texts show. So, though the Bayeux Tapestry includes a rare image of a horse being used to pull a plough, it also shows men carrying weaponry, bales and dragging a four-wheeled cart with the aid of a harness. According to his *Life*, a harness was also used by St. Cuthman to help him lift a cart-like contraption on which he carried his invalid mother (Figure 26).

Figure 26 Keeping a lookout at the port.

Rivers provided an important routeway into Anglo-Saxon England from the coast and provided a network of local and regional communications along which goods and people could be transported. The importance of rivers for building economic and social links is exemplified by distributions of distinctive regional artefacts in the early Anglo-Saxon period. This distribution shows, for example, that in the modern county of Buckinghamshire, which came into existence as an administrative unit in the late Anglo-Saxon period, the early Anglo-Saxons in the west of the county were linked with their neighbours in Oxfordshire, while the people living in the north of the county were in close contact with Northamptonshire, and the people in the east of the county were linked, through the Thames Valley, with Bedfordshire, Hertfordshire and, ultimately, London. Roads and other land routes connected directly to important harbours. In Kent, landing places at the terminus of roads are often marked by place names with the element *ora* (shore), such as Oare and Great Stonor. In a grant by Frithuwold, sub-king of Surrey, to Chertsey in AD 672/674, he described the port of London, where ships came in to land 'by the public way'. The local and regional river and land routes in England were connected to ports, all of which were under the ultimate control of the King, as part of an effective transport system.

The extent to which the navigability of rivers was of economic importance is illustrated by the documentary sources – and rare but growing archaeological evidence – for maintenance and work on rivers. The monks at Abingdon Abbey, at the request of the men of Oxford, cut a large canal across one of their meadows to ease the traffic of goods. A mid-Anglo-Saxon channel marker has been found in Holy Brook at Coley Park Farm, and excavations by the Thames at Oxford at a main crossing of the river have shown significant channelling to control the river from the eighth century. The settlement at Glastonbury, Somerset, was dominated by the wealthy Abbey, which was almost certainly responsible for a series of works designed to facilitate access and trade to the Abbey. These included a causeway made up of a thick layer of boughs and brushwood lain over the peat surface, onto which mortar was spread. Large timber structures found overlaying the brushwood and filled in with limestone and lias may represent the footings of a bridge recorded in the documentary sources. In addition, an artificial waterway over 1 mile (1.6 kilometres) in length ran from the Abbey to Northover River. Radiocarbon dates place the use of the waterway to the end of the Anglo-Saxon period. The channel may be a mill leat, but documentary evidence suggesting that the Abbey was accessible by boat and the archaeological evidence for the length and path of the waterway suggest that it was a canal. By the late Anglo-Saxon period, the Foss Dyke, north of Lincoln, was also a managed waterway.

The first Anglo-Saxons came to England in ships – Gildas used the Germanic word *keel* to describe them – and ships were always important in allowing Anglo-Saxons to travel up rivers and along the coast. We know relatively little about the appearance, technology and capacity of Anglo-Saxon boats, however. To date, only a handful have been discovered by excavation – the 88.6-feet-long (27-metre-long) clinker-built boat buried in Sutton Hoo Mound 1, which probably dates to the turn of the sixth century; the Graveney ship, built around AD 900 as a cargo boat, also clinker built; some log boats, including the 9.84-feet-long (3-metre-long) example used as a coffin in an early Anglo-Saxon grave at Snape, Suffolk (not far from Sutton Hoo), and another log boat from the river Calder near Wakefield, Yorkshire, which has been radiocarbon dated to the early eleventh century. The Graveney ship, 56 feet (17 metres) in length, was carrying a cargo of hops, indicative of the agricultural specialisation, production and trade characteristic

of tenth-century Anglo-Saxon England; it may have been bound for
Canterbury, Rochester or London when it sank.

Until the eighth century, boats were powered by oars, although it is
possible that some boats had an additional sail – the Sutton Hoo Mound 1
ship, for example, which had rowlocks, has been reconstructed with a sail,
though there is no archaeological evidence that it was used as a sailing
vessel. Poems and other texts give an intimate picture of the hardships
suffered by early medieval sailors and seafarers, 'a weary crewman rows
against the wind', a late Anglo-Saxon poet noted.

Although ships and seafaring appear to have been important in
Anglo-Saxon life and poetry, in practice, a large part of the long-distance
trade and seafaring voyages may have been left to foreign traders and
merchants, particularly the Frisians. When Alfred wanted to counter
the Viking supremacy on the sea, he relied on Frisian shipbuilders to
construct a fleet for him, typically to Alfred's own design. The inventive
Alfred reasoned that the bigger, the better; so he commissioned ships
twice as long as the Viking warships, with sixty or more oars for
propulsion, to make them swifter and more stable than the Viking ships.
To an extent, Alfred's 'arms race' was successful, but, as with any new
design, there were unexpected drawbacks. In their first engagement, the
ships successfully blocked Viking raiders in an estuary on the Dorset
coast, but the size of Alfred's ships made them heavy and difficult
to manoeuvre. Not only did they run aground, giving the Vikings an
opportunity to engage in hand-to-hand fighting with the beached English
ships, resulting in the deaths of two important Anglo-Saxons and three
Frisians whose seamanship was being used by Alfred (Wulfheard, Æbbe
and Æthelhere), but, when the tide turned, the lighter Danish boats were
re-floated more rapidly and were able to row away unchallenged. In the
end, though, the wounds inflicted on the Viking crew during the land
battle were so severe that they were only able to row the ships with
difficulty; two of them were wrecked on the coast at Sussex, leaving
one to limp back to the Viking stronghold of East Anglia. Nonetheless,
a pattern of large shipbuilding had been set. When Bishop Ælfwold
of Crediton died in 1016, his bequests to the king included a boat with
sixty-four oars lying in the port. The boat was nearing the end of
construction, and Ælfwold apologised that the rowlocks had not been
fitted yet and hoped that the work would be finished before he died.

Chapter 8

Death and Religion

From the beginnings of Anglo-Saxon England, until the arrival
of Christianity in the seventh century, the Anglo-Saxons were, as far
as the evidence suggests, pagans. Though traces of their religious beliefs
are still present in everyday English – Easter, and some of the days
of the week, are named after Germanic pagan deities – our knowledge
of Anglo-Saxon paganism is limited. When Christianity was introduced
to Anglo-Saxon England, the documentary and archaeological sources
show that the Anglo-Saxons readily incorporated this new religious
system to their own social and religious framework. However, a rigid
separation between 'religious' and 'secular' is anachronistic to Anglo-
Saxon society, where religion was a part of everyday life, and where
the distinctions between 'church', 'family' and 'society' are almost
impossible to draw.

Pagan religion

We have only the sketchiest idea about the framework for early
Anglo-Saxon religious, spiritual and supernatural beliefs. There
is plentiful evidence for artefacts and patterns of behaviour that might
be interpreted as part of a spiritual belief system, but how that system
was organised – indeed, whether it was organised at all or whether
religious belief was an aspect of personal, private behaviour – is open
to question. It is particularly problematic that all the evidence is
embedded in layers of cultural change and later agendas, which have
buried our knowledge of the period in wrappings of interpretation and
re-presentation. Christian writers who offered the first proper written
evidence for the period, for example, were not interested in explaining
earlier pagan beliefs or belief systems, only in eradicating them
(illustrated by the decision taken at the Synod of Clofesho in AD 747
to ban 'divines, soothsayers, auguries, auspices, amulets, enchantments
or any other filth of the ungodly') or in adapting and subverting pre-
Christian practice to bring it into the church, a policy famously promoted
by Pope Gregory the Great, one of the main actors in bringing about the

conversion of the Anglo-Saxons. According to Bede, one of Gregory's letters to his missionaries working in England advised them that, after 'long deliberation about the English people', he thought it best that 'the idol temples of that race should by no means be destroyed, but only the idols in them…. For if the shrines are well-built, it is essential that they should be changed from the worship of devils to the service of the true God.' This was quite a break from previous practice, but Gregory argued that the Anglo-Saxons would be more willing to come to a church if it was located in a familiar place. It also reveals Gregory's actual ignorance about Anglo-Saxon England, for such evidence as we have suggests that nothing related to paganism would have been 'well built' in Gregory's terms. An added layer of complexity, however, is that one of the biggest headaches for Gregory's missionary to England, Augustine, was the surviving Christian British clerics, who disagreed vehemently with key current Roman Christian practice, such as the method for calculating the date of Easter, and the correct way to tonsure hair. It may well be British or former Romano-British churches, rather than Anglo-Saxon pagan temples, that Augustine was hoping to reuse for his new churches.

In common with other Old English documents referring to Anglo-Saxon paganism, part of the problem with this passage telling us about Gregory's instructions about the conversion of pagans is that, at the time that the Anglo-Saxons were writing about themselves, the 'official' religion was Christianity, and all writings were framed in the context of a long tradition of patristic and religious literature, from the Bible onwards. We cannot be sure, therefore, that the document produced by the Synod of Clofesho, which talked about soothsayers and amulets, was banning any current practice; it might have been continuing a formulaic pattern laid down in late antique Christian literature from the Old Testament onwards about abolishing witchcraft and sorcery. Even out-and-out 'pagan' heroic poems, such as *Beowulf*, were written down within a Christian framework and may be read in Christian terms as an allegory of good and evil and the workings of God's plans on earth. By the later Anglo-Saxon period, there were certainly secular readers and scribes, but the majority of the surviving written sources were created within monastic scriptoria, the writing factories of the time. The very concept of the written word was intimately connected to Christianity, and so most Anglo-Saxon writing was created with the consciousness that a document in some way expressed God's work in a Christian world. One late Old English medical charm from a text known as *Lacnunga*, for example, is for a sudden stitch (*wið færstice*). The remedy begins by listing ingredients and instructing that they should be boiled in butter and then provides a chant to be recited before the liquid medicine is to be applied. The whole incantation is entirely pagan, referring to grave mounds, gods, elves and witches: 'Six smiths sat, wrought battle-spears. Out spear, not in, spear. If herein be a bit of iron, work of witches, it shall melt...', except the last line: 'Be thou healthy; may the Lord help thee.'

It is clear from occasional references in the literature, and to charms such as the one cited above, that knowledge of the pagan past, and stories about old gods and heroes, circulated even after England had converted to Christianity. There was still a shared, common pool of knowledge about old religious practices. Unfortunately, because this knowledge was so integral to Anglo-Saxon folk culture, writers assumed that a mere reference to pagan deities, heroes or behaviours would suffice; readers and listeners did not need the obvious explained to them. In a poem called *Widsith*, an old poet told his audience more and more unlikely and impossible stories about himself and his part in famous mythological/ historical events. The audience may have been impressed by the writer's range and breadth of knowledge, but the poet knew that a knowledgeable audience would recognise that he could not possibly have been present at the events he described. Some of the characters catalogued by the 'far-travelled' Widsith are recognisable figures from Germanic legend, but others are completely unknown. Similarly, the beautiful love poem 'Wulf and Eadwacer' reads as a desperate lament from an abandoned lover, but the identity of the characters remains inaccessible, as do the references to an underground habitation and an island. The poem can be read as an evocation of human love and longing, but it may also be possible that Wulf, Eadwacer, the reference to the guarded island and the underground house were part of a well-known mythological or religious story, now lost.

Pagan gods and spirits

Our best evidence for the names of pagan deities lies embedded in our most prosaic modern nouns – the days of the week, which have their origins in pre–Anglo-Saxon Germanic belief systems, which were shared by Scandinavian and other Germanic tribes. Tuesday recalls the god Tiw;

Wednesday recalls Woden; Thursday recalls Thor and Friday recalls Frey/Freya/Frig. A few other gods are known from other modern words; Easter, the most important Christian festival, is named after the goddess Eostra, who presumably had an important festival at this time of the year in the early Anglo-Saxon world. She was so important that her name survives to this day, but we know absolutely nothing else for certain about her, nor about how her festival was organised. Hretha, mentioned by Bede as the goddess whose month preceded that of Eostra, is equally obscure.

Place names offer some of our best evidence for the importance of deities to the early Anglo-Saxons (Figure 27). Sacred places survive in the landscape – places with an 'eccles' (from the Latin *ecclesia*, meaning church) component marked pre–Anglo-Saxon churches, such as Eccles (Kent) and Beccles (Suffolk), founded by the Christianised Romano-British. On the other hand, place names containing the element *hearg* (Harrow, Harrowden), or *weoh, wih* (Weedon, Weoley, Willey), suggest the location of a heathen shrine. There are also a number of place names in the landscape that are associated with Old English gods or other supernatural beings: the gods Tiw, Woden, Thunor and Frig are commemorated in place names such as Tysoe (Oxfordshire), Wednesbury (Staffordshire), Thursley (Surrey) and Friday Street (Suffolk).

Some place names contain the element *Grim*, meaning 'the masked one', a nickname for Woden. This element is particularly associated with the prehistoric ditches and other earthworks crossing the English landscape: Grims Ditch, Grimsdyke, Grimsbury (Oxfordshire) and Grimes Graves (Norfolk). Lesser deities are also present in the landscape: goblins (*puca* and *hob*) are both attested in place names, and there are documentary references to the *feldelve* (field elf). Elves were also evoked in personal names with the element *ælf*: Alfred (elf-counsel) and Ælfric (elf-power), for example.

A few fertility rituals survive in late Anglo-Saxon contexts. In one, to protect the land if it has been blighted by sorcery or witchcraft, you are to drip oil, honey, barm and milk of every animal on the land, every tree and plant known to man (except *glappan*, possibly buckbean) and holy water was to be dripped in four places where turfs had been cut. Further rituals were to be carried out, including a visit to the church, and a chant which began with an invocation to *Erce, Erce, Erce* – this perhaps naming an earth or fertility deity.

Figure 27 Place names which probably refer to pagan religious practices.

Temples and places of worship

Bede, writing about the Anglo-Saxon conversion to Christianity, offered only the most sketchy references to belief systems in pre-Christian England. Two well-known episodes, however, hint that early Anglo-Saxons had specific buildings or temples dedicated to their gods. In one, Bede explains how the pagan priest Coifu, disillusioned with his own useless gods and attracted to the new religion of Christianity, defiled the sacred temple which he had once protected by riding a stallion (which was forbidden to priests of his old pagan religion) and throwing a spear into the temple area. The second story described the half-hearted conversion of the powerful King Redwald of East Anglia, whose Christian wife wanted him to convert, but who was worried about how his powerful warriors and supporters would react. Accordingly, he built a church next to his pagan temple and worshipped at both altars. Add to this Gregory's opinion, discussed above, that the Anglo-Saxons had places of worship sufficiently well built to be converted into churches, and the implication is that the pre-Christian Anglo-Saxon landscape was dotted with built structures used by Anglo-Saxons for their pagan worship.

Given this documentary evidence, archaeologists have long expected to find some material evidence for Anglo-Saxon temples. Comparison with earlier British sacred sites would suggest that a temple or sacred area would be marked by one or more of the following features: a special structure, not similar in form to those in ordinary settlements; 'special' deposits, possibly votive offerings, gold or silver, or human or animal burials or sacrifices; and a special location, close to wells, springs, rivers or significant monuments in the landscape. A temple site would also show signs of prolonged, though possibly seasonal, use, perhaps marked by special pits, or the rebuilding of one structure on the same spot as a previous building.

Place-name evidence has encouraged the belief that there should be Anglo-Saxon temples and sanctuaries to be found in the landscape. Two Old English words seem to have indicated religious sites: *hearh* and *weoh*, examples of which have been given above, support the idea of a specific place or structure for pagan worship. In practice, however, archaeological evidence for any such structures has been hard to come by. Early Anglo-Saxon buildings, as discussed earlier, fall into two simple types: sunken-featured buildings and timber-framed buildings. It is extremely hard to point with certainty to any excavated examples which fall outside the 'normal' Anglo-Saxon range, in layout, structure or associated artefacts, which might qualify as 'temples'. The most interesting buildings, from this point of view, have been found at Yeavering, Northumbria. Yeavering is the place called *ad Gefrin* by Bede, where, he recorded, the missionary Paulinus preached to King Edwin and his people and carried out mass baptisms in the nearby river. Excavations at Yeavering by Brian Hope-Taylor in the 1970s revealed a range of uncommon structures. A complex of timber-framed buildings was identified as the site of the royal palace at Yeavering. An enigmatic semi-circular structure with a central post-hole was interpreted as an Anglo-Saxon version of an amphitheatre. Perhaps this was the place where Paulinus preached, but perhaps the central pole also acted as a totem for pagan worship – Edwin was a powerful pagan king before his conversion. There are a number of exceptional buildings at the site, including one building which was apparently encased by a second structure. The common practice at this time, when a building became structurally unsound, was to erect a new replacement structure at a new site. The striking exception to this practice was in church building, in which case it was the actual ground on which the building stood that held the sacred power and resonance. Is the 'double' building at Yeavering evidence of sacred pagan ground? Or is it perhaps more reasonably interpreted as an early, wooden, rebuilt church?

Archaeologists and historians have come to the conclusion that, armed with a Latin vocabulary for churches and temples, the writers of the documentary sources probably presented a pagan religion which mirrored Christianity in terms of structures and attitudes to sacred space, whereas the archaeological evidence suggests that daily worship of pagan gods did not require special built structures. The place-name evidence needs to be treated with caution. When Anglo-Saxons designated a site as a *hearh* or *weoh*, were they referring to their own temples or to places they recognised as having been important to their predecessors? Research has indicated that *weoh* sites, for example, are linked to sites of Romano-British activity.

Pre-Christian death and the afterlife

Archaeological evidence for pre-Christian burial rituals is plentiful in terms of the treatment of the body at the point of placement in the ground. With very few exceptions, Anglo-Saxon burial grounds are characterised by new foundations, not in any way continuing to use existing Romano-British cemeteries. They were usually located at some distance from settlements, and burials rarely encroached on living spaces, just as houses were rarely built over cemeteries (though exceptions, such as one of the two cemeteries associated with the settlement at Mucking, Essex, do occur). The cemeteries were usually situated on a rise or prominence, so that they were visible from a distance. Early Anglo-Saxon cemeteries were like early Anglo-Saxon settlements; they tended to sprawl over the landscape, apparently without any marked boundaries or enclosures, unless there were pre-existing monuments in the landscape, such Romano-British boundary ditches. To this extent, there was apparently no sense of a delineated 'sacred ground' for burial – that concept came much later, with the introduction of Christianity. A number of cemeteries seem to have deliberately reused old markers in the landscape, such as Bronze Age barrows, perhaps using old monuments to appropriate ancestors or to reinforce and legitimise new ownership of the land.

There were two main forms of the burial ritual – inhumation with grave goods, where the body was placed in the ground, usually, but not always, in a single grave; and cremation, where the clothed body was burnt before being placed in a pot or other container and placed in the ground, sometimes with additional small burial items. Generally, the cremation ritual predominated in the Anglian, eastern and northern parts of the country, while inhumation predominated in Kent and the south, though it is becoming increasingly apparent that cremation, though much less common than inhumation, was also a prevalent ritual in the southern parts of Anglo-Saxon England, too. Many fifth- and sixth-century inhumation cemeteries also contain a few contemporary cremations. At Lechlade, Gloucestershire, the excavated Anglo-Saxon cemetery, in use from the fifth to the seventh century, contained 219 excavated bodies (in 199 graves) and an additional 29 cremations. In Berinsfield, Oxfordshire, a similarly large inhumation cemetery contained 118 excavated bodies in 100 graves, and 4 cremations, though the excavators noted that a number of cremation burials might have been destroyed in the topsoil before the excavation began (Figure 28).

Cremation and inhumation, as ways of disposing a body, seem dramatically different, and the treatment of bodies in the grave also shows enormous variety in orientation, size of the grave, grave furnishings (post-holes, mounds and ditches, barrows), grave goods (of which more later), body position (prone, on the side, crouched or supine) and in the number of bodies in one grave. Most burials are single, but two or more bodies are found buried in the same grave (and all buried at the same time) with sufficient frequency for multiple burials to have been a significant minority ritual.

Why is there so much variation in the Anglo-Saxon burial ritual? It is possible that different burial rituals reflect different social status amongst the dead. The Anglo-Saxon settlements serving inhumation cemeteries

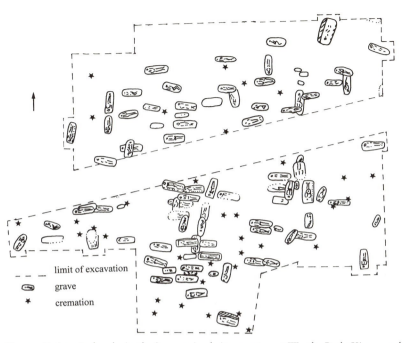

limit of excavation

grave

cremation

Figure 28 A typical early Anglo-Saxon mixed-rite cemetery at Worthy Park, Kingsworthy.

were small and supported only a few families. Buildings do not show any particularly strong sense of hierarchy, rather they are all similar in terms of size, and settlements are also similar across the country in terms of layout and types of building. Early Anglo-Saxon settlements do not indicate a strong hierarchy – prince, thane, freeman, slave and so on – these social categories seem to have developed more strongly later in the seventh century. William Filmer-Sankey, trying to make sense of the variety of cremation and burial he had found at the sixth-century cemetery at Snape, Suffolk, suggested that perhaps burial ritual reflected allegiances to different deities. The Anglo-Saxons appear to have respected a pantheon of deities, so the suggestion is attractive.

There are also hints that burial grounds were places where some ritual activity took place. Mounds and posts were placed over some graves, suggesting that there was a wish to remember or commemorate the dead. Some burial grounds include small structures, such as the little four-post building erected over cremations in Alton and Apple Down, Hampshire; Lechlade, Gloucestershire; and Berinsfield, Oxfordshire. It also seems likely that burials were places for communal displays and gatherings, which may be particularly relevant in a society which seems to lack any obvious communal ritual structures or buildings.

Reconstruction of what happened between the death of a person and their final deposition in the ground is difficult, because little survives archaeologically, and the documentary sources are sketchy. Evidence from inhumations suggests that bodies were not kept above ground long before burial, certainly not to the extent of any significant decomposition, though occasionally insect pupae have been found preserved by the mineralisation of belt buckles or brooches on clothing, so there may have been a short period during which the body was displayed above ground. Given the number of clothing artefacts found on bodies, it is likely that corpses were displayed, dressed in their funeral clothing, so that everyone could see the artefacts they were going to be buried with.

This 'display' aspect was socially significant in a number of ways. It has been suggested that the artefacts placed with bodies were there to demonstrate the power and wealth of the family or community doing the burial; this was conspicuous consumption of material wealth. It is difficult, otherwise, to find reasons why small farming communities, such as the Anglo-Saxons were, would have wanted to remove so many precious items – brooches, beads, belts, clothing, pots, weaponry – from everyday circulation by placing them beyond use by the living community in the ground. Given that artefacts were going to be placed out of reach in the ground, a period of display would also have made sense so that everyone in the community could see exactly what was going to be buried. This would have been a handy mechanism to prevent grave robbing – it would be extremely difficult to wear or to try to sell an artefact if everyone in the community knew that it had last been seen heading to the cemetery on a body. In fact, Anglo-Saxon cemeteries are remarkable because bodies were almost never robbed after death in spite of the value of some of the material placed in the graves. The dead and their objects were respected.

The cremation ritual, though less impressive from an archaeological point of view, was more complex and dramatic for the burying community. Burnt and melted objects found in cremation urns suggest that bodies destined for cremation, like those which were inhumed, were laid out fully clothed before being incinerated. Successful cremation of a body, as many murderers have found to their cost, is not a simple matter. Considerable quantities of wood are required, and there is a technique to building a pyre which will reach the kind of temperatures required to burn a body. The journey of the body to the funeral pyre on the *adfaru* (path to the funeral pyre) may have been a ceremonial affair. Cremation cemeteries, such as the one at Spong Hill in Norfolk, are often much larger than inhumation cemeteries – Spong Hill contained over 1,000 excavated individuals – suggesting that they served a much wider community than the inhumation cemeteries. It may be that corpses were carried some distance to reach the cremation cemetery. After cremation, the charred remains were collected and placed in a container, often a decorated pottery urn. Analysis of cremated remains shows that the same location may have been used for several pyres, because cremated remains often contain partial bones from more than one body.

Cremation urns tend to be much more highly decorated than the pottery found in domestic circumstances. The intricacies of decoration suggest that they were unlikely to have been made for an individual immediately after death. It may be possible that they were made or chosen some time before death, perhaps kept aside in the house ready for future use. It is also possible that cremated remains were kept in urns for some time before the urns were placed in the ground. The decorative element on cremation pots concentrates on the upper surface, so that the full decorative scheme is best appreciated from on top, and the fact that cremation urns were often found in groups and clusters at Spong Hill suggests that the top of the urn may have been exposed in the ground, marking the site of the burial and allowing other urns to be placed next to it in due course. In addition to the cremated remains and fragments of the melted grave goods, cremation urns sometimes contain extra items which have not been burnt, such as tweezers, miniature combs or other small artefacts, suggesting an extra phase of mourning and remembrance before the body was placed in the ground.

Archaeology cannot tell us much more about the burial ritual, but documentary sources do offer a few glimpses of a more spiritual and ritual process. The poem 'Maxims 1' from the *Exeter Book* stated that 'holly has to be burned, and a dead man's legacy divided'; the materials used for cremation and inhumation may have had more significance than we know. *Beowulf* famously described several different forms of burial ritual, including placing a body in a ship and sending it out to sea, burying a body in a mound with treasure and cremating the body of Beowulf and placing it in a mound which took ten days to build. The poet noted that 'a Geatish woman [Beowulf's wife?], sorrowful,

her hair bound up, sang a mournful lay'. When Beowulf imagined
the possibility of being killed and eaten by the monster Grendel, he
commented that there would be nothing of his corpse to care for and
that there would be no need to 'hide his head'. The references to the
bound hair of the female mourner and the covered head of the dead
imply a range of funerary rituals for both cadaver and mourners which
are now lost.

In addition to any other rituals, feasting may have been an important
aspect of the funeral. Though they are not common in Anglo-Saxon
graves, some burials did include food and drink amongst the grave
goods. It is not possible to tell what the purpose of these deposits was.
They may represent part of a wake, or meal for the dead, which the
mourners ate at the graveside – such wakes have been recorded in
medieval and early modern England. Alternatively, deposits of food may
have been intended to provide the spirit of the dead person with food
in the afterlife, though this is unlikely, only because food deposits would
be found more commonly if providing sustenance for the dead was part
of pagan Anglo-Saxon ideology. Alternatively, the food may have been
present in the grave as a votive offering to a deity or as part of the general
display of wealth and status which the burial ritual offered. In any event,
it seems likely that the food offerings associated with the burial ritual
represent special, ritual or celebratory food.

Examples of food included within the grave assemblage are disparate
and occasionally surprising. Parts of edible animals, such as sheep, cattle
and goose, have been found placed in bowls in the grave, as well as eggs,
nuts, fruit and, in the case of one burial, a cooked lobster.

In the context of funeral feasting, it is notable that many Anglo-Saxon
inhumations contain fragments of pottery and animal bone in the soil
above the grave. Such fragments are usually interpreted as accidental,
secondary deposits of material which just happened to be in the soil
which was put back on top of the burial, but it is likely that some of
these fragments represent vessels which were used as part of a funerary
feast, and which the mourners around the graveside broke and threw
into the grave as it was being filled, perhaps taking some sherds away
with them as a *momento mori*, a token by which to remember the
dead. Such speculations serve as a sharp reminder that, though we have
a mass of data from Anglo-Saxon inhumations, the rituals that may
have occurred before, during and after burial are largely a matter
of conjecture.

Why were the dead buried or cremated with artefacts? The idea that artefacts related to social status or displays of conspicuous consumption has already been discussed. It has also been suggested that grave goods may have been intended to serve the dead in the afterlife. There are problems with this suggestion, not least that a number of bodies – about 50 percent of most excavated inhumation cemeteries – were buried without any archaeologically visible grave goods. What little is known about pre-Christian ideas of the afterlife is limited and characterised by the idea that what happens after death is unfathomable. The *Beowulf* poet's comment on the hero Scyld Scefing's elaborate ship burial as it floated off on the tide was that 'no-one can honestly say, neither advisors in the hall nor heroes under heaven, who received the cargo'.

As Christianity was brought to Anglo-Saxon England, there were changes in the burial ritual. New, 'Final Phase' cemeteries were introduced, in which more bodies were buried without grave goods, weapon burial became less common and a few burials were given a spectacular excess of grave goods. Part of this change in ritual was marked by the introduction of cruciform jewellery in gold and garnet, particularly in association with the graves of rich women. Perhaps these women were wearing a new, fashionable form of jewellery, but there is increasing evidence that rich seventh-century burials, rather than being the last gasp of paganism, were actually the burials of Christians, at a time when burial within a churchyard had not yet been introduced. In this context, it is important to bear in mind that the church never condemned burial with grave goods in this period. Burial with grave goods cannot be equated with paganism. St. Cuthbert himself, for example, was buried with his bible, his portable altar covered in decorated silver, his clothing, a comb and other artefacts including a gold and garnet cross. More recently, the find of the 'Prittlewell Prince' at Essex has confirmed that rich seventh-century burials, including that of the Sutton Hoo Mound 1, might have been Christian. The 'Prittlewell Prince' was buried in a chamber, elaborately furnished with the same range of grave goods as have been found with the princely burial at Sutton Hoo and Taplow, such as weaponry, drinking and feasting equipment, exotic imports, gold and garnet decorative items, and two gold foil crosses placed on the body. In this case, the crosses were not part of a decoration on an imported item, like the silver bowls from Byzantium at Sutton Hoo, or part of a costume. The crosses were placed on the body with deliberation and intent, to symbolise the Christian affiliation of the dead. It may be that the grave goods from earlier pre-Christian burials, rather than representing the wealth of the deceased, or in any way equipping them for the afterlife, were actually votive offerings to pre-Christian deities beyond the grave.

Animals

Amongst the burials within Anglo-Saxon cemeteries were a number of animals whose bodies were unlikely to be food offerings, particularly dogs and horses. Animals were also conspicuous in early Anglo-Saxon animal art, and a number of surviving Anglo-Saxon myths and illustrations suggest that some animals were considered to be sacred or to have ritual significance (Figure 29).

Sketchy documentary evidence suggests that horses held a special place in early Anglo-Saxon society. The mythical founders of Anglo-Saxon England were called Hengest and Horsa. Their names translate as 'horse and gelding', and these epithets may recall early Anglo-Saxon twin horse deities or horse worship. A number of horses have been found in burial contexts. At Lakenheath, Suffolk, excavators discovered the burial of a horse with richly decorated trappings in a grave next to a young warrior male. At Great Chesterford, Essex, horses and dogs were

Figure 29 Eagle shield decoration, from Grave 81, Mill Hill, Kent.

given separate burials, not associated with humans. Their presence in this early cemetery is enigmatic. They may have been buried as part of a ritual sacrifice, but because their graves are not associated with any human burial, they may have been buried as if they were people. In this context, it is not surprising that the earliest documentary evidence hints at horse riding as a special, status-linked activity, which was perhaps alluded to in Bede's description of the priest Coifi's actions. Anglo-Saxons were also noted for having a taboo about eating horse flesh. An illustration on the enigmatic, early eighth-century Frank's Casket shows a seated human figure with a horse's head, holding branches and greeting a helmeted figure carrying a spear and shield. The figure is called 'Hos', and the legend in runic writing around the scene in which it appears says (though the translation is not certain) 'Here Hos sits on a mound of sorrow' (Figure 30).

The boar also seems to have had a special place in Anglo-Saxon folklore, being particularly associated with battle: a boar figure decorates the crest of the helmet found buried with a sixth-century Mercian warrior at Benty Grange, Derbyshire, for example. According to surviving mythological evidence, the boar was sacred to the Vanir, Germanic fertility gods.

Figure 30 'Hos sitting on a sorrow mound': an obscure reference to a lost mythical figure, from the Frank's Casket.

Beowulf, unusually for an aristocrat, had a name which did not alliterate with any in his family. His name may have been a nickname: Beowulf means 'bear', and Beowulf is characterised by his extraordinary physical strength which enabled him to fight Grendel with his bare hands. 'Wulf', by contrast, was a common element in male and female names (Wulfwaru, Wulfric, Æthelwulf), and *heorot* (stag) also occurs in names (Heorogar), and was the name given to Hrothgar's royal hall, which Grendel attempted to destroy. At Sutton Hoo, a stag figure surmounted a whetstone (a royal insignia), and an illustration of the palace of King David in the *Utrecht Psalter* shows a stag's head crowning the gable.

Birds had a special place in Anglo-Saxon ritual, too. They occur as beaked heads in early Anglo-Saxon metalwork, or as bird-shaped brooches, imported from the Continent. Eagles and ravens had particular resonance within heroic warrior mythology: birds could move between this world (middle earth) and the worlds above and below. Images of biting birds occur in particular association with images of warriors: the Sutton Hoo helmet, for example, has images of dancing warriors on the helmet plates, who are themselves wearing helmets adorned with beaked heads. The early seventh-century gilt-bronze buckle found in a grave at Finglesham, Kent, depicts a man carrying two spears. He is naked except for a buckled belt and a helmet topped by two opposing bird heads. Another grave at the same site included an enigmatic metal object depicting a bearded man's head wearing a similar beaked-head-decorated helmet.

Ubiquitous in early Anglo-Saxon art is the dragon. Snake-like dragons writhe and crawl across Anglo-Saxon metalwork in complicated woven patterns, from the finest gold metalwork found in the richest graves to simple, inexpensive disc brooches worn in daily life. In literary sources, dragons are associated with treasure: 'the dragon belongs in its barrow, cunning and jealous of its jewels' wrote the poet of 'Maxims II'. Barrows are burial mounds: the dragon was the symbolic guardian of the world's hidden treasures and, by association, of the dead (Figure 31).

The conversion to Christianity did not mean the abandonment of animal symbolism. Instead, animal images were converted for use within Christian iconography, so that the eagle represented the apostle John, the bull was transferred to represent Luke, the dragon became a symbol of the devil, to be trodden upon by images of Christ, and birds inhabited the vines of a Christian paradise.

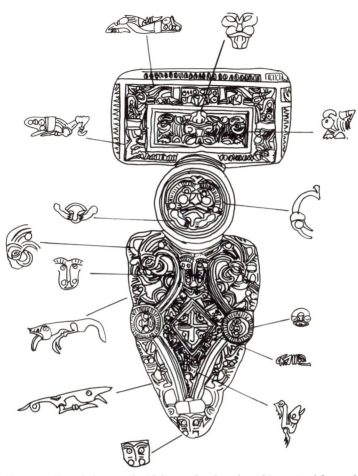

Figure 31 Brooch decorated with human heads and writhing animal figures from Grave 41, Bifrons, Kent.

Witchcraft

Burial 67 at Buckland was of a woman, whose grave goods include a lump of iron pyrites, who was buried face down in a contorted position, possibly as a result of having been buried alive. Gruesome though it may appear, this burial is by no means without parallel in the Anglo-Saxon archaeological record. An example comes from the poorer Anglian cemetery site at Sewerby, Yorkshire. Grave 41 contained the burials of two women, one on top of the other. The upper was lying face down, her head to the right, her legs and arms raised, with one large

stone under her shoulder and part of a beehive quern on her pelvis. She
was around thirty-five to forty-five years of age at the time of her death.
Her grave goods included a buckle, knife, jet spindlewhorl, two annular
brooches – one bronze, one gilt – some bronze sheet which may have
been for suspension, a wooden container and a string of fifteen beads,
including amber. She was one of the richest burials in this community,
bettered only by one or two burials, including that of the woman buried
beneath her – a seventeen to twenty-five year old, neatly laid out in
a wooden coffin. She had sleeve clasps of bronze and gilt (although not
a pair) and two strings of beads, one containing 117 beads, including
amber and gold, and the other of 88 beads, also including amber and
gold.

What is the explanation for this double burial? The prone woman may
have been a slave, thrown into the grave after the burial of her owner, but
the rich grave goods associated with the upper burial would normally
be associated with a wealthy woman and undermine this theory.
She may have been a sacrifice, although again, her wealth makes this
a less-attractive theory. Alternatively, she may have been considered
responsible in some way for the death of the young woman. The
sacrificed woman was buried with a number of items which may have
been amuletic: the jet spindlewhorl, the amber beads and the wooden
container. These may have been part of the equipment of a witch, and
the excavator believes that the most plausible explanation for the events
is that the older woman was accused of having caused the death of the
younger by misuse of her special knowledge, and her punishment was
burial alive.

In the Old English text *Prognostications*, a list of predictions based
on a child's date of birth, the fortunes of the male and female child
are told. A child born on the fifth moon of the year will, it is predicted,
be lucky to survive; after five years 'he often dies useless. A girl will die
worst, because of her evil deeds and witchcraft [*wyrt-gaelstre* – literally
"knowledge of herbs"].'

The archaeological evidence may provide evidence for women's roles
as witches/healers within early Anglo-Saxon society. The first problem
posed by the archaeological evidence would rest on how we are
to identify the symbols of the magical/religious woman. Bags, pouches,
plants and possible amulets do occur in later Anglo-Saxon medical
recipes, as do runes. In archaeological terms, the expectation would be
to find items of this sort in the grave assemblages of those whose social

persona was defined by their special medical skills. A woman in the seventh-century cemetery at Orsett, Essex, for example, has been identifed as a possible 'witch', because she had tied up in a cloth bag a miscellaneous collection of oddments whose significance is difficult to explain in terms other than amuletic. The bag contained two copper-alloy pieces from a hanging bowl, three or more iron rings, an iron guard mount from a knife, a large bead of lignite or shale and an iron chatelaine. Was such a collection 'normal' in female graves of this period?

An analysis of one rich Kentish cemetery at Buckland, excavated between 1951 and 1965, offers the following results. The excavated area contained about 165 burials, of which 62 were male and 71 were female. The site was in use between c.475 and c.750. Precious materials such as amber, crystal and garnet were found in the grave goods on the site, predominantly with women, because these materials tend to be associated with necklaces which men, within the cemetery ritual, did not possess.

'Amuletic' items from the site included fossils, stones not natural to the area, such as iron pyrites, cowrie shells and various small boxes. Workboxes, or small containers, may have had significance for the materials they enclosed. Twenty-three burials contained one of the above items, of which only two were male burials – Grave C, the burial of a high-status male (indicated by the sword included in his grave) whose disturbed grave contained small pebbles, and Grave 150, who was buried with a bronze box. It was possible to ascertain the contents of the boxes in only two cases – the remnants of a wooden box apparently enclosed a fossil in the case of Grave 55, the burial of a female; and in female Burial 60, the box contained a key, two spindlewhorls, an amber bead and a large horse tooth. The cemetery site can be divided into chronological plots, according to the dating suggested by the artefacts. Boxes or amulets crop up with women in plots from the earliest phases of the site to the latest. If one or two women were operating as 'wise women' or 'doctors' within any one generation in a given Anglo-Saxon community, and amuletic items indicated the burials of the community's 'wise woman', then this is precisely the distribution of items that we would expect with females. The evidence from the Buckland cemetery would indicate that, while men are not excluded from this behaviour, it would appear to be women whose ritual reflects their medical or magical skills.

It is difficult to distinguish between keepsakes and amulets, and it may be that items archaeologists might interpret as 'amuletic' actually had no superstitious significance for their owners, in which case we may say that women, rather than men, were perceived to be the accumulators of such knicknacks in the Buckland burial ritual. There is slender corroborative evidence, however, to indicate that these trinkets may be more than trivial.

Trepanning

Trepanning – the deliberate removal of a disc of bone from the skull of a living person – was not common in Anglo-Saxon England, but it occurs in a range of contexts from sixth-century cemeteries to church cemeteries, and in a range of sites in Anglo-Saxon England, from Kent to Yorkshire, with a particular cluster of cases around the fenlands, possibly the work of one practitioner. There is no certain evidence that trepanning was carried out for 'medical' reasons, in that almost none of the known cases exhibit any sign of head wounds or other ailments which might have prompted this form of surgery. There are other explanations for the practice. This particular form of body modification may have had ritual or symbolic purpose, or the roundel of cranial bone removed from the skull may have been the object of the exercise. It has also been hypothesised that trepanning was connected with exorcising devils from the sick, or it may have been a treatment for epileptics. The fact remains that, while there are a number of plausible suggestions, we still do not have any good explanation for this particular activity.

Typically, the trepanned Anglo-Saxon skulls healed before death, suggesting skill and confidence on the part of the trepanners. The surviving trepanned skulls also indicate that it was not for lack of ability that other forms of surgery were not common in the Anglo-Saxon medical repertoire.

Domestic rituals

Only recently Anglo-Saxon archaeologists have come to suspect that some of the evidence from early Anglo-Saxon settlements may point to a ritual dimension to everyday Anglo-Saxon domestic life. The evidence is still being assessed, and needs further investigation. An example is provided by the quotidian loom weights. They are ubiquitous on Anglo-Saxon sites – spinning and weaving was a daily activity for most, if not all, women. Some sunken-featured buildings seem to have been used just to hold the loom and for cloth making, because some have been found with the loom weights in situ on the floor of the structure, exactly where they had fallen when the woollen threads that held them rotted on the loom. Loom weights seem to have been entirely domestic and non-religious in nature – they are very rarely found in cemetery contexts, although spindlewhorls, shears, beating pins and cloth beaters occasionally are. Given that the rest of the paraphernalia of textile production found its way into the graves, though, why should loom weights have been excluded from this context? And why should loom weights, so easy to reuse, have been left abandoned in sunken-featured buildings when they could so easily have been retrieved? Although the making of loom weights did not take the same investment of energy as other forms of pottery, such as creating a decorated urn, work was still required to collect and shape the heavy clay, and useful combustible material had to be collected and burnt to fire the loom weights. Do abandoned loom weights represent an unwanted commodity? Or was there some taboo associated with reusing them, re-stringing a new loom with them or even reusing a weaving shed? It is speculative, but it is not beyond the bounds of possibility that, when a woman died, the weaving shed in which she had worked and the loom and unfinished cloth within were also abandoned as a token of mourning.

Given the lack of obvious religious buildings or sanctuaries found by archaeological excavation, domestic buildings may have served as special or hallowed spaces, and this may explain some of the material, usually assumed to be rubbish, which is found placed in sunken-featured buildings and timber-built halls, because the animal bones and pottery found in association with these structures are not always the casual deposits they seem. When St. Augustine came to England, King Æthelbert of Kent (who already had a Frankish Christian wife, of course) insisted that the meeting with the newcomer should take place in open air. The pragmatic reason was probably that he wanted all his followers to be able to witness the meeting, but the reason Bede gave was that Æthelbert held to the superstition that magic traps could have been laid for him if he had held the meeting in a building.

Other evidence hints at everyday superstitions and rituals. The *Beowulf* poet referred to the ancient art of sortilege, and a collection of animal *astragali* (foot) bones found in a later fifth-century cremation urn at Caistor-by-Norwich, Norfolk, might have been intended for use in foretelling the future by osteomancy. This collection of bones has only drawn attention because of its unusual context, but it raises the question of how many other domestic items may have been put to an occult purpose.

Christianity

The earliest Anglo-Saxons settling in England would have come into contact with Christianity through pockets of surviving Romano-British Christians, and when Augustine arrived in Kent to convert King Æthelbert and his people, he began to worship in a pre-existing church. St. Augustine's mission from AD 597 is traditionally credited with the official conversion of the Anglo-Saxons, since his mission came directly from the Pope, but Christianity filtered into England through different routes. Frankish Christians certainly came to England, and the heroic efforts of the ascetic Irish, such as Fursey, who converted parts of East Anglia, had a significant part to play. Bede himself was much influenced by St. Cuthbert, who himself followed the Irish model of Christianity. Bede, who had a deep dislike and distrust of native British Christians (for reasons that are not clear), is spectacularly silent about the conversion of the Midlands, and it may be that the parts of England bordering Wales had an active Christian population, converted by the British.

Conversion in Anglo-Saxon England was a top-down process, which is to say, kings converted and their people followed. Apostasies occurred, notably in times of famine, or when usurping kings took the throne, but by the end of the seventh century, the majority of the population would have been nominally Christian.

What was the impact of Christianity on daily lives? Christianity brought with it specific ideas which had an impact on family and inheritance strategies, because marriage between close kin was prohibited, limiting the pool of available spouses. The church was sometimes able to acquire land through implementation of these rules. The church at York, for example, gained lands in Northumbria because of an illicit union – there were two brothers who had one wife. There was

a problem with children too – they now needed to be baptised – not
necessarily an easy proposition, when there were very few bishops
to go around. Even one of Bishop John of Beverley's own retinue was
discovered not to have been properly baptised when he fell off a horse
he had been racing (against the Bishop's advice) and could not be cured
by John's intervention. The introduction of Christianity also brought
some benefits. Sunday was to be a day of rest, even for slaves, and early
legislation made sure that owners were held responsible for making sure
that the rule was upheld.

The church may have taken on some of the roles traditionally carried
out by extended family. Anglo-Saxons were used to the idea of fosterage,
where children would be sent into other households – often the
households of close kin – partly for their education, and partly because
fosterage strengthened ties and obligations between families, and was
a mechanism to create and maintain social bonds, just like the marriage
contract. With the introduction of Christianity, children were also
'fostered' into the church, which took on the reciprocal obligations
of foster parents. Bede himself was given into the care of Benedict Biscop
at the age of seven (the same age that Beowulf says he was fostered). Such
ecclesiastical fosterage or oblation need not have been a matter of parents
giving up their children to strangers, however. Bede says of himself that
he was born in the territory of the monasteries of Monkwearmouth and
Jarrow, and it is perfectly possible that Bede's family was connected
to Benedict's in some way. When Willibald's parents decided to give him
to the church at the age of five, in fulfilment of a vow they had made
when he recovered from an illness two years previously, they consulted
all their relatives and appointed the 'honest and trustworthy' Theodred
to accompany them to the monastery at Bishop's Waltham, where, after
discussion with Abbot Egwald, and with the permission of the other
monks, the child was accepted. Child oblation was often a family affair.
King Edgar dedicated his young child Edith to a life in a convent, but
he was the patron of the institution and Edith's mother was its abbess.
Keeping ecclesiastical institutions in the family was a common practice
in Anglo-Saxon England, and one followed by the Irish too (Figure 32).

The distinction between secular and religious life was not always clear-
cut. Monastic houses, often founded by nobles or royalty, to be run by
and accommodate their own kin, were in many ways very similar to elite
secular households. This, at least, was the view of the Synod of Clofesho
in 746/747, which condemned the keeping of poets, harpers, musicians

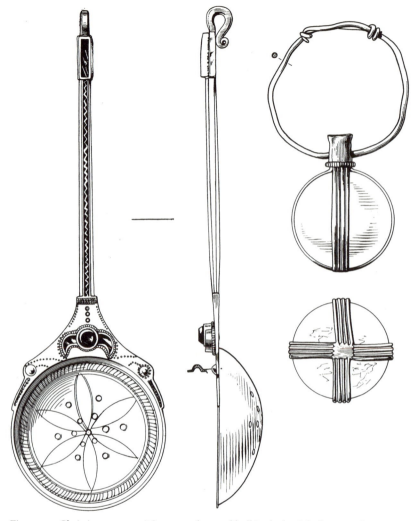

Figure 32 Christian or pagan? Spoon and crystal ball in the burial of a seventh-century woman, Grave 51, Bifrons, Kent.

and jesters in religious communities, and additionally criticised the staging of horse races at religious festivals. The cleric Alcuin later criticised clerics who went fox hunting, and Bede records the critical reaction of St. John of Beverley when one of his young monks, in an excess of youthful enthusiasm, raced his horse with predictably nasty consequences. Archaeological evidence corroborates the view that a clear distinction between secular and Christian settlements is not always obvious. Excavations at Flixborough, Lincolnshire and other middle to late Anglo-Saxon sites, have led to much discussion and argument about whether they are ecclesiastical sites or secular sites. Finds include writing styli, and inscribed lead plates. There are burials associated with these sites, and they have imported pottery. Continental imports are a marker of Christian sites, not least because Christian rituals require wine and oil, usually brought in from abroad. But these sites also show evidence for craft production, and it can be argued that the secular elite had access to writing and exotic imports too. It is not clear whether these are ecclesiastical sites which sometimes had secular functions, or vice versa.

By the tenth century, most people living in England had access to a local church, and burial within the churchyard, without grave goods, was the norm. One of the best excavated examples of the manorial church and surrounding burials is the site at Raunds Furnells, Northamptonshire, where a simple two-celled church is surrounded by closely packed, east–west orientated, aligned burials within a rectangular enclosure. Christian burial did not mean everyone was treated the same in death, however; there was still tremendous variation in the ritual, which may have been related to social status. Differences included the presence or absence of coffins, stones in the grave and burial location. Burials of infants, for example, were clustered around the walls of the church at Raunds, and fewer burials were found to the north of the church, traditionally a less-favourable area for burial. Christian Anglo-Saxon England was a hierarchical society, even in death.

Chapter 9
Health, Sickness and Survival

In pre-modern societies, life expectancy was short, diseases and
disabilities were beyond medical help, and coping with disease was part
of everyday life. This said, a number of surviving medical texts, including
the earliest medical book in the English language, dating from the tenth
century, and the skeletal evidence from Anglo-Saxon cemeteries, show
that there was a strong and lively tradition of health care in Anglo-
Saxon England and that some medical interventions were surprisingly
pragmatic and sophisticated. At the same time, texts such as the *Lives*
of the saints and the grave goods associated with the dead from the
earlier Anglo-Saxon period provide evidence about Anglo-Saxon
attitudes towards health, sickness, the causes of illness, the way sickness
might influence the status of the sufferer – for both the better and the
worse – and the care due to those who were sick, even within dispersed
agricultural societies where the sick and infirm might be considered
a burden on the community.

Stature

Estimates of stature based on the skeletal evidence from cemeteries offer
a surprisingly consistent story across Anglo-Saxon England. The earliest
cemeteries, from the fifth to the sixth century, show that the population
buried in these Germanic burial grounds was a little taller than the
population associated with the late Romano-British cemeteries, with
males standing at about 5.68 feet (173 centimetres) and females
at around 5.31 feet (162 centimetres) on average.

It has been suggested that there might be a genetic dimension to the
increase in height in the earlier Anglo-Saxon population over the native
British population, but height is also related to diet. The evidence from
the early Anglo-Saxon inhumation cemeteries shows that the population
was relatively healthy, with little bone evidence for diseases caused
by malnutrition or deficiency in the diet. Skeletal evidence and stable-
isotope analysis show that there was no significant difference in diet
between men and women; although there is some evidence from the little

stable-isotope analysis that has been done to suggest that, at the site of Berinsfield in Oxfordshire, at least, young adult males enjoyed a diet rich in the best proteins – sheep and cattle – while older males ate more fish and pork.

Life expectancy

Documentary sources indicate that average lifespan in secular aristocratic life could be brutally short, and not from natural causes. A case in point is the family history of King Æthelwulf of Wessex, who died in AD 858 fighting the Vikings. He was succeeded by his four sons in turn (the fifth and eldest having predeceased him), the first three of whom also died fighting the Vikings. The fourth and youngest was King Alfred, who died at the age of fifty-one, in AD 899, after a long and famously sickly life.

Skeletal evidence from cemeteries does not offer a more positive view for the general population, either. Mortuary populations are not complete populations (few Anglo-Saxon cemeteries have anything like the expected number of infants for a pre-industrial population, for example), but the statistics are sobering. At Berinsfield, Oxfordshire, more than half the females represented by the buried population had died by the age of thirty. Males did rather better, as only eight of the twenty-six had died before the age of thirty. On average, only 10 percent of the population represented by the skeletons found in early Anglo-Saxon populations survived to live for more than forty-five years.

Physical health and disease

On a more positive note, Anglo-Saxons had remarkably healthy teeth when compared with earlier Romano-British and later medieval populations, probably because there was little access to sugar in the average daily diet. At Berinsfield, no one had lost teeth through dental decay before the age of thirty, and caries was rare. When teeth did become infected, however, there was little remedy for the pain. One skeleton at Berinsfield had defective enamel on the molars, which lead to a number of untreated caries, which would have caused the individual to suffer from constant discomfort and debilitating low-level infection.

Another individual from the same site had a large carious cavity on one side of the jaw. The teeth on this side were noticeably less worn than on the healthy side, showing the care the sufferer had taken not to chew on that side.

One affliction to which almost all Anglo-Saxon adults were prone, to a lesser or greater degree, was vertebral degeneration, probably as a result of the wear and tear of daily life. Males seemed to suffer from back trouble at an earlier age than females, perhaps as a result of a heavier workload. Osteoarthritis in joints is also visible in a significant number of Anglo-Saxon skeletons, with hips being the most common joint to suffer, but cases of osteoarthritis at wrists, elbows, knees, ankles and shoulders are also prevalent.

Skeletal evidence is not particularly useful for identifying the cause of death, except in rare cases, but occasionally, chronic diseases left their mark on bones. Several cases of tuberculosis and leprosy are recorded for the Anglo-Saxon period. Assessment of the treatment of those identified with leprosy (or a similarly disfiguring, chronic disease) in the early Anglo-Saxon period suggests that they were given special rituals at death, which imply enhanced social status. At Edix Hill, Cambridgeshire, for example, three cases of females with disfiguring tubercular diseases are also amongst the richest in the cemetery. At Beckford, two burials identified as being leprous were buried slightly away from the main cemetery (though the site was only partially excavated), and both, again, were given rich grave goods. Interestingly, the Beckford and Edix Hill burials were associated with infant or juvenile burials. Similarly, in Grave 10 at Berinsfield were the remains of a female whose back was badly damaged, probably through tuberculosis, and who would have had to have walked bent double in life. Her grave had been disturbed by a modern dragline, but some grave goods, including amber and glass beads, were discovered, in addition to the bones of two other bodies, one of which was in its very early teens. Whether diseased adults were associated with other burials, particularly infants and children, because disease had given the sufferers a childlike status, or whether the disease gave the individuals enhanced status which drew children to them (like later infant burials surrounding the special place of the church), remains speculative.

Though invisible in the archaeological evidence, the documentary sources report outbreaks of 'plague' devastating parts of the country. Bede records that one outbreak in AD 664 depopulated southern Britain first, before moving northwards and then into Ireland. Bede named various monks who were killed by the plague, but he also offers cases of survivors. An Anglo-Saxon monk called Egbert, living in Ireland, who may have been known to Bede, caught the plague of AD 664, but recovered, and in spite of (or perhaps because of) a life of great abstinence, characterised by regular fasting, lived to be ninety, dying in AD 729.

Sanitation and water supplies

Early Anglo-Saxon rural settlements were sited next to clean, running water. Comparative studies of the earliest archaeological evidence for Anglo-Saxon settlement and associated Old English place names suggest that the earliest settlement names were topographical, and many were based on the theme of water, relating to water supply, water control, crossing points and dry places. Mucking, Essex, the site of a major early Anglo-Saxon settlement, seems, at first, to belong to the *ingas* type of place name. But a reassessment of its etymology suggests that its 'ing' element is derived from the singular suffix, *ing*, meaning 'place of', found in place names such as Docking (place where dock grows) and Clavering (place where clover grows), both in Essex. The 'ing' suffix could also be attached to watercourses, such as Frating, Matching and Tendring, also in Essex, and it is likely that Mucking fits into the early chronology of place names, being named after a small creek or stream close to the settlement.

Access to clean drinking water in urban settings was problematic. Excavations at Anglo-Saxon York have revealed a well shaft close to the river Foss, constructed out of a hollow, black-poplar tree trunk, revetted with wattle and daub, and such moderately unhygienic water supplies would have provided water for the community. As in the later medieval period, it was probably safer to drink alcoholic beverages than to risk drinking urban well water.

Personal hygiene

There is not much evidence for Anglo-Saxon cleanliness and personal hygiene. Early Anglo-Saxon mortuary costume sometimes included small metal items hanging from belts which have been interpreted as ear scoops and tweezers. They are found with adults of all ages, but are relatively more common in the graves of older people. Perhaps water was too valuable a commodity to waste on washing unless you belonged to the elite, because in the eighth century, Benedict Biscop sent Boniface a bath towel, a face towel and a little frankincense (*sabanum unum et facitergium unem et modica thymiana*), but it may be that the cloth in this gift was of particularly high quality, and the inclusion of frank- incense in the gift implies that the items were intended to be used in a ritual or specialised way. Evidence for head lice still caught in the teeth of abandoned bone combs from ninth-century Coppergate tells an evocative tale of everyday discomfort due to lice infestations (Figure 33).

The surviving evidence suggests that Anglo-Saxon sanitation was rudimentary. Examples of latrine pits are rare in early and rural Anglo- Saxon settlement contexts. At West Stow, Suffolk, for example, three abandoned sunken-featured buildings (SFBs) contained cess, though it was impossible to be certain whether the material was of human or animal origin. If it was human, it means that people were defecating

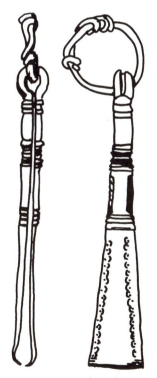

Figure 33 Anglo-Saxon tweezers, a relatively common grave good accessory.

in limited and selected areas. It is probable that much human waste was collected for manuring the fields. The Old English word *feltun* meant both privy and dunghill. Still, the dunghill provided the normal growing conditions for two useful plants, the *feltwurma* (wild marjoram) and *feltwyrt* (mullein), both of which were used in Old English medicinal recipes.

In urban contexts, disposing of waste material was problematic, as the Old English word *adelseath* [sewer] suggests. The first part of this Old English word still survives in modern English as 'addle'. Excavations at Anglian York revealed a number of cess-filled pits, where coprolitic material was interspersed with fragments of textile – Anglo-Saxon toilet paper? But the tenth-century houses at York seem to have been noxious by modern standards. The earthen floors of the houses rose over time, as mud and dirt built up on them, and analysis of the floor material at these houses has shown that domestic rubbish was trampled into the floors. Outside the houses, conditions were, if anything, worse – rotting vegetation, windblown soil and domestic rubbish, including animal remains, appear to have been simply dumped at the back of the houses. The situation, and the smell, can hardly have been improved by the occasional flooding of the nearby river Foss. In addition, the area at the end of the tenement plots was cratered by pits. Some of these had been wells, and some had been used for cess and rubbish from the outset. Repeated digging and dumping meant that rubbish was left lying on the surface, attracting animal and bird scavengers, whose bones were also found amongst the deposits.

As indicated above, the general health of early Anglo-Saxon populations, based on the skeletal evidence, was good. A few studies of rare coprolite evidence have reinforced this general picture. At West Stow, Suffolk, for example, coprolites of mixed human and animal origin, taken from SFBs and pits, provided relatively little evidence of parasites. In the samples which did contain parasites, the main forms were whip worms and the large round worm, though the very low number of eggs found suggests that any infection was light. Unfortunately, the preservation of the evidence meant it was impossible to be sure whether the parasite eggs were associated with human or animal infection, though the analyst thought it likely, based on the size of the samples, that they came from adult humans. This might also help to explain the apparently very light levels of infection illustrated by the skeletal evidence.

Later medieval, urban communities show rather more signs of
disease and physical stress. Coprolite analysis from a medieval cess pit
at Winchester showed a concentration of parasitic eggs more than thirty
times that from West Stow, while the inhabitants of Anglo-Scandinavian
Coppergate, York, were infested with whip worm and maw worm. Given
the levels of cess and rubbish inside and outside the dwellings at York,
close to the water wells, conditions there were ideal for the constant
transmission of these gut worms and the contamination of the water
supply.

Accidents and injuries

The archaeological and documentary sources agree that accidents were
a hazard of daily life and could lead to fatal consequences. The poem
'The Fates of Man' reminded parents (as if they needed reminding) that
unexpected misery could befall their grown children at any moment –
one might be killed by wild animals, and another may be killed in battle.
Less dramatic, but equally unpleasant domestic accidents might occur.
The Old English word *adloma* (one crippled by fire) implied the comparative dangers of the open fires which heated Anglo-Saxon settlements.
The hagiographic literature is replete with victims of domestic and
workplace accidents. Bede recounted the story of a mason's child who
received a crushing fall while helping his father at work. A law of King
Alfred's discussed the case of one man killing another unintentionally by
allowing a tree to fall on him while they were working together. The dead
man's relatives were to get the tree. A record for the year AD 977 stated
that the upper floor of a building collapsed, causing all those in it to fall,
apart from Archbishop Dunstan, who was left miraculously standing
unhurt on a surviving beam. The collapse of this building's upper storey
was unlikely to have been an isolated case of an insecure building,
because the poem 'The Gifts of Men' included, amongst the talents given
out to different people, the description of one who was trained to craft
every sort of building: 'He knows how to truss the spacious construction
securely against sudden collapses.'

Injuries found on Anglo-Saxon skeletons cannot be ascribed with
certainty to accident, rather than to violence, but some fractures are
more likely to be caused by mishaps. The late Anglo-Saxon population
at Raunds exhibited a number of bone injuries suggestive of accident.

Twenty-four skeletons had bone injuries, of which the majority were Pott's and Colles's type of fractures to the shafts of the fibula and radius – injuries usually sustained from an awkward sideways fall injuring the leg in the first case, and a fall leading to an awkward landing on an outstretched arm in the second. Males had more fractures than females at this site. Other injuries are less easy to categorise as accidental. A male from the late Anglo-Saxon rural cemetery at Chimney Farm, Oxfordshire, had had his front teeth knocked out. It is possible that this was accidental, but this injury is more characteristic of a punch to the mouth.

Deliberate violence is certainly the cause of a range of depressed fractures and blade injuries to skulls, as well as blade injuries to bones of the body. Both male and female skeletons have been found with weapon injuries, though, as might be expected, males were more usually implicated in such violence. It has to be stated that the majority of Anglo-Saxon burials, including those males buried with weapons in the early Anglo-Saxon period, show no signs of having been involved in fighting or warfare. However, when fighting did occur, the results could be dramatic. At the late Anglo-Saxon/early Norman cemetery site associated with the church and priory of St Andrew, Fishergate, York, nineteen males had fatal injuries made by sharp implements with no evidence of healing, and the majority of these injuries were from blows to the head and upper body. The devastating consequences of weapon injury where the individual survived are illustrated by one of Alfred's laws, which offered compensation for injury causing 'damage to the muscles in the neck, so that he has no control over them but nevertheless continues to live'; the compensation was to be a hefty 100 shillings, by far the largest sum to be given in compensation, 'unless the witan deem a juster and greater sum'.

Care in the church

The importance of the church as central to the process of curing disease for the Anglo-Saxons should not be underestimated. According to the teachings of the church, many illnesses were caused by the devil, so a monk, rather than a lay practitioner, was the obvious person to bring health. Equally, God was considered responsible for punitive illnesses. For example, when thieves attempted to break into the church of the saint and martyr St. Edmund, the Old English text records that the thieves were struck down with paralysis through the night, until they were apprehended in the morning and taken away for execution. Small wonder, then, that some afflicted with chronic illness hoped that a visit to the church to atone for their sins, or a prayer for the mediation of a powerful saint, might lead to a cure. One of the most effective saints of the late Anglo-Saxon period was, according to his biographer Ælfric, St. Swithun. Prolific miracle cures emanated from his tomb and shrine at the Old Minster, Winchester, which were too numerous in range and quantity for even the keen pen of the hagiographer to record. Amongst Swithun's most noteworthy achievements were the curing of three blind women and their dumb guide, the curing of a paralytic and the curing of a man who had multiple fractures after a riding accident. According to Ælfric, sick and disabled people would travel considerable distances to seek a cure at Swithun's shrine. One blind English man who had lived for four years in Rome in the hope of a miracle from St. Peter even travelled back from Rome after being told in a dream that St. Swithun would cure him. The power of St. Swithun was clearly something of a phenomenon, and crowds gathered at the church for cure. There are indications that Ælfric was not exaggerating the popularity of this saint, because he described a scene any of his readers could visit for themselves – a church hung about with crutches and cripples' stools from one end to the other, and there were so many of these tokens of Swithun's healing powers that not half of the crutches and stools could be hung up, according to Ælfric.

While individual saints gained a reputation for being able to effect miraculous cures, living churchmen were practising medicine and might reasonably be described as doctors. Bede cites a doctor named Cynefrith, who attended the saintly Queen Æthelthryth before her death, and who was present at her body's exhumation from the grave and translation into a church in a new coffin some sixteen years later. Cynefrith had lanced a tumour on her jaw before her death, but when her body was exhumed, the gaping wound had miraculously healed. The best recorded of these ecclesiastic Anglo-Saxon doctors was St. John of Beverley, who died in AD 721. His life, written by Bede, is interesting for the way it shows St. John distinguishing between cures effected by simple medicine and miracles. A dumb boy, who was also suffering from a severe skin condition, was brought to the saint to be healed. The hagiographer records that John asked the boy to stick out his tongue. Having made the sign of the cross over the tongue, John asked the boy to repeat after him the sounds of the alphabet, which the boy duly did. Astonished at having found his tongue, the boy, so the hagiographer describes, then spent the rest of the day talking to anyone who would listen. The boy's skin condition, however, was dealt with by 'a physician' (*medico*), who was ordered by Bishop John to undertake the cure of the boy's scabby head. This is medicine. In fact, it is possible that the boy's dumbness was also cured by practical means: if the boy was suffering from the condition known as 'tongue tied', the action of putting his tongue out – particularly if John grasped it to make the sign of the cross – might have broken the frenulum, thus effecting a cure.

On another occasion, John's learning was made even more explicit. Visiting an abbess, he was informed that her daughter was fatally ill with a swollen arm and was asked to make her better. Inquiring into the circumstances of her illness (asking for a history, as any modern family doctor would before attempting a diagnosis), John discovered that the girl had been bled, to which he retorted that it had been a foolish and ignorant action to bleed her on the fourth day of the moon, and he recalled that Archbishop Theodore had taught that it was dangerous to bleed a patient when the moon was waxing and the tide flowing.

Archbishop Theodore was sent to England in AD 668 by Pope Vitalian. Theodore was a native of Tarsus in Cilicia and was described by Bede as 'well trained in secular and divine literature, both Greek and Latin'. It was through foreign ecclesiastical scholars that Greek and Latin literature, including medical literature, were first brought to the Anglo-Saxons, and Bishop John was a product of their training. John's miracles, as recorded by Bede, illustrate that the Greek and Roman medical tradition was alive and working in seventh-century Anglo-Saxon England and that it was a first course of action in the case of illness. Only when it was clear that 'conventional' medicine would fail, was John credited with miraculous healing.

There is some further archaeological evidence to suggest that the church functioned as the primary carer for the sick in some circumstances. One cemetery associated with a nunnery at Nazeingby, Northamptonshire, included the burial of a severely disabled older adult, suffering from possible congenital dislocation of the hips. According to the site report, there was no way in which this man could have reached the age of fifty without a great deal of help. Skeletons with relatively high levels of bone pathology were also found in this cemetery, including a female aged over fifty years with severe osteoarthritis, a female over fifty with osteoarthritis and bone changes typical of tuberculosis, a male aged between thirty-five and forty-five with fatigue fractures of both feet, a case of hydrocephalus aged between twenty-five and thirty at the time of death and a case of Down's syndrome. The population within this cemetery is highly unusual in many ways. There was a preponderance of females, high levels of pathology and an unusual proportion of the burials had reached old age. Survival into old age of some of the highly pathological individuals suggests a degree of care for the sick and that this site was the cemetery of a hospice run by a religious order.

Bede's description of St. Hilda's famous double monastery at Whitby in the seventh century included a building where the sick and terminally ill were kept. Bede further records a number of monks and nuns who were victims of paralysis or extremely debilitating illness who were nonetheless cared for and kept alive for considerable periods of time, including Torhtgyth, a nun who had been severely ill for nine years, and another 'certain nun, of noble family' who had been 'so disabled that she could not move a single limb' for many years.

The majority of people who fell seriously ill, however, would have relied on their immediate family, kinsmen and even neighbours for support, as the *Lives* of the saints indicate. One man struck by a paralysing illness was taken to St. Swithun's church by his friend, while another, who had been paralysed for many years, consulted his friends and kinsmen about whether he should make the journey to St. Swithun. A mad youth, Hwætred, who had killed several men in his frenzies, was being cared for by his miserable parents, who were so desperate when they took him to a saint for a miracle cure that they would almost rather he had died than that things should carry on as they were, according to the hagiographer. Another law of King Alfred, stating that a man who was born deaf and dumb could not be held responsible for his crimes, but that his father had to bear the responsibility instead, corroborates the impression given by the story of the mad youth that parents were legally responsible for the behaviour of children who were considered incapable, through illness or impairment, from taking up an adult place in society.

Doctors

Though doctors (Old English *laece* [leech]) do not figure prominently in the documentary sources, the surviving evidence does suggest that ordinary people in the later Anglo-Saxon period were expected to have access to people with special medical knowledge. A ninth-century law of King Alfred, for example, states that 'if anyone strikes his neighbour with a stone or fist in such a way that he can still get about on a stick, the assailant is to get a doctor for him and do his work as long as he cannot do it himself'. Identifying these doctors and the medicine they practiced is more difficult. The problem of identifying medicine in a non-ecclesiastical setting in Anglo-Saxon England is compounded by the fact that all known scriptoria were within monastic contexts, so it would seem likely that the surviving Old English medical texts were produced in a monastic setting. However, the people mentioned by name in the surviving documents who appear to have special medical knowledge may well have been secular. The four most likely contenders for the role of doctor in late Anglo-Saxon England are all found in the Old English medical text known as Bald's *Leechbook*. The style of Bald's *Leechbook* indicates that it was intended as an aide-memoire for someone familiar with the subject matter. A great deal of knowledge on the part of the reader is assumed, to such an extent that it seems very likely that the book represents the personal text of a medical practitioner, probably Bald himself. The skill of the scribe or copyist, a person named Cild, suggests that he, too, may have had some medical knowledge or training. Bald's *Leechbook* was not an original work, any more than a modern medical textbook is, and its acknowledgement within the text of the work of other doctors provides us with two more personal names, Oxa and Dun, both males. However, although no female doctors were recorded by name in surviving texts, an entry in the *Prognostications* indicates that female doctors were known: 'The twenty-second moon is good for buying servants. A child born on it will be a doctor (*laece*). A girl likewise. And poor.'

'Other doctors' mentioned in Bald's *Leechbook* were not always Anglo-Saxons. Parts of the *Leechbook* were derived from the *Medicina Plinii, Practica Alexandri* and other texts. In Book II of the *Leechbook*, the contents list says that information on the liver is provided by 'doctors [who] teach this remedy for swelling and injury to the liver', and 'doctors say these are the symptoms of a swollen and damaged liver, and remedies for that, and for hardening of the liver'. Malcolm Cameron has shown that these remedies are a close translation of the *Epitome Altera* of Vindicianus. Sometimes, the sources are acknowledged within the text. In *Leechbook*, Book I, 87:1, the 'Great Doctor Plinius' is referenced. However, Bald does not particularly discriminate between the medical knowledge and authority of his native and continental sources.

Bald may not have had direct access to the Mediterranean works
he translated, and he may have been drawing on other Old English
translations of translations. However he came by his information, Bald
was pulling together the known and tried knowledge of all doctors,
pooling sources to provide an up-to-date compendium of tenth-century
medical practice. It is impossible to tell to what extent Bald dictated
the collection of material found in the text, or whether the scribe Cild
understood the source material he was copying, although comparing
some of the original sources to the Anglo-Saxon versions, it would seem
that both had some knowledge of what they were about – foreign
ingredients have been swapped for herbs available in England, and
selection and editing of the original sources have taken place.

Bald's *Leechbook* provides an invaluable insight into the medical
knowledge base of the day, showing that, while there was a strong
influence from the Graeco-Roman system of medicine, the Anglo-Saxon
practitioner was not an ignorant or uncritical follower of foreign texts.
Bald's carefully organised collection of remedies drew on experience
and other native medical traditions, too. The scriptorium at Winchester
may well have been responsible for producing Bald's *Leechbook*. The
surviving copy of the *Leechbook* (there may once have been many) is
in the British Museum, MS Royal 12 D.xvii. The surviving manuscript
of Bald's *Leechbook* consists of three sections or books, the first two of
which are thought to belong together, and appear to form an intentional
whole. The third book may have been a later addition.

Book I follows standard Graeco-Roman practice in being divided
up into a logical sequence, starting with illnesses of the head and moving
progressively around the body. Sections 1–13 of Book I cover diseases
of the head, including eye problems, coughs, deafness and nosebleeds.
Sections 14–22 discuss diseases of the body, from coughs and vomiting to
unspecific pains in the sides up to 'pain in the loins'. This leads on to leg
problems, which are dealt with in Sections 23–30, again ranging from
the relatively minor (chilblains and over exercising) to severe (splinting
a broken leg). Sections 31–44 give information on how to treat diseases
that affect the whole body, such as jaundice, cancer and gangrene. The
odd exception is Section 34, where remedies for apparently trivial nail
problems nestle in between remedies for ulcerating skin and remedies
for 'blackened and deadened body'. Sections 45–54 are about 'worm'
diseases; that is, illnesses that either were caused by insects or parasites
or were believed to have been. Sections 55–61 are concerned with

paralysis of one sort or another, while Sections 62–67 are about fevers and madness. The remaining sections are an eclectic group, made up of the 'leftovers' – diseases or problems that do not obviously fit into any of the other categories, such as dog bite, impotence and bloodletting. Book II is concerned with internal ailments.

Although the books seem to be given a logical order, the actual remedies for any given problem are offered in a heap, with no way of differentiating between them. In the first section of Book I, for example, there are twelve remedies for 'a headache', each offering a different range of herbal treatments, including drinks, pastes and creams derived from both native and exotic plants:

> Rub a penny weight of the plant called myrrh in a mortar, add
> a bucket full of wine to the pulp, rub the head with it and drink it
> at night fasting. For headache, take rue and wormwood, pound and
> mix with vinegar and oil, sieve through a cloth, rub it onto the head,
> or make a paste with the same ingredients, apply it to the head, and
> cover it with bandages when you want to go to bed. For the same
> thing, take betony and pepper, rub thoroughly together, leave them
> hanging up in a cloth overnight, use as a cream.

There is no hint that one of these – and the list goes on for another nine remedies 'for the same thing' – is any more efficacious than another, nor any hint of differentiation between these headaches, yet headaches are caused by a variety of illnesses and lead to a variety of associated symptoms (though there is a different section for 'half a headache'). Headaches may be throbbing, persistent, sharp or associated with dizziness and nausea. Headaches may be caused by anything from a trivial hangover to a life-threatening brain tumour. This may offer an explanation for the wide range of remedies for what are seemingly the same diseases. For headache, which could have a variety of causes, a range of remedies was appropriate, because one or the other of them might eventually be efficacious. Read in this way, the *Leechbook*, if it is supposed to offer advice, advocates a muddled 'lottery methodology' in medicine – keep trying, because one day you might hit the right combination.

However, what a reading of the whole manuscript shows is that there may have been a conscious choice not to include the details we might expect, because occasionally they *are* included: remedies for nausea and swelling were described as 'noble', those for spider bite as 'excellent', and that for 'blackened and deadened body' (gangrene) were described as 'powerful and noble remedies'. It may well be, then, that the Old English medical text appears muddled because it was written for a trained doctor who would know how to differentiate between the remedies in a way lost to the modern, ignorant reader.

It is also clear from the descriptions within the *Leechbook* that the Anglo-Saxon doctor was perfectly capable of observing symptoms and the progress of some diseases. The accurate descriptions of gangrene and jaundice are testimony to this skill, as is the following useful and reasonable treatment for a fractured skull: 'For a fractured skull, and if the brain is visible, mix a little egg yolk with honey, fill the wound with it, cover with a bandage of hemp. Then leave it alone, and after about three days look at the wound. If there is a red ring in the healthy skin around the wound, then you will know that it is incurable.' Bald has prescribed a useful paste to seal the wound, with honey to act as an osmotic agent, and his prognosis is broadly correct. Furthermore, there are some remedies where distinctions between types of ailment are made by simple tests. For a swollen throat, windpipe and mouth, the reader is advised that

> There are two types of the disease. One is in the jaws: when you look into the open mouth it is swollen and is red about the uvula, and the patient cannot breathe easily and feels suffocated, also he cannot swallow or speak easily, and has lost his voice. However the disease is not dangerous. The other is when the throat is swollen and pussy, the patient cannot speak, and the swelling is in both the neck and the tongue. The patient is unable to breathe easily and cannot turn his neck, or lean his head forward to see his navel, and unless he is treated immediately he will be dead in about three days.

Here, there is advice on how to predict the progress of the disease, and how to distinguish between serious (probably meningitis) and less serious illnesses, when the patient presents similar symptoms. A final example of this, and perhaps the most impressive, is the section on the treatment of gangrene:

> If the swelling skin eruptions or the red mould come externally from wounds or cuts or blows, treat the condition immediately with scarification and applications of barley, in the way that knowledgeable doctors well know how; you will make it better.

If the blackened area is so deadened that there is no feeling in it,
then you must immediately cut away all the dead and numb parts
to the living body so that none of the dead area is left of that which
could feel neither ice nor fire before. After that, treat the wound
as you would the part that still has some sensation and is not
completely dead. You must draw the blood from the deadened place
with frequent scarifyings, sometimes severe, sometimes light. If you
must chop or cut an unsound limb from a healthy body, then do not
cut on the border of the healthy area, but cut into the well and
healthy area so that you will make it better and cure it more quickly.
Treat the cuts like this: take bean meal or oat meal or barley meal,
or such meal as you think will do to apply, add vinegar and honey,
cook together and apply and bandage on to the sore places. If you
want the ointment to be more powerful, add a little salt to it and
bandage it up now and then, and bathe with vinegar or with wine.
If needs be, give a herbal drink occasionally.

Such careful and accurate instructions, asking the doctor to use discretion
and observation, are well within the Mediterranean tradition of 'rational'
medicine. Aspects of Anglo-Saxon medical knowledge mirrored the best
available anywhere in the pre-modern world. If other remedies did not
describe illnesses in detail, or differentiate remedies for the same illness,
it would seem that it was not because the compiler of the *Leechbook* was
incapable of such thought processes, but that he chose not to in most
cases. Further evidence for the sophistication of the Old English doctor
comes from the well-known injunction in the *Leechbook* to doctors:

always consider when you are giving potent medicines what the
strength and condition of the patient is. Are they strong or vigorous,
so that they can cope with strong medicine, or are they delicate and
frail and weak, so that they will not be able to stand the medicine.
Apply the medicine according to the condition of the patient,
because there is a great difference between the bodies of men,
women and children, and in the strength of the daily labourer and
the leisured, of the old and the young and of those used to hardships
and those who are unused to such circumstances. It is a fact that
a pale body is weaker and more tender than tanned and sunburnt
ones. If you intend to cut a limb from the body, then consider the
condition of the area and the strength of the place, because some

areas fester more readily if they are not carefully attended. Some react to the treatment later, some sooner.

As Bald's *Leechbook* makes clear, those who had access to medical knowledge in Anglo-Saxon England were expected to behave, in many ways, like their modern counterparts. Case histories might be taken, and the doctor was supposed to use discretion and observation in the prescribing of dosages: for gangrene, the medical practitioner is counselled to take stock and to think about the patient rather than mechanically prescribing according to the book. This medical advice appears startlingly modern and rational, and on one level, it is. However, this very same advice is echoed in a tenth-century law code of King Æthelred, who was strongly influenced by Archbishop Wulfstan of York:

> And always the greater a man's position in this present life, or the higher the privileges of his rank, the more fully shall he make amends for his sins, and the more dearly shall he pay for all misdeeds; for the strong and the weak are not alike, nor can they bear a similar burden, any more than the sick can be treated like the well. And therefore, in forming a judgment, careful discrimination must be made between age and youth, wealth and poverty, health and sickness, and the various ranks of life.

The similarities between the medical text on the one hand and the law code on the other are a timely reminder that physical health, mental health, spiritual health and the health of the kingdom were not separate entities to the Anglo-Saxon mind. The elite of Anglo-Saxon society, trained in Latin and Greek by the church and through church schools, but writing confidently and fluently in their own language too (a rarity in early Medieval Europe), viewed medical knowledge, the ability to heal the physical body, not as a skill separate from political skill or religious knowledge but as an intrinsic part of the wider pool of all human knowledge.

Medical equipment

Artefactual evidence for any medical practice beyond basic nurturing of the sick is difficult to identify in the earlier Anglo-Saxon period. Small metal tool sets known as 'toilet instruments' are found amongst the grave goods of males and females in this period. They include tiny spoons, tweezers and little picks discussed earlier in this section. Perhaps these implements were used to maintain personal appearance, or it may be that there was awareness that personal hygiene was linked to general health. Absent from the Anglo-Saxon archaeological record, however, is anything to compare with the surgical instruments found in Roman contexts. The Anglo-Saxons had some contact with Roman culture, and Germanic troops served in the Roman Army where surgeons practiced their trade, but the Anglo-Saxons do not seem to have copied this aspect of Roman medical practice. In the later documentary evidence too, references to surgical interventions are very few and far between (Figure 34).

MEASURING AND DOSING

Old English name	Artefact
Mele	A measure
Steap fulne	Stoup, beaker, flagon
Pening gewege	Penny weight
Ane yntsan	An ounce
Cucler fulne	Spoon full
Healfne cucler	Half spoon
Bollan fulle	Bowl full
Godne bollan fulne	Good bowl full
Lytle bollan fulne	Little bowl full
Ceac fulne	Jug full
Hand fulla	Hand full
Fæt ful	Vat, vessel
Scenc fulne	Sconce/cup full
Micelne scenc fulne	Big cup full
Ambre fulne	An amber full
Tynamberne ketel	A ten amber kettle
Mele fulne	Basin full

MANUFACTURING AND APPLYING

OE name	Artefact	Use
Mortere	Mortar	Pounding
Feþere	Feather	Applicator
Smael sife	Small sieve	Sieve
Hæwenne clað	Blue/grey cloth	Sieve
Linenne clað	Linen cloth	Sieve
Crocc	Pot	Boiling
Æren fæt	Brass vessel	Simmering
Cyperenum fæt	Copper vessel	Simmering, boiling

Figure 34 Medical equipment in Bald's *Leechbook* I and II.

Ceac ofnete	Jug with lid	Boiling
Grate	Grate	Grating
Toþ gare	Tooth pick	Applicator
Bleda	Saucer	Catching worms
Niwum cytele	New kettle	To make steam
Micelne citel	Large kettle	Boiling and reducing into smaller kettles
Pann	Pan	Boiling
Ane brade pann	A wide pan	Heating fat
Foþorne	Lancet	Cutting
Seolc	Silk	Sewing
Bydene	'Bidet'/bucket big enough to sit on	Sauna equipment
þorne	Thorn	Digging out pus
Brocen glaes gearn gegrunden	Finely ground glass	Ingredient
Tige horne	Cupping horn	Drawing blood

STORAGE

OE name	Artefact
Croccan	Pot
Croccan gepicod utan	Pot pitched on the outside
Calic	Chalice
Aerene ampullan	Brass flask
Horn	Horn
Glaes faet	Glass vessel
Faet	A vessel
Blede	Saucer
Ciricbellan	Church bell
Pohhan	Pouch/purse

Figure 34 Medical equipment in Bald's *Leechbook* I and II. (continued)

The collection of artefacts which a medical practitioner would have required to make Bald's preparations and carry out his procedures includes methods of weighing (spoonfuls, handfuls, bowlfuls and kettlefuls), methods of storing ointments (metal vessels, horn vessels, vessels with lids, pots and bags) and methods of applying the medicine (feathers and picks). What is striking about the list is that almost everything in it could have been found within an Anglo-Saxon domestic setting. However, the context in which a full range of materials – especially metalwork, horn, silk and the variety of pots – are found in one place are high-status sites such as the manor house at Goltho, Lincolnshire; urban contexts; and ecclesiastical sites, and it is in these places that we should assume the majority of doctors plied their trade.

Chapter 10
Slaves, Criminals and Outcasts

'Daily life' evokes a picture of domesticity, of regular, familiar occupations, of comfort and companionship. For the majority of Anglo-Saxons, daily life, even if it was sometimes hard, was at least bearable. Not everyone was so lucky, however. A proportion of Anglo-Saxons lived at the very bottom of the social scale as slaves. A proportion also found their daily lives dramatically changed through their own crimes or through violence towards them. Daily life in Anglo-Saxon England was also hedged about and constrained by the imposition of law, which could offer security, but also represented a force to deprive individuals of their life or their freedom.

Slavery

When Anglo-Saxon aristocracy made wills to redistribute their wealth after their death, they counted humans as their assets. The assets at Bishop Æthelwold's estate at Yaxley, Cambridgeshire, in AD 963 consisted of

> thirteen able-bodied men and five women and eight young men and sixteen oxen, a stalled ox and three hundred and five sheep and thirty swine and a hundred flitches of bacon [a flitch is a salted and cured side of bacon] and all the delicacies that belong to them and thirty cartloads of corn and eighty acres sown and one harrow and six barrels and two tubs and three troughs and a cauldron and a trivet and nine year-old stallions and one fat pig.

At least the humans came at the top of this list of farming assets.

Slavery was part of Anglo-Saxon society, and a significant proportion of the population were born, lived out their lives and died as slaves in Anglo-Saxon England. Slaves were also traded abroad: Anglo-Saxon slaves were one of the commodities exchanged for the exotic imports that came in to the country. Tradition has it that Anglo-Saxon slaves in the marketplace at Rome inspired Pope Gregory's mission to the island on the edge of the known world, and another female Anglo-Saxon slave, Balthilde, was sold overseas and found herself in the possession of an elite Merovingian Frank: eventually, she became a Frankish Queen. Yet, by the time of the Norman Conquest, slavery had all but ceased to exist. The demise of slavery in Anglo-Saxon England was not as a result of Christian horror at the idea, though freeing slaves was considered to be an act of piety. On the contrary, towards the end of the institution of slavery, ecclesiastical landholders owned by far the largest number of slaves. But what did slavery mean in Anglo-Saxon England? What were the lives of the least noticed and recorded section of Anglo-Saxon society? And what were the changes in society that led to the abandonment of slavery?

At the close of the Anglo-Saxon period, only 12 percent of the population recorded in the *Domesday Book* were slaves, though records suggest the proportion in the preceding centuries had been higher. There were a number of ways an Anglo-Saxon could become enslaved: they could be born into slavery, they could be made slaves as a legal penalty for criminal behaviour, they could be taken as captives of war, children could be sold into slavery and adults could choose to enslave themselves. Bede records the case of a man enslaved after having been taken captive, and the story implies the existence of a regular and efficient slave market: a young Northumbrian, wounded in battle, was captured and became the property of a Mercian, who then sold him in London to a Frisian trader.

Some people sold themselves and their children into slavery, probably as a desperate attempt to avoid starvation or debt, though within higher-ecclesiastical and aristocratic circles, at least, there was a suspicion that unscrupulous parents were raising revenue by selling their children: the Latin *Penitential* of Theodore, Archbishop of Canterbury (d.690), noted that 'if he is compelled by necessity, a father has the power to sell his son of seven years age into slavery; after that he has not the right to sell him without consent'. Theodore, however, was a Greek by birth and had come to England as part of the mission to Christianise the pagan Anglo-Saxons, so this comment may be a reflection of Mediterranean practice, rather than showing any knowledge of Anglo-Saxon life. A few centuries later, Archbishop Wulfstan of York preached a sermon which was highly critical of Anglo-Saxon morality (he argued that the Viking depredations were God's punishment for the sins of the Anglo-Saxons), and he included the crime of selling off family members to the Vikings in his polemic against the sins in the daily lives of his congregation.

This method of becoming a slave – selling oneself or one's kin into slavery – is a reminder that slavery in Anglo-Saxon England was not exactly comparable to the states of slavery in other societies. There is no doubt that slaves had more or less the lowest social status in Anglo-Saxon society, but there were actually worse things to be, and a society in which individuals and their communities were mutually dependent for their daily survival, slavery brought with it obligations upon the slave owner to provide the slave with a minimum of sustenance and personal protection.

Slavery could also be a temporary, rather than a permanent, state. Some slaves were freed, some married out of slavery and some could buy themselves out of slavery, because slaves could own money. Two women, one historical and one literary, highlight how Anglo-Saxon society could encompass great social mobility. Both women were queens: Queen Balthilde was one of the more successful Merovingian queens, according to the writings of Gregory, bishop of Tours, who recorded a largely unflattering history of the Frankish royalty. Balthilde, an Anglian by birth (she was quite probably a relative of the East Anglian royal family), was spotted by King Clovis II of Neustria and Burgundy when she was in the retinue of his mayor as an Anglo-Saxon slave. She was given to Clovis, and she went on to exert influence over the Merovingian court, including a period of regency after the death of her husband and before the accession of her son. She died in 680 and is buried in the church at Chelles. Her ornate funeral costume survives, with embroidered skeumorphs of Byzantine-style necklaces in place of the gold and garnet jewellery she probably wore in life.

One of the ways in which Gregory tried to show that the Merovingians were unfit kings was by highlighting the ways in which they married unsuitable women, far below them in social status. It is possible that Gregory exaggerated Balthilde's status for effect. Though she may never have been a slave, her rags-to-riches story seemed sufficiently plausible to be given a place in Gregory's historical record.

Wealtheow appeared in the story of *Beowulf*. She was the wife of Hrothgar, king of the Geats. She is described as a great lady, bedecked with jewels, who graciously passes drink around the mead hall to her husband's guests, but her name translates as 'foreign slave'. The first element of Queen Wealtheow's name comes from the Old English *wealh*, meaning foreign, but also used with the connotation of slave. It still survives in modern English, in the English word for the people living in the country west of Offa's Dyke – the Welsh. It also survives in place-name evidence – the usual original meaning of most 'Walton' place names, for example, is 'settlement of the *Wealh*'. There has been a suggestion that some of the burials found in early Anglo-Saxon furnished cemeteries may be the burials of these *wealh*, the native Welsh-speaking Romano-British inhabitants of Anglo-Saxon England who were overrun and enslaved by the usurping Anglo-Saxon invaders. According to this theory, the bodies within the inhumation cemeteries buried without grave goods or buried in an unusual position – curled up and contracted, rather than laid out on their backs, for example – may represent a surviving British element in the Anglo-Saxon population, whose burial shows that they had low, possibly slave, status, amongst the Anglo-Saxons. Not all archaeologists share this interpretation of the mortuary evidence. Amongst the problems of reading the archaeological evidence in this way is that many grave goods, especially those made of horn, wood or material, would not have survived in the archaeological record, and so we cannot be sure that anyone without archaeologically recoverable grave goods was necessarily buried without any accompanying artefacts. A case in point is a burial from the sixth-century site at Snape, Suffolk. Excavations here by William Filmer-Sankey found a number of high-status burials, including the burial of a young male with two drinking horns at his feet. Normally, drinking horns are associated with most high-status burials, such as that of Sutton Hoo Mound 1 and Taplow. In cases where evidence for drinking horns survives, they are usually inferred from the metal fittings decorating the horns. In the case of the Snape burial, there were no associated metal decorations, and the organic outline of the horns only survived because of the unusual preservation conditions of the acidic East Anglian soil. Had this burial been in Oxfordshire or Kent, for example, no trace of the drinking horns would have survived, and the burial would have been assumed to be low status. At some excavated sites, such as Berinsfield, Oxfordshire, the unaccompanied burials are distributed so evenly among burial groups that it is hard to argue that lack of grave goods marked people out as belonging to different ethnic or familial groups.

While it may not be possible to assert that all burials without grave goods from the fifth and sixth centuries represent a surviving, enslaved element of the Romano-British population, where there is good skeletal preservation, there is some evidence from the inhumation furnished cemeteries to suggest that those given the poorest burials also had the hardest lives. At the fifth- to seventh-century site of Worthy Park, Hampshire, the five burials whose skeletons showed the most evidence of difficult lives in terms of trauma and osteological wear (Graves 20, 40, 57, 70 and 73) had very few grave goods. Grave 20 contained a female aged over fifty at the time of her death, with no grave goods; Grave 40 was of a male aged thirty-five to forty, whose only grave goods was a bead, apparently clutched in his right hand. Grave 57 was an old male, aged fifty or more, with no grave goods, and Grave 70 contained another male, aged between forty and fifty years at the time of death – his only grave good was a single iron nail by the right side of his left thigh, with very degraded traces of wood preserved on its underside. The male skeleton in Grave 73 was aged about thirty-five to forty-five years at the time of death and had no grave goods. As a whole, the population of the Worthy Park cemetery showed relatively little sign of sickness and trauma, which is usual for cemeteries of this period. These five skeletons, though, were severely affected by arthritic lesions (Graves 20, 57, 70 and 73) and periodontal lesions (40, 57 and 73), both of which point to strain and stress on the body, particularly in adolescence. Burials 20 and 70 had forearm fractures of the sort that can be associated with warding off blows, and Burial 57 had a deformity on the metacarpal shaft, probably the result of a well-healed fracture. Burial 57 had a healed fracture of the rib, and Burial 73 had suffered a deformity of the metatarsal, possibly as a result of a compound fracture. In addition, Burial 70 had a well-healed fracture on the right shoulder. These five skeletons exhibited further pathologies, including a small, linear depression on the skull of Burial 57, probably caused by a shallow wound inflicted by a sharp implement.

The five low-status burials at Worthy Park are all relatively long-lived for an Anglo-Saxon population, and it may be that their lack of grave goods may have more to do with their age than their status. On the other hand, their bodies, atypical for this cemetery, show signs of a hard, stressful and sometimes violent life, and they have been identified as 'the overworked drudges of the community', perhaps the slaves.

The *Domesday Book* makes it clear that, amongst the tasks carried out by slaves, a number of occupations needed specialist knowledge and training. Slaves are recorded working as ploughmen, stockmen, swineherds, beekeepers, dairymaids, seamstresses, weavers and priests, all activities which were also carried out by free men and women. The ploughman of Ælfric's *Colloquy* sums up the attitude to work of an Anglo-Saxon slave: '*hig! hig! micel gedeorf ys hyt, geleof, micel gedeorf hit ys, forþam ic neom freoh'* [oh, oh, great hardship is it, dear one, great hardship it is, because I am not free].

The end of slavery

By the end of the Anglo-Saxon period, slavery was already in decline, and it died a natural death with the arrival of the Normans. To understand why slavery came to an inevitable end is to understand the extent to which Anglo-Saxon society was constructed on a system of mutual obligations and kindred trust which had become outmoded by the late Anglo-Saxon period. First, as has been made clear above, slavery brought with it rights and obligations. The advantage of slavery for those without any other resources was that it brought with it legal and social entitlements – entitlement to food, protection, clothing and basic needs. It is true that slaves were punished by whippings and beatings for their crimes where other classes of society were fined, but this was only because slaves, by default, had little money to pay fines, not because they were less valued as human beings than other social classes. Slavery also brought with it the possibility of betterment – training for specialised work, and the possibility of saving money. For slave owners, however, particularly with the fragmentation of large estates in the later Anglo-Saxon period, and with availability of free men to carry out estate work, slavery became something of an economic liability. Slaves had to be provided for, even after they became old and less productive. It was less of a drain on estate resources to hire free men, without any long-term obligations and responsibilities, than to have slaves. The enthusiastic freeing of slaves illustrated in the late Anglo-Saxon wills may have had less to do with altruism than with finance; those making their wills had an opportunity to unburden their heirs of financial responsibilities to unproductive old slaves by (cruelly?) freeing them in their wills. It is probably for this reason that, at the time of the *Domesday* census, by far the largest proportion of slaves worked on church estates. It was not that the church exploited slaves, but that the church effectively provided welfare for a group of people who would otherwise have been completely destitute and without protection.

At the lower end of the Anglo-Saxon social scale, there was a range of classes of people who hovered just above the 'slave' category, all of whom were, in one way or another, tied in service to their lords, but also dependent on them for protection. Just above slaves were cottars, the majority of whom may have been freed slaves, who worked on the estate land in exchange for smallholdings, usually on previously wild or unexploited land. Place-name surveys have shown that 'cot' sites (Wolvercote, Oxfordshire, and Nethercot, Devon, for example) are usually on marginal land and could represent the deliberate granting of small plots of land to cottars to encourage the development and cultivation of previously uncultivated land, particularly on the edge of uplands and woodlands.

Next, above cottars came bordars, or *geburs*, slightly richer peasants, also tied to the estate and with obligations of service to the lord. Their rented smallholdings provided them with produce, but they also worked for the lord; they are recorded as brewers and bakers, as well as working on the land. Groups of bordars may have given their names to some of the Burton and Bourton place names in England. Above the bordars were the ceorls, free smallholders who paid taxes and owed public service, acting as jurymen in courts, for example, and who also owed service to their lord. Charlton and Carlton place names denote settlements of ceorls, who are also memorialised in the modern English 'churl'. Like cottars, ceorls settled on marginal lands, as the number of place names in England combining ceorl and cot to form variants of Chalcot and Charlcot indicate.

The differences between the slaves at the bottom of the social pile and the ceorls, the lowest of the free, may have been acute to an Anglo-Saxon, but to the new Norman overlords, fine distinctions of degree and obligation were of no interest. All these classes of men were tied to the lord's estate in one way or another; they were all Anglo-Saxons, they were all peasants and therefore they were all unfree. Slavery may have finally disappeared in England because the slight social differences between slaves and other classes of peasant were invisible to the Normans, which in itself emphasises the way in which Anglo-Saxon slavery was in many ways a variation on other forms of lower-class status.

Justice

From the earliest recorded law codes, the church and kings were working together to define wrongdoing and to create a workable system of punishment and compensation. The earliest kings to write down their laws suggested that they were following Roman legal systems, but in practice, Anglo-Saxon law codes enshrined a largely Germanic legal system of compensation for misdeeds by payment of a fine. In this system, each person had a value (wergild) according to his social status, with the king's life being worth the most and a slave's worth the least. Every transgression required compensation in proportion to the worth of the person wronged or the object stolen or damaged. In the earliest laws, physical violence was the last resort as a punishment, even when it was a case of homicide, and was usually reserved only for those who had no way of paying a fine. Because they were utterly dependent on their masters for their food, shelter and protection, and rarely (by definition) had any personal wealth, slaves were the single social group who received corporal punishment in the early Anglo-Saxon period, though whipping, trial by ordeal, judicial mutilation and execution spread into other social groups towards the end of the period, particularly when England was under the rule of Scandinavian kings. Slaves were not singled out for physical punishment because they were considered less human or less worthy than other groups, but because Anglo-Saxon justice was based on a principle of honour and payment, and slaves had no way of paying for their crimes.

To understand the Anglo-Saxon judicial system is to really understand the way in which Old English society was, at heart, communal, local, co-operative and familial. Behaviour was regulated by the power of shame; bad behaviour – theft, assault and worse – was limited by the difficulty of maintaining secrecy, because everyone in the neighbourhood was known to everyone else, and the community gossiped about everyone's business – a practice fostered by communal feasting. Neighbours almost certainly had an intimate knowledge of each other's personal possessions. There is little evidence for locks on doors in early Anglo-Saxon settlements, though personal chests and boxes were kept locked. However, a determined person could probably break through a wall or enter a window opening (glass in windows was a rarity). Theft would be easy under such circumstances, but what would a thief do with the stolen goods? Anyone in the community would instantly recognise stolen artefacts, and neighbouring communities would look with suspicion at a stranger. In any event, guilt or otherwise was not necessarily judged on evidence, rather it was judged on character. If a person was suspected of a crime, they would be brought before a court of their free neighbours. They were required to produce character witnesses, as was their accuser. The court, which almost certainly knew both the accused and the adversary, would then decide which of them was most likely to be telling the truth, based on the status and testimony of the witnesses. In other words, if a person had a bad reputation, they were likely to be deemed a criminal even if they were innocent of a crime. However, if the accused belonged to a high-status family, fear, or respect, might lead a court to declare them innocent. The complexities of these transactions are illustrated by a law of Ine, which stated that if a man was accused of theft, and could not buy his way out of trial by ordeal, but then another man stood surety for him until the accused could pay him back: 'Then if he is accused a second time ... and he who had pledged for him will not continue to stand ... he who had given the pledge shall lose his goods' (Figure 35).

Once found guilty, if a person were of high status, they would be fined, even for relatively serious crimes. A fine might seem an ineffective and unrepresentative punishment for a serious crime, but the guilty verdict would have called the honour of both the accused and their family into question in public, and their personal humiliation would then affect their social standing and that of other members of the kin group and their witnesses, whose oaths had been disregarded.

The majority of Anglo-Saxon law codes enshrine a principle of personal responsibility for criminal actions. Several lay stress on the fact that wives cannot be accused of a husband's crimes, unless there was specific evidence that they condoned their husband's actions. First offenders were treated more leniently than repeat offenders. Actions carried out in secret were treated more harshly than those that were open and public. Destroying someone's trees by fire, for example, was considered a crime, because fire is quiet, whereas for cutting down a tree with an axe, the maximum fine payable was 90 shillings: 'he need not pay for more, however much there may be, because the axe is an informer and not a thief'. More seriously, if a man killed another whom he thought to be a thief, and immediately declared it, the presumed thief's relatives had no redress. If, however, the murderer concealed the killing, but it was afterwards discovered, the relatives had the right to go to court.

Much violent crime seems to have been sparked by drunken quarrels. Those who resisted the temptation to get involved were compensated: 'if two men quarrel over their cups and one endures it patiently, the other who was violent shall pay a fine of thirty shillings.'

Figure 35 Taken prisoner: an illustration of the Biblical account of Lot being seized.

The blood feud

One characteristic of Anglo-Saxon society, in common with many other communities with kindred-based social control, was the *fæhth*, the blood feud. The payment of wergild in compensation for damage or death, so important in the law codes, might seem to support James Campbell's description of Anglo-Saxon society as 'brutally commercial', but wergild was a better alternative to protracted interfamilial blood feuds. Nonetheless, where a murderer refused to offer wergild, a family would pursue vengeance. A law of King Edmund (d.946) tried to limit the potential bloodletting arising from a feud by insisting that the relatives of an unlawfully killed man could only legally exact vengeance on the killer himself, and then only if he, with the help of his friends, had not been able to raise the wergild within twelve months. Furthermore, anyone who killed another in a feud pursued in a legitimate way had to carry out penances before he could be admitted to the king's presence. In another effort to control and regulate the repercussions of a feud, Alfred's law insisted that 'the man who knows his enemy to be living at home, that he is not to fight before he asks him for what is due'. A wronged family could legally fight and kill their enemy, but only if they waited twelve months and were seen to give their enemy clear opportunity to exculpate himself. Secret or sudden vengeance on an unsuspecting enemy was not legally tolerated, but revenge on an enemy who had been given all proper and legal chances to pay a wergild was.

In spite of legal efforts to control blood feud, it is clear that it persisted within Anglo-Saxon society throughout the period. The extent to which honour regulated society is revealed in two law codes, one of Æthelbert (d.616), and a late ninth-century code of Alfred, which lists a range of compensations for personal injury. Though, as might be expected, the most serious injuries receive high levels of compensation, there are instances where compensation is based not on the extent to which your injury was disabling, but the extent to which it could be seen. The reason for this probably relates to honour or worth. If you had been assaulted, it showed that your attacker not only did not fear your reprisals, but also did not fear the collective reprisals of your family. To bear visible signs of assault was to signal that your family was not of sufficiently high status to deter attack. The only way to avoid prolonged tit-for-tat bloodletting, which could span generations, was by a clear and public system of financial compensation. The humiliation for the attacker and the public act of admission of guilt inherent in providing compensation was a way for the wronged family to maintain honour without resorting to further violence.

Execution

Corporal punishment, particularly in the extreme form of execution, was rarely evoked in the earliest law codes, and there was almost always a clause allowing a wergild to redeem a life, but it is noticeable that, as the centuries wore on, and particularly during and after the Viking

incursions, levels of violence in the law codes began to increase. When
the famous 'pagan' royal burial site at Sutton Hoo was re-excavated
by Professor Martin Carver in the 1980s, an unexpected and gruesome
facet of Anglo-Saxon death came to light. In addition to the prestigious
barrow burials, there were two separate areas containing the shadowy
traces of less-grand inhumations. The acidic Suffolk soil had eaten away
almost all the bone, but a dark stain in the sands served to show how
the bodies had lain in their graves. It quickly became apparent that
these were no normal inhumations. Many of the bodies were in
contorted positions, or were buried face down, apparently with their
hands tied behind their backs. Some had their decapitated heads placed
on their legs.

The first interpretation of these burials was that they were human
sacrifices associated with the barrow burials, thus confirming the 'pagan'
nature of the mound burials at Sutton Hoo. Dating evidence, however,
quickly established that these burials post-dated the use of the cemetery
as a royal burial ground. In fact, the burials were found to date over
a century later, fixing them firmly in the Christian period. A new
explanation was required, and it was quickly realised that these deviant
burials represented the bodies of victims of later Anglo-Saxon justice.
Once the true nature of these burials became apparent, the date and
origin of similar collections of deviant burials were also revised. The
burials of prone males around an earlier seventh-century barrow burial
at Cuddesdon, Oxfordshire, fall in this category, as does the group
of males interred in the prehistoric dyke at Aves Ditch, Oxfordshire,
and the nine or more males buried in the Roman Villa at Shakenoak,
Oxfordshire. In some of these cases, it was possible to tell the cause
of death. Burial 1 at Shakenoak, for example, had died because a sharp-
edged implement had been applied to the neck. More than twenty
execution sites dating to the late Anglo-Saxon period have now been
identified across England. The majority of these date to the tenth century
or later, though execution cemeteries were in use from the seventh
century. They were often associated with pre-existing monuments, such
as prehistoric ditches, Roman villas or earlier Anglo-Saxon barrows – all
prominent and visible sites for judicial violence. The most prominent
site used for execution and burial was Stonehenge, Wiltshire. Several
skeletons had been found during excavations at Stonehenge in the early
part of the twentieth century. Recent radiocarbon dating of one of these
skeletons dated it to the seventh or eighth century, and a careful study

of the bones revealed that the man had been killed by a blow to the back of the head with a sharp implement. It is likely that some of the other skeletons will also date to the Anglo-Saxon period, and in this context, the name of this world famous prehistoric site takes on a new meaning: *stan hencge* means 'stone gallows' in Old English.

Occasionally, there is evidence of judicial violence taking place at known meeting places. There is a single prone male burial at the royal palace site of Cheddar, Somerset, and there are execution burials at the eighth- to ninth-century complex settlement at Higham Ferrars, Northamptonshire. This site, consisting of enclosures, buildings and a large malting oven, has been interpreted as a purpose-built centre for the collection and redistribution of royal tribute, while the burials indicate that the site had a judicial, as well as an economic, function.

Not all of the examples of deviant burial from the middle and late Anglo-Saxon periods need have been victims of public executions, but, given the prominent locations of many of the execution sites, it is likely that the majority of these burials were public – either the burials of judicially executed criminals or the burials of other people who had been denied a resting place within a church. The documentary sources describe the categories of people who were denied burial in consecrated ground, including adulterers, oath breakers, homicides, those who refused to pay church dues and, according to a law of Edmund dating to around AD 942, 'those who have sex with nuns (unless they make amends)'. In addition, those whose manner of death meant that they had neither confessed nor received absolution might be denied consecrated burial, such as women who had died in childbirth, children who had died unexpectedly, strangers and men who had died in battle. The latter case might perhaps offer an explanation for a curious eleventh-century burial at North Elmham, Norfolk, of a man who had died a violent death and whose body was buried beneath the boundary wall of the churchyard – neither within nor outside consecrated ground.

It seems from the law codes that the bodies of some of those who were the victims of legal execution might leave no archaeological record at all. According to the laws of Æthelstan, a free woman who was to be killed for her crimes was to be thrown from a cliff or drowned, while in the case of a female slave who committed a theft, she was to be burnt. According to the laws of Edward and Guthrum, the bodies of people, mutilated for their crimes, were to be abandoned, unless, three days later, they were still alive, in which case their friends or relatives were allowed to help them if they had permission from the bishop. That these laws were implemented is suggested by the story recorded by the late tenth-century Frankish scholar Lantfred, who was at one point a monk of the Old Minster, Winchester. In his Latin *Translation and Miracles of St Swithun*, he told the story of a man who had been wrongly convicted of robbery and had been punished by mutilation. He was scalped, had his eyes gouged out, his hands, ears and feet cut off, his nose mutilated and then he was abandoned in the open fields 'dead in respect of nearly all his limbs, to be devoured by wild beasts and birds and hounds of the night', until he was saved through the miraculous intervention of the saint.

A suggestion as to the crimes of some of the men found in execution cemeteries may be hinted at in an Anglo-Saxon charter which names Shakenoak Villa as the place 'where the *cnihtas* lie'. *Cniht*, which gives us the modern English 'knight', had a range of meanings, and in this case, the best translation might be 'the place where the lads lie'. Anglo-Saxon law codes indicate that gangs looking for trouble could be a problem. A law of Ine defined a gang of thieves as being up to seven men. More than seven represented a threat to society: if the number of men was between seven and thirty-five, they were a *hloð* or troop (though with a sense of being wild and unregulated: a *hloðere* was a robber), and more than thirty-five was an army. Anyone accused of being in a troop could clear himself by oath or pay compensation (*hloðbot*). To be killed by a gang was to suffer *hloðslit*.

Outlaws

In early Anglo-Saxon law codes, the ultimate secular deterrent for misdeeds (apart from execution) was to be outlawed. We have already seen how important it was for a man to have family and supporters around him; without the protection of a lord or a kin group, a man was vulnerable to assault or murder with no expectation of reprisal. 'The unbefriended man gets wolves as his comrades, beasts abounding in treachery; very often that comrade will savage him,' wrote the poet of 'Maxims I'. The extent to which outlawry reduced a man's status is made clear by the fate of King Cyneheard of the West Saxons, who, the *Anglo-Saxon Chronicle* recorded, was deprived of his kingdom by his witan (the aristocratic group who gave counsel to the king) for his 'evil deeds'. Forced to flee the kingdom, this royal male was murdered by a swineherd

who came upon him. In normal circumstances, a swineherd would
not have dared to touch a king, but an outlaw could be killed without
retribution. This story also shows that the principle of co-operative
self-regulation within communities operated even at the level of the
aristocracy. The Anglo-Saxons did not recognise a 'divine right' of kings,
or at least not until the tenth-century reforms of the church encouraged
a new view of the relationship between royal and ecclesiastical power.
Even being the eldest son of a reigning monarch was no guarantee
of attaining the throne, and a king was always vulnerable to being
deposed by his witan, if they had the power and courage to do it.

Strangers and foreigners

Exotic finds from the early Anglo-Saxon graves and from middle
and late Anglo-Saxon contexts, as well as the documentary sources,
suggest that everyday life in Anglo-Saxon England included contact
with a number of people who were not Anglo-Saxons. In the tenth
century, archaeological evidence demonstrates that York was a thriving
mercantile city, with visiting traders from Ireland, Sweden, Denmark,
Germany and Holland. Recent excavations from the football stadium
at Southampton have uncovered a range of burials, including cremation
burials, persisting into the seventh century, when cremation had
elsewhere given way to inhumation. The objects found buried with the
dead at Southampton may explain why cremation burials persisted at
this site. Some of the artefacts, including a small gold crescent-shaped
pendant only directly paralleled by one at a royal site in Frisia, have an
overseas origin. It may be that the people buried in this site, within the
important port of Hamwic, were either an elite who had close contact
with Continental traders or actually members of a foreign enclave
of traders based at Hamwic.

In addition to traders, documentary sources record a number of
craftspeople brought to England to make artefacts for the elite or to bring
new technology to Anglo-Saxon England. Bishop Benedict famously sent
for glassmakers and stonemasons from Gaul to help him build his new
monastic establishments at Monkwearmouth and Jarrow in the seventh
century. Later, an equally desperate King Alfred brought in foreign
specialists who could read and write in Latin, lamenting that the Viking
depredations had lead to a deplorable state of learning in England. Royal

courts naturally included visitors and courtiers from abroad who would enhance the reputation of the king. Alfred was pleased to record the visit to his court of the merchant Othere, whose account of distant voyages to Norway were written down for posterity. Kings, nobles and the elite were also able to travel abroad: Alfred was first taken to Rome when he was four, according to his *Life* (written by the Welsh monk, Asser). Though direct contact with the Continent was not readily available to non-elite Anglo-Saxons, nonetheless, foreign influences had an impact on daily life. Most noticeably, this influence was in art styles, and to an extent in fashion: the headdresses, small necklaces and linked pins found in burials of the seventh century owe their origins to Byzantine dress. Foreign influence could have a more lasting impact, too. Edward the Confessor spent much of his youth in a Norman court and brought many of his Norman friends to England when he became king. There is evidence of French settlement in some key English sites before the Conquest and of the building of the characteristic motte-and-bailey Norman castles on the borders with Wales before the Conquest, too.

If a stranger came into your community, how could you be sure that he was not an outlaw? A stranger represented instability, untrustworthiness and a possible threat to the local community. Legislation attempted to mitigate the problem by defining ways in which a stranger could be accommodated or demonstrate his credentials. An early Wessex law code offers clear evidence of the risks taken by anyone who left their own territory – it stated that if a stranger left the road, and 'neither shouts, nor blows a horn', then he would be assumed to be a thief, and either put to death or put up for ransom. To look after a stranger was also to take responsibility for the good character of that person. In the laws of Hlothhere and Eadric of Kent, it was decreed that if a man gave hospitality to a stranger (a trader or anyone else who had come over the border) for three days in his own home, and if the stranger then did harm to anyone, the host must bring the other to justice or make amends on his behalf. When Beowulf came to the court of Hrothgar, a member of the king's entourage quickly established that Beowulf and his troop were legitimate visitors: 'I have never seen so many men, so brave in bearing. I perceive that it is for glory and courage, not because of outlawry, that you have sought out Hrothgar.' Hrothgar himself noted, however, when Beowulf was announced, that it was precisely as an outlaw seeking refuge that Beowulf's father had come to him many years before, and that Beowulf owed Hrothgar an old family debt, because Hrothgar had sheltered Ecgtheow and settled the feud by payment. But hosts had to be wary: by the time of Alfred, the penalty for harbouring outlaws was loss of all possessions and loss of life.

If the presence of a stranger in a community raised suspicion and doubt, how much worse to actually be that stranger. Anglo-Saxon poetic records leave no doubt that the situation of a man alone, without friends or kin, especially through no fault of his own, was utterly desperate. Poems such as 'The Seafarer' and 'The Wanderer' portray this desperate isolation and sense of wretched alienation from the world in powerful terms. The Wanderer described himself as a man remembering hardships, the violence of his enemies and the loss of his loving family. He fell asleep 'when grief and sleep combine together' and dreamed that he was once again afforded the protection of his lord, only to awake to cold seas and snow. '*Sorg bið geniwad*' is his lament: 'sorrow is renewed'. The Seafarer, too, comments on the pain of being alone. He contrasts his life of hardship with that of a man living in wealth and comfort and adds bitterly that 'the prosperous man does not understand this – what those suffer who journey furthest in exile'. Although both the Wanderer and the Seafarer keenly feel the loss of friendship and comfort, and the pain of being strangers, there is a sense in which they have both undertaken voluntary journeys, and of course, their pain is an image of Christian renunciation and the idea that the soul is a wanderer on earth until it finds its true home in heaven. The Old English word *wræcca* encompassed this range of meanings: a *wræcca* could be translated as an adventurer or a stranger, or as a fugitive or an exile, but all these states involved, in the Anglo-Saxon mind, the feelings of misery so powerfully evoked in 'The Seafarer' and 'The Wanderer' that it is no surprise that the word survives in modern English vocabulary as wretch.

Chapter 11
Conquest and Conclusions

For an Anglo-Saxon, family and kinship were at the heart of a contented daily life. In the earliest rural communities, survival was a family effort: every hand was needed for the labour of growing or catching food, building houses, making cloth and clothes and creating the equipment required for daily life. With the introduction of Christianity, the church took on some of the functions of the family, buttressing it in many ways, not only by affirming the importance of marriage and preventing the fragmentation of family units, but also compromising it by banning marriage within degrees of relationship – difficult for a population tied to the land and to a local community to fulfil.

Daily life in Anglo-Saxon England moved with the rhythm of the seasons, with their agricultural rounds of planting and harvesting, shearing and culling; religious rounds of festivals, fasts and observances; and taxes. Depending on the social status of the individual, many of the major historical events may have had little impact on daily life. Serfs and slaves, for example, may have noticed little change in their lives before and after the Norman Conquest, though other political events – the extortions of the Vikings or the drafting of labour to build dykes and fortifications around the new *burhs* – may have been more disruptive. Documentary sources suggest that natural events, such as plagues, droughts and famines, had a far greater impact on the daily lives of Anglo-Saxons.

The steady functioning of Anglo-Saxon life depended on transparency and honesty in all transactions, which resulted in the assumption that anything which took place out of the public eye was to be viewed with suspicion. Trust was built on kinship, friendship and a complex system of obligations owed and paid. At its worst, this system led to prolonged blood feuds and enmity, but at its best, it was the foundation for the effective system of government which flourished in Anglo-Saxon England from the seventh century on. By the time of the Norman Conquest, English kings could recall and replace their currency with confidence every six years, they could call up an army in the south of the country and march it hundreds of miles north (and back again), and they could promulgate laws which were expected to be observed in every part of the country.

Even at the end of the Anglo-Saxon period, England was not a homogenous kingdom. Different parts of the country kept their own identity, and although dress may have become similar across the country, dialects certainly remained local. The north and south were united, but uneasily – during the Conquest, the north came close to separating from the south and might have succeeded had it not been for William the Conqueror's violent suppression of the northern rebellion.

Given political stability, daily life in Anglo-Saxon England was more than a long and hard struggle for survival. There was room for art, decoration, games and play and especially storytelling and history, which were often interwoven. There was also room for drunken violence and assaults, on men and women. Women played an active role in Anglo-Saxon daily life, not only managing private and domestic life, but taking a place in public life and commerce too.

Daily life in Anglo-Saxon England has left a legacy – of place names, boundaries, buildings, literature and, above all, a vocabulary with which daily lives in English-speaking countries are still explained and described.

To an unmeasurable but significant extent, the Norman Conquest of Anglo-Saxon England was accompanied by a rewriting of Anglo-Saxon history which has coloured our understanding of the late Saxon period. After the defeat of King Harold, the last Anglo-Saxon king, at the Battle of Hastings in 1066, William the Conqueror embarked on a campaign to control and subjugate his new country. As part of the campaign to overawe the Anglo-Saxons, and to discourage any resistance, he organised the dismantling of many of the most important Anglo-Saxon buildings, replacing them with new, Norman structures, with a special focus on church buildings. As a result, the Anglo-Saxon churches that have survived tend to be small, rural buildings. Only rare traces remain of the buildings which underlie substantial Norman structures at the most important ecclesiastical centres, such as York, Canterbury and Worcester. As a result, we have only a limited idea about the scale of Anglo-Saxon architecture in the tenth and eleventh centuries, and about the extent to which Anglo-Saxon England was a cultural backwater, or was reproducing new building styles on the Continent.

Recent excavations, and reviews of surviving evidence, are leading to a reassessment of late Anglo-Saxon England. There is now some support for the hints given by surviving contemporary sources of ambitious building programmes carried out by Anglo-Saxon bishops in the closing decades of the Anglo-Saxon period. At Worcester Cathedral, for example, a recent archaeological excavation has drawn attention to the possibility that a large Anglo-Saxon rotunda, or round church, may have existed at the site. If so, this might resolve the long-standing mystery of the circular Chapter House at Worcester. This Norman circular Chapter House has no precedent, though it was later copied: chapter houses were always rectangular, until the Normans built a circular one at Worcester. Was it constructed by a Norman, though? Worcester is also unique in that it housed the only Anglo-Saxon bishop to retain his ecclesiastical post after the Norman Conquest. Bishop Wulfstan, though a friend and counsellor to King Harold, successfully transferred his allegiance to King William. As part of his role as 'Norman' Bishop, Wulfstan, so his *Life* informs us, was obliged to pull down the three existing Anglo-Saxon churches at the site and to replace them all with a new Norman cathedral. According to the written account, Wulfstan wept as the buildings of his predecessors were razed to the ground, an experience which must have been particularly painful since the last Anglo-Saxon church had been constructed only a few decades earlier. However, at the time of the millennium, round churches were increasingly fashionable across Europe, and at least two were constructed in Anglo-Saxon England at Abingdon and at Canterbury. Archaeologists have speculated that one of the Anglo-Saxon churches at Worcester may have been a rotunda and that the Norman Chapter House at Worcester may have been constructed on the foundations of a pre-existing Anglo-Saxon rotunda church.

Wulfstan's survival as Bishop of Worcester raises the question of whether 1066 marked an absolute and abrupt halt to the Anglo-Saxon way of life. It is certain that it marks some major changes amongst the elite, the majority of whom lost their lands and status, and many of whom fled the country. In some parts of the country, the Conquest marked a devastating end to the Anglo-Saxon way of life. The north of England, which still tended to look to the Scandinavian world, was in danger of breaking away from William's control. His response was swift and ruthless. The 'harrying of the north' led to the permanent destruction of many settlements, and to a significant movement of population, as refugees escaped from the burnt and devastated lands. The impact of William's actions is painfully evident in the *Domesday Book*, which compares the value of the northern estates before the

Conquest to their value in 1084. In village after village in the north, lands were recorded as waste, valueless and unoccupied.

In other respects, daily life must have continued relatively unchanged, particularly for the lower classes. It is now clear that, to a large extent, the parochial, tenurial and manorial infrastructure of Norman England was already in place in before the Conquest. Though the elite may have spoken French, and though laws were in French, other groups continued to speak Old English. The last entries in the 'E' version of the *Anglo-Saxon Chronicle* were written in Old English in 1154, nearly a century after the end of Anglo-Saxon England.

In the fifth century, when the Germanic invaders overran what became Anglo-Saxon England, their language and culture obliterated the language and culture of the native Romano-British. It is remarkable that the Norman Conquest did not replace English with French in the same way. One reason why it did not was that Anglo-Saxon England, unlike other western kingdoms, had a well-established tradition of writing in the vernacular. Elsewhere, Latin was considered to be the pre-eminent and appropriate language of literacy: Latin was a universal language, and it was considered that anything written in Latin could be transmitted widely in time and space. To waste valuable vellum and ink on a local dialect such as English was unusual. Circumstances, such as a lack of scholars who could read Latin, particularly after the Viking invasions, may have contributed to the flourishing of a written English language, but, by writing laws, wills, charters, histories and other texts in English, the rulers and leaders of Anglo-Saxon society, both lay and secular, were able to ensure the wide transmission of texts. Even if local lords and shire reeves ('sheriffs') were illiterate, they could certainly understand what was read out to them, and there is no doubt that the content of many Anglo-Saxon texts was intended for a listening audience, rather than for a private reader. When the Normans conquered Anglo-Saxon England, they may have established a French court with French laws, dispossessing and destroying the major Anglo-Saxon political leaders in the process, but they relied on the collaboration of local Anglo-Saxon leaders to run the business of the shires. Surviving evidence shows that some Anglo-Saxons were prepared to take advantage of this to improve their status. One Æfsige of Faringdon, for example, held only two hides of land before the Conquest, but by 1086, he is recorded as being in possession of estates in Oxfordshire, Gloucestershire and Berkshire. Two generations later, there is a record of his grandson, Robert of

Astrop – a 'Norman' gentleman and country squire of the twelfth century, of Anglo-Saxon parentage and grandparentage, still speaking English.

Not just the local leaders but many of the businessmen of early Norman England were also English. All but one of the forty householders recorded as living and working in Oxford in 1086 had Anglo-Saxon names, as did all the moneyers. Even by the 1130s, nearly half the recorded names for the town were English or Scandinavian, even though, as we have seen for Robert of Astrop, there was a growing tendency to give Norman names to English children. Effectively, the businessmen and local leaders of Norman England were literate Englishmen who continued to write and speak their own language, because it was already the language of government and literature. The continued use of written English for the purposes of business and local affairs, combined with the lack of any further effective invasions of England in the centuries following the Conquest, is probably the reason why, compared to the rest of Europe, there has been such a remarkable continuity of institutions and land boundaries from Anglo-Saxon England to the present, and why English, rather than Norman French, is still the national language.

Timeline

407	Last Roman legion withdrawn from Britain
408	Britain attacked by Picts, Scots and Saxons
410	Last Roman officials removed from Britain
c.449	Traditional date for the arrival in Britain of Hengest and Horsa
477	Ælle, leader of the Saxons, lands on the Sussex coast and begins to dominate Sussex, according to the *Anglo-Saxon Chronicle*
c.495	Cerdic and Cynric land on the south coast; their followers ultimately establish the kingdom of the West Saxons (*Anglo-Saxon Chronicle*)
c.496–550	Period of British resistance to Anglo-Saxon incursions (giving rise to the legend of Arthur)
c.493	Date of British victory at 'Mons Badonicus', according to Bede
c.547	Gildas writes *De Excidio Britanniae*
560–616	Æthelbert, king of Kent
563	St. Columba of Ireland founds a Celtic monastery on Iona
597	St. Augustine, sent by Pope Gregory, brings Roman Christianity to Kent
605	Death of Augustine
613	Completion of the first stone abbey church of Sts Peter and Paul at Canterbury
614	Birth of St. Hilda
616–632	Edwin, king of Northumbria
623	St. Aidan founds a Celtic monastery at Lindisfarne
625	Probable date of the Sutton Hoo ship burial

627	Conversion of King Edwin to Christianity through his wife, Ethelburga of Kent, and her chaplain Paulinus
657–680	St. Hilda is abbess at Whitby; the first religious verse using Germanic alliterative style composed by Caedmon
664	The Synod of Whitby, at which the customs of the Celtic church are rejected in favour of those of Rome
673	Birth of Bede
c.693	Law codes of King Ine of the West Saxons promulgated
c.700	'Wic' site of Hamwic founded
731	Bede completes *Historia gentis Anglorum ecclesiastica* (*Ecclesiastical History of the English People*)
735	Death of Bede
c.735–804	Alcuin
757–796	Offa, king of Mercia
790	First Viking raid on England at Portland, Dorset
793	Viking raid on Lindisfarne
c.800	Only four Anglo-Saxon kingdoms remain: East Anglia, Mercia, Northumbria and Wessex
851	First time the Danish Viking army overwinters in England
867	Kingdom of Northumbria falls to the Danes
870	East Anglia overrun by the Danes
871	King Alfred of Wessex comes to the throne
877	Vikings settle in Mercia
878	Viking army defeated by Alfred at the Battle of Edington; King Guthrum of the Vikings baptised
c.886	Alfred agrees boundaries with the Danes: the area of Danish settlement (Danelaw) is established
c.891	Earliest surviving version of the *Anglo-Saxon Chronicle* begins

899	Death of King Alfred. His son, Edward the Elder, succeeds throne and begins the reconquest of the Danelaw
924–939	Athelstan, king of Wessex. He completes the reconquest of the Danelaw (except York) and becomes the first king of England
937	Battle of Brunanburh
954	End of the Viking kingdom of York
c.950–1000	Period of monastic revival led by Dunstan, Æthelwold and Oswald. Flourishing of Winchester and Canterbury scriptoria: the four major surviving books of English poetry (including the *Exeter Book* and the *Beowulf* manuscript) are written
959–975	Reign of Edgar
978–1013	Reign of Æthelred 'the Unready'
991	English defeat by the Danish army at the Battle of Maldon
1002	Æthelred orders the killing of Danes living in England (the St Brice's Day Massacre); Swein 'Forkbeard' attacks England
1013	Swein acknowledged as king of England
1016–1042	Reign of Cnut the Danish king and his sons
1042–1066	Reign of Edward the Confessor, son of Æthelred
1066	Death of Edward and coronation of King Harold
1066	Battle of Stamford Bridge, at which Harold's army defeats that of Harold Hardrada; Battle of Hastings, at which William defeats Harold. End of the Anglo-Saxon state
1153	Last vernacular entry in the Peterborough version of the *Anglo-Saxon Chronicle*

List of Illustrations

18. Deviant burial: Grave 43, young female, buried prone, Kingsworthy (from Hawkes and Grainger 2003, courtesy of Oxford University School of Archaeology).

19. Stone fragment of an Anglo-Saxon animal head from excavations at Worcester Cathedral Chapter House (photo: Graham Norrie).

20. The Norman motte and bailey castle, Oxford, which blocked the main western approach to the town, forcing a deviation still called 'New Road' (photo: author).

Figures

1. Map of Anglo-Saxon England and its kingdoms in the seventh century.

2. The Roman town of Dorchester-on-Thames and early Anglo-Saxon presence: 1, Dorchester; 2, site of Iron Age Dyke Hills; 3, site of Iron Age *oppidum*; 4, river Thames. Scale in metres (after Sonia Chadwick Hawkes 1986, courtesy of the Oxford University School of Archaeology).

3. Shropshire: ancient Celtic names and names which refer to British people (courtesy of Margaret Gelling, from Gelling 1992).

4. Female clothing items showing contrasting regional variation: (a) Anglian brooches and wristclasp from a female grave at Morning Thorpe, Norfolk, and (b) Kentish brooches from a female grave at Finglesham, Kent (after Green *et al.* 1987 and Hawkes and Grainger 2006).

5. Elite seventh-century Christian grave goods: 1, gold pendants from Milton Regis, Kent; 2, gold and garnet necklace, Desborough, Northamptonshire; 3, gold and garnet pendant cross from Ixworth, Suffolk; and 4, gold, silver and garnet composite brooch from Boss Hall, Ipswich, Suffolk (drawings by Harry Buglass).

6. An example of runic writing on the back of a mended composite disc brooch from a burial at Harford Farm, Norfolk. The runes read, '[L/T]uda mended this brooch.'

7. Sword with sword ring, Grave 204, Finglesham (after Hawkes and Grainger 2006).

8. Spear length and age at Great Chesterford, Essex.

9. Reconstructed plan of the late Anglo-Saxon fortified thegn's residence at Goltho: 1, probable site of gate; 2, probable location of ditch; 3, probable location of pallisaded embankment; 4, latrine; 5, weaving sheds; 6, kitchen; 7, bower/private sleeping quarters; 8, hall; 9, stone path; and 10, water pit. Scale in metres (after Beresford 1987).

10. Paying taxes to the reeve: from a manuscript illustration showing Joseph's brothers offering him payment in his capacity as Pharaoh's reeve (after British Library Cotton MS Claudius B.iv ff144 63v).

11. Keys from Anglo-Saxon burial contexts: scale in centimetres.

12. Part of the excavated area at West Stow, Suffolk, showing the sprawling layout of huts, buildings and halls: scale in metres (after West 1985).

13. Anglo-Saxon houses in the Bayeux Tapestry. 1–3, rural houses; 4, higher status house; and 5, royal house (after the Bayeux Tapestry).

Selected Bibliography

Site reports

Beresford, Guy. 1987. *Goltho: The Development of an Early Medieval Manor c.850–1150*. English Heritage Archaeological Report 4. London: HMBC. The site report of the excavations at this important late Anglo-Saxon/Norman settlement.

Boddington, Andy. 1996. *Raunds Furnells: The Anglo-Saxon Church and Churchyard*. English Heritage Archaeological Report 7. London: English Heritage. The best example of a fully excavated late Anglo-Saxon village church and churchyard, with full skeletal analysis to show age, sex and pathology of a late Anglo-Saxon population.

Boyle, Angela, David Jennings, David Miles and Simon Palmer. 1998. *The Anglo-Saxon Cemetery at Butler's Field, Lechlade, Gloucestershire. Volume 1: Prehistoric and Roman Activity and Anglo-Saxon Grave Catalogue*. Thames Valley Landscapes Monograph 10. Oxford: Oxford University Committee for Archaeology. A catalogue of the finds from a well-excavated early Anglo-Saxon cemetery with good skeletal preservation and some rich burials.

Drinkall, Gail, and M. Foreman. 1998. *The Anglo-Saxon Cemetery at Castledyke South, Barton-on-Humber*. Sheffield Excavation Reports 6. Sheffield: Sheffield Academic Press. The site report of sixth- to seventh-century cemetery site with a rich material culture and good skeletal preservation.

Evison, Vera. 1988. *An Anglo-Saxon Cemetery at Alton, Hampshire*. Hampshire Field Club and Archaeological Society Monograph 4. Gloucester: Alan Sutton Publishing. The site report for an early Anglo-Saxon cemetery containing inhumations and cremations with buckets, jewellery, swords, spears, etc. with full illustration.

Evison, Vera. 1994. *An Anglo-Saxon Cemetery at Great Chesterford, Essex*. Council for British Archaeology Research Report 91. York: Council for British Archaeology. Site report of a mixed inhumation and cremation cemetery with horse and dog burials.

Filmer-Sankey, William, and Tim Pestell. 2002. *Snape Anglo-Saxon Cemetery: Excavations and Surveys 1824–1992*. East Anglian Archaeology Report 95. Bury St Edmunds: Suffolk County Council.

Foreman, Stuart, Jonathon Hiller and David Petts. 2002. *Gathering the People, Settling the Land: The Archaeology of a Middle Thames Landscape, Anglo-Saxon to Post-Medieval*. Thames Valley Landscapes Monograph 14. Oxford: Oxford Archaeology. The report includes an intriguing middle Saxon temporary market site.

Green, Barbara, Andrew Rogerson and Susan White. 1987. *The Anglo-Saxon Cemetery at Morning Thorpe, Norfolk*, vols 1 and 2. East Anglian Archaeology Report 36. Dereham: Norfolk Archaeological Unit.

Hamerow, H. 1993. *Excavations at Mucking. Volume 2: The Anglo-Saxon Settlement*. London: English Heritage. An important publication of an early Anglo-Saxon settlement excavated in the 1970s, though unfortunately the associated cemeteries have still not been published.

Hardy, Alan, and Peter Lorimer. 2004. *The Roots of an English Town: Exploring the Archaeology of Higham Ferrers*. Oxford: Oxford Archaeological Unit. Report on an important recent excavation which sheds new light on mid- to late-Anglo-Saxon economy and hierarchy.

Hawkes, Sonia Chadwick, and Guy Grainger. 2003. *The Anglo-Saxon Cemetery at Worthy Park, Kingsworthy, Near Winchester, Hampshire*. Oxford University School of Archaeology Monograph 59. Oxford: Oxford University School of Archaeology.

Hawkes, Sonia Chadwick, and Guy Grainger. 2006. *The Anglo-Saxon Cemetery at Finglesham, Kent*. Oxford University School of Archaeology Monograph 64. Oxford: Oxford University School of Archaeology.

Hawkes, Sonia Chadwick, Esther Cameron and Helena Hamerow. 2000. 'The
    Anglo-Saxon Cemetery of Bifrons, in the Parish of Patrixbourne, East Kent'.
    Anglo-Saxon Studies in Archaeology and History 11: 1–94.
Hey, Gill. 2004. *Yarnton: Saxon and Medieval Settlement and Landscape*. Oxford: Oxford
    Archaeology. A specialist site report which includes evidence from the eighth- and ninth-
    century rural settlement and cemetery.
Hope-Taylor, Brian. 1977. *Yeavering: An Anglo-British Centre of Early Northumbria*.
    London: Her Majesty's Stationary Office. The royal palace of King Edwin – a key site
    for the seventh century.
Malim, Tim, John Hines and Corinne Duhig. 1998. *The Anglo-Saxon Cemetery
    at Edix Hill (Barrington A), Cambridgeshire: Excavations 1989–1991 and
    a Summary Catalogue of Material from 19th Century Interventions*. Council
    for British Archaeology Research Report 112. York: Council for British Archaeology.
    An early Anglo-Saxon inhumation cemetery.
Museum of London Archaeology Service. 2004. *The Prittlewell Prince: The Discovery
    of a Rich Anglo-Saxon Burial in Essex*. London: Museum of London Archaeology
    Service. A lovely illustrated volume on this rich burial and its grave goods. An easy read.
West, Stanley. 1985. *West Stow: The Anglo-Saxon Village*, 2 vols. East Anglian
    Archaeology Report 24. Hadleigh: Citadel Press. A good example of an early
    Anglo-Saxon settlement and its associated artefacts.

Old English sources
Bradley, Sidney. 1995. *Anglo-Saxon Poetry*. London: Orion Publishing Limited.
    A new edition of Sidney Bradley's collection of translations of the most well-known
    Old English poems, as well as some less well-known poems and riddles.
Colgrave, Bertram, and Roger Mynors. 1969. *Bede: Ecclesiastical History of the English
    People*. Oxford: Oxford University Press. The authoritative edition of Bede's Latin text
    with English translation.
Crossley Holland, Kevin. 1999. *The Anglo-Saxon World: An Anthology*. Oxford World's
    Classics. Oxford: Oxford University Press. A collection of Old English texts, sensitively
    translated into modern English with well-written introductions to each text.
Dumville, David, and Simon Keynes (eds). 1983. *The Anglo-Saxon Chronicle:
    A Collaborative Edition*. Cambridge: D.S. Brewer. A scholar's edition of editions
    of the Chronicle in Old English and Latin with notes in English.
Heaney, Seamus (tr.). 2007. *Beowulf (Bilingual Edition)*. London: Faber and Faber.
    A beautiful translation of the famous Old English poem, with the original Old English
    text on facing pages for reference.
Hodges, Richard. 1989. *The Anglo-Saxon Achievement: Archaeology and the Beginnings
    of English Society*. London: Duckworth. An important and readable book by
    a controversial and stimulating scholar.
Keynes, Simon. 1984. *Alfred the Great: Asser's Life of King Alfred and Other
    Contemporary Sources*. London: Penguin. A fascinating insight into Alfred and
    his world through translations of contemporary Old English texts and an excellent
    introduction.
Sherley-Price, Leo (tr.). 1991. *Bede: The Ecclesiastical History of the English People*.
    London: Penguin. An accessible translation of the most important account of early
    English history.
Swanton, Michael. 1984. *Three Lives of the Last Englishmen*. New York: Garland.
    A fascinating translation with introduction of the Old English *Lives* of Harold
    Godwinson, Hereward the Wake and Wulfstan, bishop of Worcester.
Swanton, Michael. 1996. *The Anglo-Saxon Chronicle*. London: Dent. A useful translation
    of the chronicles.

Whitelock, Dorothy. 1956. *English Historical Documents, Volume I (c.500–1042)*. Oxford: Oxford University Press. A huge, invaluable compendium of documents, including wills, charters, chronicles, letters and poetry, translated by Professor Whitelock.

General

Arnold, Christopher. 1997. *The Archaeology of the Early Anglo-Saxon Kingdoms*. London: Routledge. This is the second, revised edition of a book originally published in 1988. Offering some original approaches to the interpretation of the archaeological evidence, and the book has long provided fuel for debate.

Backhouse, Janet, D.H. Turner and Leslie Webster. 1984. *The Golden Age of Anglo-Saxon Art, 966–1066*. London: British Museum Press. The book accompanied the exhibition of late Anglo-Saxon art at the British Museum.

Banham, Debby. 2004. *Food and Drink in Anglo-Saxon England*. Stroud: NPI Media Group. A readable, illustrated account of Anglo-Saxon diet, with recipes.

Blair, John. 2002. *The Anglo-Saxon Age: A Very Short Introduction*. Oxford: Oxford University Press. A useful introduction written by a leading scholar in the field.

Blair, John. 2005. *The Church and Anglo-Saxon Society*. Oxford: Oxford University Press. A monumental work and the current last word on the relationship between Anglo-Saxons and Christianity by an eminent scholar. A well-written and lucid account.

Booth, Paul. 2007. *The Thames Through Time: The Archaeology of the Gravel Terraces in the Early Historical Period, AD 1–1000*. Thames Valley Landscapes Monograph 27. Oxford: Oxford Archaeology. A well-written account which includes descriptions of the important Anglo-Saxon cemetery and settlement sites along the Thames Valley.

Brown, Michelle. 1991. *Anglo-Saxon Manuscripts*. London: The British Library.

Brown, Michelle. 2007. *Manuscripts from the Anglo-Saxon Age*. Toronto: University of Toronto Press. A beautifully illustrated, well-written, accessible book on Anglo-Saxon manuscripts and book production, suitable for the general reader.

Bruce-Mitford, Rupert. 1968. *The Sutton Hoo Ship-Burial: A Handbook*. London: British Museum. A valuable and accessible guide to the most important excavated Anglo-Saxon burial.

Cameron, Esther. 2000. *Sheaths and Scabbards in England AD 400–1000*. British Archaeological Reports British Series, 301. Oxford: Archaeopress. A fascinating book by an expert conservationist – very useful for re-enactment.

Cameron, Malcolm. 1993. *Anglo-Saxon Medicine*. Cambridge Studies in Anglo-Saxon England 7. Cambridge: Cambridge University Press. A comprehensive study of Old English medical texts assessing the rational and physiological basis of Anglo-Saxon medicine, written with medical historians and non-specialists in mind.

Campbell, James, Eric John and Patrick Wormald. 1991. *The Anglo-Saxons*. London: Penguin. Becoming out of date, but still a very useful introduction to the archaeology of Anglo-Saxon England, with excellent illustrations and photographs.

Carver, Martin. 2005. *Sutton Hoo: A Seventh Century Princely Burial Ground and Its Context*. London: British Museum Press. A generously illustrated review of excavations at Anglo-Saxon England's riches burial site, with new interpretations on the basis of recent evidence which replace all previously published theories about the site.

Coatsworth, Elizabeth, and Michael Pinder. 2002. *The Art of the Anglo-Saxon Goldsmith: Fine Metalwork in Anglo-Saxon England: Its Practice and Practitioners*. Woodbridge: Boydell Press. A lovely book with useful illustrations.

Crawford, Sally. 1999. *Childhood in Anglo-Saxon England*. Stroud: Sutton Publishing. The only book on the subject, and it combines archaeological and documentary evidence to fill in some of the gaps in our knowledge.

Dark, Ken. 2000. *Britain and the End of the Roman Empire*. Stroud: Tempus. A good read with a persuasive argument, but controversial and not universally accepted.

Davidson, Hilda. 1962. *The Sword in Anglo-Saxon England: Its Archaeology and Literature*. Oxford: Clarendon Press. Draws on archaeological, literary and historical evidence.

Davies, Wendy (ed.). 2003. *From the Vikings to the Normans*. Oxford: Oxford University Press. A useful, scholarly set of papers for those with a good grounding in the later Anglo-Saxon period.

Dobney, Keith, Deborah Jacques, James Barrett and Cluny Johnstone. 2007. *Farmers, Monks and Aristocrats: The Environmental Archaeology of Anglo-Saxon Flixborough*. Excavations at Flixborough 3. Oxford: Oxbow Press. A book aimed more at Anglo-Saxon archaeologists than at the general reader, it offers important environmental evidence for trade, society and daily life in England between the eighth and tenth centuries at this key site.

Dodwell, Charles. 1982. *Anglo-Saxon Art: A New Perspective*. Manchester: Manchester University Press. A scholarly and well-illustrated account of the development of Anglo-Saxon art in paintings, metalwork, textiles and sculpture.

Esmonde Cleary, Simon. 1989. *The Ending of Roman Britain*. London: Batsford. Still the most erudite and accessible account of the evidence immediately prior to and following the arrival of the Anglo-Saxons.

Faull, Margaret (ed.). 1984. *Studies in Late Anglo-Saxon Settlement*. Oxford: Oxford University Department for External Studies. An important collection of essays.

Fell, Christine. 1986. *Women in Anglo-Saxon England*. Oxford: Basil Blackwell. A lively, accurate and interesting portrayal of the daily lives of women in Anglo-Saxon England. Not recent, but still an important book.

Fernie, Eric. 1983. *The Architecture of the Anglo-Saxons*. London: Batsford. A useful introduction to the subject.

Fletcher, Richard. 2002. *Bloodfeud: Murder and Revenge in Anglo-Saxon England*. London: Allen Lane, the Penguin Press. An accessible account of legal and social attitudes to violence in Anglo-Saxon England.

Foot, Sarah. 2006. *Monastic Life in Anglo-Saxon England, c.600–900*. Cambridge: Cambridge University Press. A major work assessing the links between monastic and secular life. A well-argued and accessible account.

Gelling, Margaret. 1992. *The West Midlands in the Early Middle Ages*. Studies in the Early History of Britain. Leicester: Leicester University Press. A fascinating regional study.

Gelling, Margaret. 2005. *Signposts to the Past*. Stroud: Phillimore and Company. A brilliant and well-written insight into English place names, with a large section on Anglo-Saxon place names and their relationship to Anglo-Saxon landscape and life by the leading place-name expert.

Hadley, Dawn, and Julian Richards (eds). 2000. *Cultures in Contact: Scandinavian Settlement in England in the 9th and 10th Centuries*. Turnhout: Brepols. Includes papers from leading academics in the field on ethnicity, trade, merchants and settlement.

Hagen, Ann. 1994a. *A Handbook of Anglo-Saxon Food: Processing and Consumption*. Pinner: Anglo-Saxon Books. A variety of sources have been used to produce and account for early English food production, filled with fascinating insights.

Hagen, Ann. 1994b. *A Second Handbook of Anglo-Saxon Food and Drink: Production and Distribution*. Hockwold-cum-Wilton: Anglo-Saxon Books. A complement to the first handbook, and a mine of useful and interesting detail.

Hall, Alaric. 2007. *Elves in Anglo-Saxon England: Matters of Belief, Health, Gender and Identity*. Woodbridge: Boydell Press. A book for academic readers and specialists, rather than generalists, but a useful study showing the intertwining of myth, medicine and society.

Hamerow, Helena. 2002. *Early Medieval Settlements: The Archaeology of Rural Communities in Northwest Europe from AD 400–900*. Oxford: Oxford University

Press. There are some important sections on Anglo-Saxon settlement in this important book by the leading scholar in the field.

Harrison, Kenneth. 1976. *The Framework of Anglo-Saxon History to AD 900*. Cambridge: Cambridge University Press. A technical assessment of how the Anglo-Saxons created their calendar and defined their dates.

Haywood, John. 1994. *Dark Age Naval Power*. London: Routledge. Includes much relevant material on Anglo-Saxon maritime technology and travel.

Higham, Nicholas. 1992. *Rome, Britain and the Anglo-Saxons*. London: Seaby. A radical re-interpretation of the period.

Hill, David. 1981. *An Atlas of Anglo-Saxon England*. Oxford: Basil Blackwell. An invaluable collection of maps with commentary.

Hills, Catherine. 2003. *Origins of the English*. London: Duckworth. Contains a useful summary of current knowledge on English ethnicity.

Hines, John (ed.). 1997. *The Anglo-Saxons from the Migration Period to the Eighth Century: An Ethnographic Perspective*. Woodbridge: Boydell Press. A scholarly volume including papers on British ethnic identity, settlement, social structure and kinship.

Hinton, David. 1990. *Archaeology, Economy and Society in England from the Fifth to the Fifteenth Centuries*. London: Seaby. An accessible but scholarly text, which should be read in conjunction with David Hinton's more recent work below.

Hinton, David. 2005. *Gold and Gilt, Pots and Pins: Possessions and People in Medieval Britain*. Oxford: Oxford University Press. A beautiful and fascinating look at what possessions meant to people at every level in medieval society, with the first five chapters concentrating on Anglo-Saxon England.

Hooke, Della. 1988. *Anglo-Saxon Settlements*. Oxford: Basil Blackwell. A discussion of Anglo-Saxon settlement, economy and landscape; recent excavations of new sites may have added to our views, but Della Hooke's work is still worth the read.

Hunter Blair, Peter. 2003. *An Introduction to Anglo-Saxon England*. Cambridge: Cambridge University Press. The third, posthumous reprint of this classic historical account, with a new introduction by Simon Keynes.

Karkov, Catherine (ed.). 1999. *The Archaeology of Anglo-Saxon England: Basic Readings*. New York and London: Garland Publishing. A collection of classic, exemplary or ground-breaking essays on a wide range of Anglo-Saxon subjects.

Kennett, David. 1978. *Anglo-Saxon Pottery*. Aylesbury: Shire Publications. A useful short guide to pots and potters.

Laing, Lloyd, and Jennifer Laing. 1996. *Early English Art and Architecture: Archaeology and Society*. Stroud: Sutton Publishing. A good introduction for the general reader.

Lapidge, Michael, John Blair, Simon Keynes and Donald Scragg (eds). 1999. *The Blackwell Encyclopaedia of Anglo-Saxon England*. Oxford: Blackwell Publishers. A major reference work with contributions from an impressive range of experts and leaders in the field. An asset to students.

Leahy, Kevin. 2003. *Anglo-Saxon Crafts*. Stroud: Tempus. A detailed explanation of how things were made in Anglo-Saxon England, including production, technology, tools and materials.

Lee, Christina. 2007. *Feasting the Dead: Food and Drink in Anglo-Saxon Burial Rituals*. London: Boydell Press. A book examining the Anglo-Saxon wake from the fifth to the eleventh century through archaeology and documentary sources.

Leeds, Edward Thurlow. 1913, reprinted in 1970 with an introduction by John Nowell Linton Myres. *The Archaeology of the Anglo-Saxon Settlements*. Oxford: Clarendon Press. A ground-breaking and influential work by the founding father of modern Anglo-Saxon archaeology, drawing attention to the importance of Anglo-Saxon settlement for understanding society. Must be supplemented with recent scholarship.

Lucy, Samantha. 2001. *The Anglo-Saxon Way of Death*. Stroud: Sutton Publishing. An accessible overview of changing Anglo-Saxon attitudes to death and burial.

Matthews, Stephen. 2007. *The Road to Rome: Travel and Travellers Between England and Italy in the Anglo-Saxon Centuries*. British Archaeological Reports International Series 1680. Oxford: Archaeopress. A revealing account of the extent of, and purpose of, international travel in this period.

Meaney, Audrey. 1981. *Anglo-Saxon Amulets and Curing Stones*. British Archaeological Reports British Series 96. Oxford: British Archaeological Reports. The best guide to Old English amulets.

Musset, Lucien. 2005. *The Bayeux Tapestry*. Translated by Richard Rex. London: The Boydell Press. Reproduces the whole of the Tapestry, including the borders with their details of everyday life.

Myres, John Nowell Linton. 1986. *The English Settlements*. Oxford: Clarendon Press. A classic assessment of the earliest Anglo-Saxon settlement. Now out of date, but an important milestone.

Owen-Crocker, Gale. 2004. *Dress in Anglo-Saxon England*, rev. edn. London: The Boydell Press. An encyclopaedic and scholarly book – not light reading, but well illustrated and the best guide to Anglo-Saxon costume.

Reynolds, Andrew. 1999. *Later Anglo-Saxon England: Life and Landscape*. Stroud and Charleston: Tempus. An accessible and readable account of the later Anglo-Saxon period, using copious archaeological evidence and with illustrations and reconstructions.

Richards, Julian. 1987. *The Significance of Form and Decoration of Anglo-Saxon Cremation Urns*. British Archaeological Reports British Series 166. Oxford: British Archaeological Reports. The first, and still the best, attempt to understand the relationship between Anglo-Saxon cremation ritual and social structure.

Rogers, Penelope. 2007. *Cloth and Clothing in Early Anglo-Saxon England*. Council for British Archaeology Research Report 145. York: Council for British Archaeology.

Scragg, Donald (ed.). 1989. *Superstition and Popular Medicine in Anglo-Saxon England*. Manchester: Centre for Anglo-Saxon Studies. A useful collection of essays on this interesting topic.

Stafford, Pauline. 1989. *Unification and Conquest: A Political and Social History of England in the Tenth and Eleventh Centuries*. London: Edward Arnold. A good book to read to help untangle the complexities of late Anglo-Saxon politics.

Stenton, Frank. 2001. *Anglo-Saxon England*. Oxford: Oxford University Press. The third edition of this seminal work of historical and archaeological synthesis. This book, first published in 1971, marks an important stage in Anglo-Saxon studies and is still worth a read.

Stephenson, I.P. 2007. *The Late Anglo-Saxon Army*. Stroud: Tempus. Useful information on military equipment and chapters on the battles of Maldon and Hastings.

Strickland, Matthew. 1992. *Anglo-Norman Warfare: Studies in Late Anglo-Saxon and Anglo-Norman Warfare*. Woodbridge: Boydell Press. A useful text.

Thompson, Victoria. 2004. *Dying and Death in Later Anglo-Saxon England*. Woodbridge: Boydell Press. A thoughtful and important review of evidence for Anglo-Saxon attitudes to death and burial in the Christian period.

Tipper, Jess. 2004. *The Grubenhaus in Anglo-Saxon England: An Analysis and Interpretation of the Evidence from a Most Distinctive Building Type*. Yedingham: Landscape Research Centre. A new and negativist view of this building form. Should be read in conjunction with Helena Hamerow's authoritative work on early medieval settlement.

Ulmschneider, Katharina. 2000. *Markets, Minsters and Metal-Detectors: The Archaeology of Middle Saxon Lincolnshire and Hampshire Compared*. Oxford: Archaeopress. Metal detected finds are problematic and have had an increasing influence on interpretations of middle Saxon settlement and economy. This judicious volume reviews and interprets the evidence and its implications and has provided a template for other scholars.

Underwood, Richard. 2000. *Anglo-Saxon Weapons and Warfare*. Stroud: Tempus. A useful introduction to the subject by a defence specialist.

Webster, Leslie, and Janet Backhouse. 1991. *The Making of England: Anglo-Saxon Art and Culture AD 600–900*. London: British Museum Press. A beautifully illustrated catalogue of an exhibition at the British Museum, divided into useful chapters, and with expert analysis of each artefact.

Welch, Martin. 1993. *Discovering Anglo-Saxon England*. University Park, Pa.: Pennsylvania State University Press. Includes illustrations and bibliographical references.

Whitelock, Dorothy. 1980. *From Bede to Alfred: Studies in Anglo-Saxon Literature and History*. London: Variorum reprints. A reprint of thirteen articles published by Professor Whitelock, showing her startling insights and intellect. Still relevant and important in the debate about the Anglo-Saxon past.

Young, Simon. 2005. *A.D. 500: A Journey Through the Dark Isles of Britain and Ireland*. London: Weidenfeld and Nicolson. An entertaining fictional account drawing on archaeological and documentary records.

Web pages

http://pase.ac.uk/

The Prosopography of Anglo-Saxon England – a database covering all of the recorded inhabitants of England from the late sixth to the end of the eleventh century, which may be searched according to name, relationship, events, occupations and other information.

http://labyrinth.georgetown.edu/

The Labyrinth. Resources for Medieval Studies sponsored by Georgetown University. The search category leads you to a variety of links, some academic and some popular, including plant-name databases, Anglo-Saxon cemetery databases and more.

http://www.reia.org/main.htm

Regia Anglorum – the webpage of the main UK re-enactment society for the late Anglo-Saxon/early Norman period.

http://www.the-orb.net/encyclop/early/pre1000/asindex.html

The Orb – an online reference book for medieval studies, offering resources for Anglo-Saxon studies, including online translations of texts, bibliographies and images.

http://web.arch.ox.ac.uk/archives/inventorium/index.php

Novum Inventorium Sepulchrale – an online digital corpus offering a searchable database of the copious collection of information on the Kentish Anglo-Saxon graves and grave goods in the Sonia Chadwick Hawkes archive.

About the Author

Dr Sally Crawford is an established scholar in the field of Anglo-Saxon studies. She is a founder of the *Society for the Study of Childhood in the Past*; a founder and general editor of the *Journal of Early Medicine* and an editor of *Anglo-Saxon Studies in Archaeology and History*. She has written extensively on Anglo-Saxon archaeology, burial ritual, childhood and medicine and has directed excavations on medieval sites in the United Kingdom. She is an Honorary Senior Research Fellow at the Centre for the History of Medicine at the University of Birmingham and an Honorary Research Associate at the Institute of Archaeology, Oxford.

Index